NUCLEAR TERROR SURVIVAL HANDBOOK
Part 1 – Within One Mile

With this knowledge you can survive.

Vern Blanchette

Rev 1 1710141

Areli Books

Copyright © 2017 V. G. Blanchette Jr
All rights reserved.
ISBN-10: 1541320972
ISBN-13: 978-1541320970

DEDICATION

This book is dedicated to my parents, Gene and Engalee, without whom I would have had a very difficult time writing this book.

 My father was a man for the time, an electrical engineer with a gentle, loving, intellectual nature, who created a love for science in his children. He is fondly remembered for playing games in our backyard with many of the neighborhood kids (Prisoner's Base), teaching details of electrical science to anyone who showed an interest, and, when the cat fell asleep and slid off the warm top of the old black-and-white television, losing himself in laughter.

 My mother, also an intellectual, warm-hearted and kind person, was an excellent home maker, actively involved in little theater and community events, and constantly involved in reading a broad variety of subjects (introducing me to Michener's *The Source* when I was fourteen). Her forte was natural science, and always sharing what she learned with her children. She was the impetus for weekend family trips to hunt agate, search out fossilized wood, and to expose her brood to places replete with local history. She made learning an adventure and a joy.

I miss them both, and dedicate this two part work to their memory.

Vern Blanchette, Space Coast of Florida, 2017

Preface

A stark white light suddenly filled the room, and over Tessie's shoulder Rob could see through their picture window what appeared to be a white-hot star rising from Yorksberg's downtown district across the river. Its brilliance kept him from looking directly at it. For a second he hesitated, and then he saw it - a circle of disturbance spreading rapidly toward them across the river. Recognizing the spreading circle as evidence of a blast wave coming from the explosion, he grabbed Tessie's arm and pulled her out from in front of the window.

"Rob! You hurt my elbow!" she said just before the window shattered into the living room and the house shuddered under a singular, loud boom. A strong, cold wind briefly blew in along with a distant, deep, horrible rumble, like continuous thunder coming from across the Taconic River.

"What happened?" she said.

"That was close." Rob shook a piece of broken glass off his shoe. His heart raced and his hands trembled from their close call.

"My fish!" Tessie wailed at the sight of their broken fish tank.

"Ten gallons of water on the rug and dying fish are nothing compared to what the folks over there are going through," he said, pointing out the window. "Forget the fish babe. Yorksberg has just been nuked."

"Nuked? You mean that was a nuclear explosion?" Tessie turned from the fish and looked at the mushroom-shaped cloud rising from the distant city. She grabbed his arm. "Rob, what do we do?"

That is the question, isn't it? What would you do? Clean up the broken glass? Save the fish? Fix the window? Pack and leave?

We will rejoin Rob and his wife in one of the stories in Part 2 of this handbook and find out what they do, but for now consider that you are living in or visiting a large metropolitan area when a terrorist organization explodes a nuclear bomb in the city. You have survived the nuclear explosion; now what will you do to survive the aftermath?

> **What you do, or fail to do, may determine whether you live or die.**

If you live in a suburb, a small town, or far from a city, don't make the mistake of thinking you are safe. In fact, you and your family could be in grave danger even if you survive the explosion.

What must you do to assure that you and your loved ones survive? This is what this survival handbook is about. Using a mixture of fiction and fact, this handbook will present you with the knowledge you need to help you survive a terrorist's nuclear attack in a city.

Note: Topics covered in this handbook are listed in Appendix E1.

TABLE OF CONTENTS

In this handbook, Chapters 12 through 22 are continued in *The Nuclear Terror Survival Handbook Part 2- Beyond One Mile.*

Introduction

If you wish to better understand what to expect if a nuclear explosion occurs in a large city near you or in a large city where you reside, you will find this book useful and informative. Reading this book will provide a clearer understanding of what it will be like to be in an attacked city and what actions you might take to enhance your chances of surviving.

Is the threat of a terrorist nuclear attack on one of our cities real? To learn more about this see Appendix C1.

The author has used as his primary reference the classic book *The Effects of Nuclear Weapons* by Samuel Glasstone and Philip J. Dolan, published by the U.S. Government Printing Office in 1977. This source, a highly technical study and report that reads like a college physics textbook, contains 653 pages that do an excellent job of detailing the effects of nuclear weapons. Unfortunately this book sets the layman adrift in multi-axis charts, non-trivial mathematics, nuclear verbiage rich in scientific-technical terms, and material that is overwhelming in both its specialized nature and volume. It leaves the average citizen asking the question "Okay, this is impressive, but what value is it to me? What is it I need to know to survive an atomic attack in my city?"

Think "hot," extremely hot, hot enough to burn your skin a mile away. [1]

---

[1] This picture is fiction. It is an altered photo of a city where buildings have been rearranged or reworked, and a Nevada atomic-test mushroom cloud has been superimposed. No humans or animals have been harmed in the creation of this photo. No radioactivity has been released.

The author has used his background (B.S. in Physics and Mathematics), his training as a teacher (M.Ed.), and his experience working in the nuclear power industry to interpret and present the contents of *The Effects of Nuclear Weapons* so that it is both pertinent to survival and understandable by the average person.

Civil defense educational material tends to be boring, so to engage the reader's interest the author has created a fictional city populated with fictional people who undergo a nuclear attack. The bomb's explosion is seen over and over again in the lives of twenty-two fictional citizens, each given his or her own chapter, with the bomb's effects correlated to the person's location and technical details of the effects ferreted out of Glasstone and Dolan's epic *The Effects of Nuclear Weapons*. By reading Part 1 and Part 2, the reader will "experience" the nuclear attack from the point of view of these twenty-two fictional lives. The stories of several people a long distance from the attacked city are included to allow discussion of the effects of the bomb at distant locations.

Following each citizen's story is an analysis section where the fictional character's experiences are explained. This analysis section also points out methods of increasing survivability and what our city fathers could be doing ahead of time to improve safety for citizens.

If you will read all twenty-two short stories, carefully consider what the analysis section says about each story, and try your hand at the self-check questions at the end of each chapter, you will be more nuclear street-smart and your chances of surviving a nuclear attack will improve.[2]

> **Some experts estimate the chance of a nuclear terror event in the United States in the next ten years is at least fifty percent.[3]**

Will an atomic bomb be exploded in a major city of the world, perhaps even in the United States? "Some experts estimate the chance of a nuclear terror event in the United States in the next ten years is at least fifty percent."[3] Your chances of survival are increased the more you know about a nuclear explosion and the better you and your loved ones prepare. [4]

---

[2] Read the footnotes, like this one. References, technical data, and knowledge-enriching content will be included in them.

[3] "Retaliation Against Nuclear Terror: A Negligence Doctrine," a paper by Ander Corr, based upon work supported under a National Science Foundation Graduate Research Fellowship.

[4] This handbook covers nuclear bomb effects from ground zero to 250 miles. You should read all the chapters and the analysis of Part 1 and Part 2 to gain a complete understanding of the issues surrounding surviving a terrorist nuclear attack in your city or in a city near you. You won't know where you will be when they strike.

Can Anyone Really Survive?

You may think there is no point in preparing to survive a nuclear attack. In your mind's eye you probably see a bleak, smoldering landscape with the ruined shells of houses standing gaunt under gray, depressing skies. You may feel you have a natural instinct that tells you that preparing to survive a nuclear attack is nonsense because the destruction would be so complete that you would rather just give up and die.

If you have had these thoughts, or if you are currently having them, you may be suffering from the propaganda found in books and movies about nuclear war. These stories were created to make money and not to make you smart. You have been conditioned to think this way, and it is far from the whole truth. Consider this - bleak, smoldering landscapes are typical of any area of intense warfare after the shelling and bombing stops, but remember that many people are not dead. Many people are not going to die. Many are well enough to help others recover and survive. Whether the attack is one hundred bombers dropping a thousand incendiary bombs over a two-hour period, or one big bomb going off in an instant, the final scene is the same. Remember that the most valuable resource to salvage from such an attack is people. The more people you can save, the quicker the city can recover.

> The most valuable resource to salvage from a nuclear attack on one of our cities is people.

What about the radiation? You may have been propagandized into thinking that recovery is impossible after a nuclear attack because radiation lingers for thousands of years, causing horrible burns and giving cancer to everyone. Nuclear radiation makes a scary story[5] and sells movies and books, but the truth is the situation is not nearly as bad as you have been led to believe. A nuclear explosion is survivable with a good quality of life, including children, grandchildren, birthdays, turkey dinners, and fourth of Julys in the park.

Not convinced? Then consider the following picture showing one of the two cities attacked with a single nuclear bomb to end the war with Japan.[6]

---

[5] Stories about radioactive mutants coming out of the sewers and chasing the bedraggled survivors of a nuclear attack are pure fiction. That has never happened and never will.

[6] Much of the following information is available on the internet. Search for "Nuclear Bomb."

Hiroshima – Did Anyone Survive?[7]

This is Hiroshima, Japan. Looks pretty hopeless, doesn't it? It looks as if no one could have survived. This destruction is particularly thorough because of the Japanese tradition of building homes of paper and bamboo. This type of construction does not withstand blast well and is extremely susceptible to fire.

> If the people living in Hiroshima, Japan, had known about the nuclear bomb and prepared, well over 95 percent of them could have survived.

At the time of the attack, the population was estimated to be approximately 255,000 people.[8] Near-term deaths due to heat burns, blast, and radiation are estimated to have been ~140,000, while long-term deaths over a period of decades due to radiation are estimated to be a few hundred. These people had no warning and no preparation, yet almost half (115,000 folks) survived. Had they known about the nuclear bomb and prepared, perhaps more than 95 percent of them could have survived.

---

[7] This photo is available in many World War II and national archives. The Hiroshima weapon released 12,500 tons of TNT (12.5 kt) equivalent energy (Ref 1 section 2.24).

[8] www.wikipedia.org This site has a good historical presentation with facts and photos donated by folks all over the world. References are cited.

Did you know that earth-covered shelters one hundred yards from ground zero[9] were not damaged? Wood-frame houses more than a mile away survived the blast[10] (though some were destroyed by the subsequent fires). The day after the blast the bridges were reopened to traffic, the second day following the blast the trains were again carrying freight and passengers, and by the third day streetcar service had resumed.[11]

There are two facts about radiation that Hollywood, scary books, and fear mongers do not want you to know. The first is that after the explosion radiation comes from bomb material mixed with the dirt and dust stirred up by the blast. These particles of dirt and dust are radioactive, but they are still just dirt and dust. You can wash it off, get away from it, bury it, and avoid it. The second fact is that the amount of radiation this dirt and dust gives off rapidly decreases.[12] That is why the site of a nuclear blast is dangerously radioactive for the first few days, but habitable later. That is why Hiroshima and Nagasaki are again cities full of people going about their normal activities of life.

Some have argued the casualties in a nuclear strike would be so horrible that preparation and defense becomes immoral. One of the best answers to this position was penned as follows:

The morality of war does not depend on the weapons with which it is fought. You have exactly one life to risk in the defense of everything that makes life worth living, and it matters little whether you lose it to a spear, a bullet, or nuclear radiation. Your forefathers risked, and often gave, that one life for your life, liberty, and pursuit of happiness. You have no right to squander their heritage, to invite war by weakness, and to leave your children to the demeaning cancer of serfdom.[13]

> Being afraid to plan and act will only hinder you and cause your worst ideas about living after a nuclear attack to come true.

Believing there is nothing you can do to survive is a self-fulfilling prophecy. Throw away that stinking thinking. You can improve your chances of surviving a nuclear attack.

---

[9] "Ground Zero" is the spot on the earth directly below the bomb when it explodes. Think of it as the center of the explosion's destructive effects.

[10] *The Effects of Nuclear Weapons*, 3rd ed., U.S. Department of Defense, 1977.

[11] L. W. Beilenson, *Survival and Peace in the Nuclear Age*, Regnery/Gateway, 1980.

[12] Nuclear scientists have found that the decrease in radioactivity (called radioactive decay) follows the seven-fold rule of nature. Every seven-fold increase in time, the amount of radioactivity decreases to 1/10 of what it was before. This will be discussed in more detail.

[13] A quote from "Some Sober Facts about Nuclear War," by Dr. Petr Beckmann, found in a supplement to the GE May 1982 *Access to Energy*, Box 2298, Boulder, CO 80306. See also: http://www.fortfreedom.org/w01.htm .

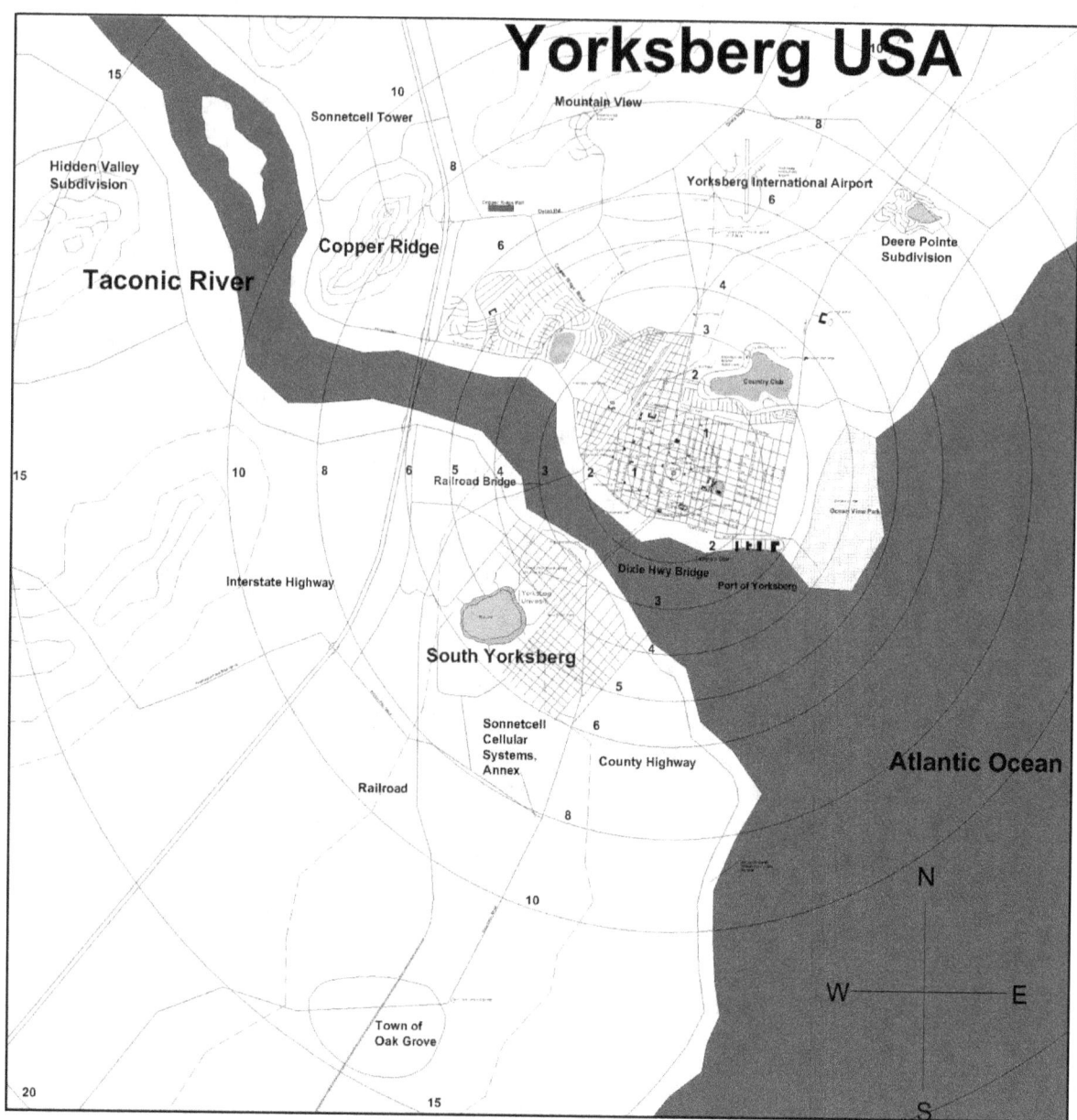

Wide View of the Yorksberg Area

Setting the Scene

Wide View of the Yorksberg Area

Before visiting our first Yorksberg citizen, let's bring our fictional city of Yorksberg to life. The *Wide View of the Yorksberg Area* is a map of Yorksberg showing features within fifteen miles of the city. Other maps of Yorksberg associated with each chapter will help you follow the stories as you read.

While some of the details in this first map may appear too small to see, they will be zoomed in on subsequent maps to reveal important details. The circular rings are centered on the location where the bomb explodes, and the rings are marked off in miles.

Note on this general view of Yorksberg that the city sits at the mouth of the Taconic River and on the Atlantic Ocean. Many of the city streets are visible as fine black lines. The double line is the interstate highway, which runs generally north to south as it passes a local elevated feature called Copper Ridge and then crosses the river into South Yorksberg. Elevations are roughly indicated by faint, dashed, contour lines.

You are encouraged to follow each story using the maps provided because distances from where the bomb explodes are critically important, and at times the fictional characters will move within the city.

The downtown Yorksberg area is shown in more detail in the map below.

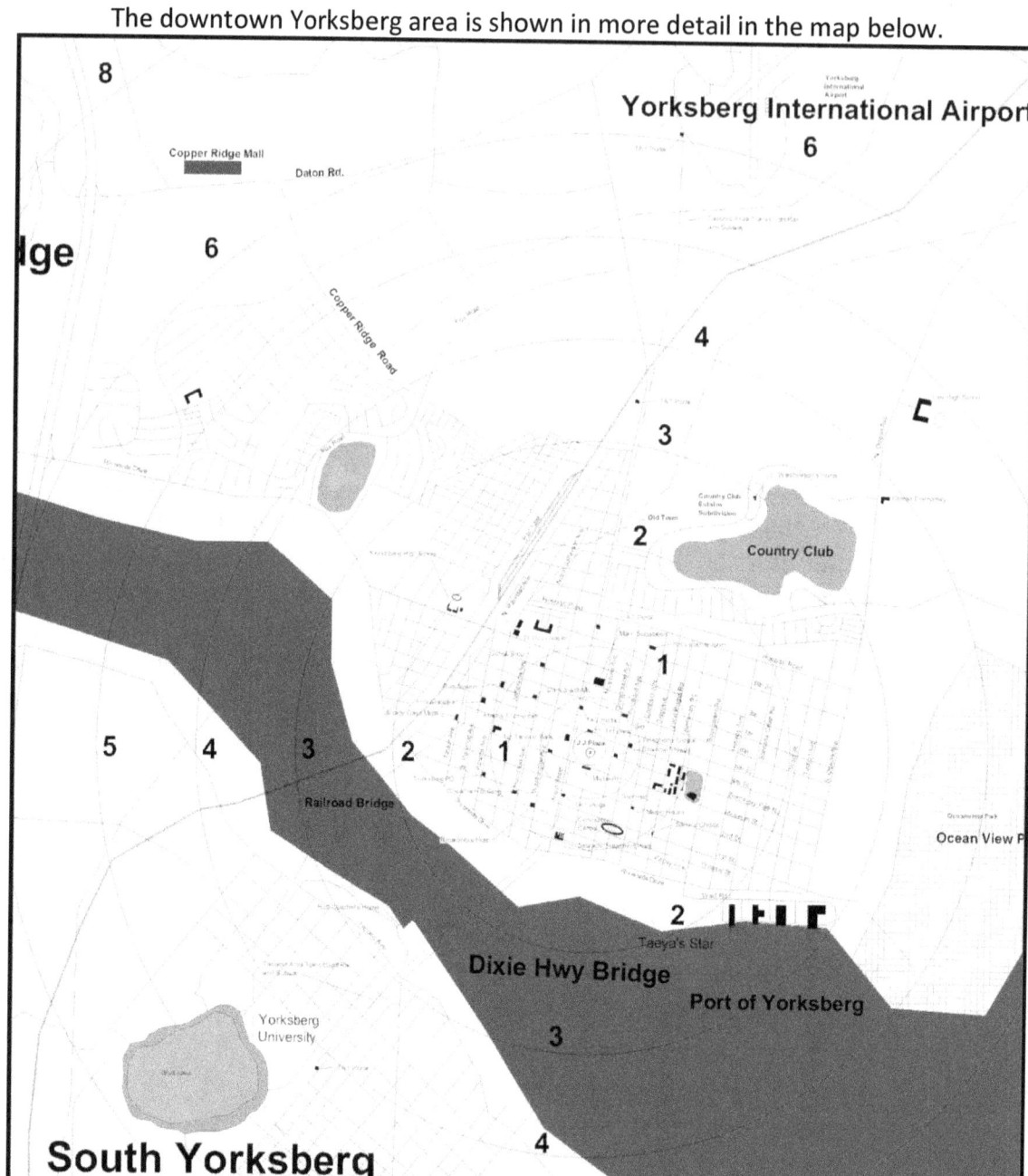

The City of Yorksberg

The City of Yorksberg

In this view we are looking at an area of the city within 5 to 6 miles of the bomb's explosion. The names of the major streets are now resolved, although still difficult to read at this scale. A railroad line crosses the Taconic River on the first bridge downstream of the interstate highway bridge. You can follow it up into the city to the railyards.

The second bridge downstream of the interstate highway carries the "Dixie Highway." This is the older state highway that carried traffic prior to the building of the interstate.

There is also a light rail subway called the Taconic Area Transit that citizens refer to as the TAT. You can see it as a dashed line next to the Dixie Highway Bridge. Follow it with your eyes as it runs from South Yorksberg under the river and then under the city up to the airport. It plays an important part in one of the stories.

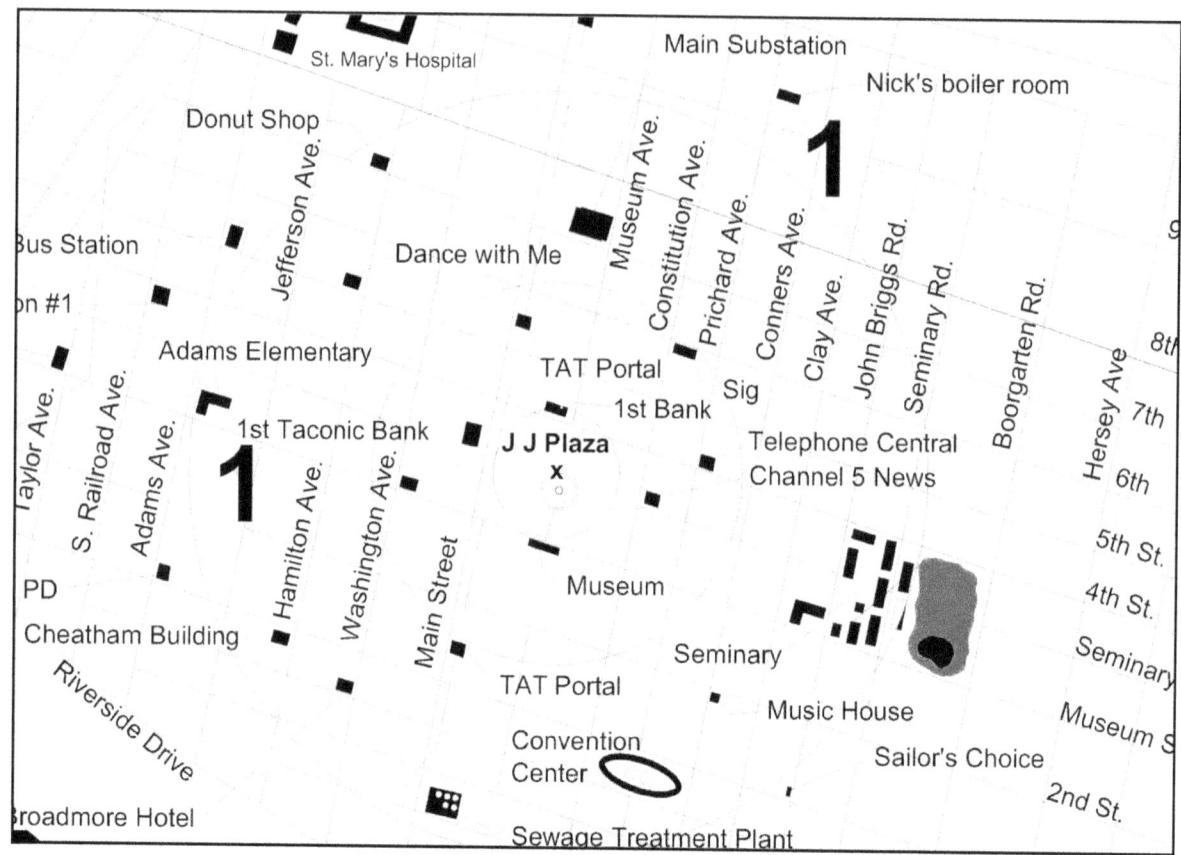

Downtown Yorksberg

Setting the Scene

Downtown Yorksberg

The map of the heart of downtown Yorksberg shows John Jay Plaza. At the center of the plaza is a fountain (the smallest circle) ringed by a circular driveway. The small "x" on the north side of the circular driveway is the location of the truck containing the nuclear bomb when it explodes.

The next larger light gray circle that almost touches the museum is the approximate diameter of the white-hot fireball the bomb creates. Just to the left of the big numeral "1" is a light gray ring one mile from the explosion. The light gray ring between this one-mile ring and J J Plaza is one-half mile from the bomb.

The small rectangles are various buildings in the city. Not all buildings and streets are shown, but most of the ones with labels will play a part in one or more of the short stories.

Look at the Downtown Yorksberg map and see if you can spot the location of the action in these chapters:

Chapter 1 – The Museum
Chapter 2 – Sigmund Johanson's (Sig's) Apartment
Chapter 3 – Sailor's Choice Restaurant
Chapter 4 – Music House
Chapter 5 – Broadmore Hotel
Chapter 6 – "Dance with Me" dance studio
Chapter 7 – Convention Center
Chapter 8 – Cheatham Building Construction Site
Chapter 9 – Donut Shop
Chapter 10 – Seminary
Chapter 11 – Adams Elementary School
Chapter 14 – St. Mary's Hospital

Throughout the narratives of each of the lives discussed in these short stories, the author has tried to keep the effect of the bomb and scale of destruction accurate to the energy released (19 kt)[14].

Ready or Not!

It is a cold December afternoon, about 35°F, with a visibility of 10+ miles and no cloud ceiling. Ground-level winds are out of the south-southwest at a fairly steady 15 mph. The roads are clear of snow, but patches of melting snow still linger along some roadways and on the north facing slopes of hills. Winds at high altitudes, 30,000 to 50,000 feet, where the heat of the explosion will carry much of the radioactive material, trend generally toward the north.[15]

---

[14] 19 kt means 19,000 tons of TNT equivalent. TNT is an abbreviation for the chemical explosive TriNitroToluene.

[15] Our bad guys have picked this day because of the weather. They have chosen a day when the upper-level winds will carry radioactive materials across as many other major cities as possible.

Can anyone survive two tenths of a mile (322 meters) from the bomb? It's time to read Chapter 1, where we learn about a young college student named Mindy Walker in the museum, and we ask "How close is safe?"

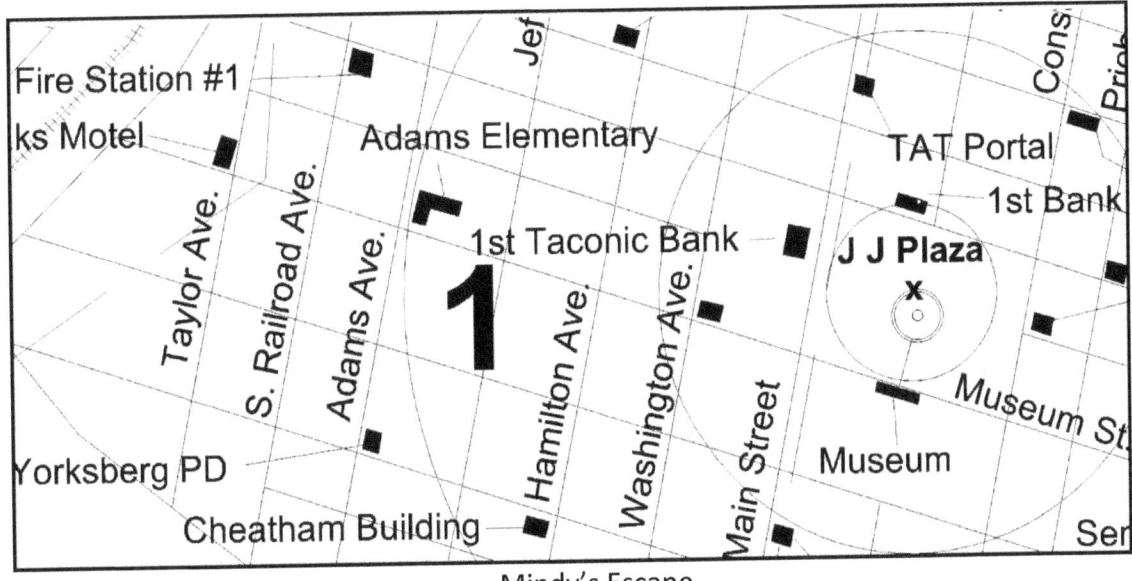

Mindy's Escape

1 – Mindy Walker – How Close is Safe? (0.2 miles)

I feel so odd... lying in the middle of South Railroad Avenue in front of Fire Station No. 1, flat on my back, a bit nauseous, shaking like a leaf, remembering the children... and remembering that I did not know all of them would be dead within minutes. My God! The children!

I have the strange sensation Mrs. Thompson is standing next to me again, and I can see the kids walking, jumping, and hopping down the broad steps of the Yorksberg Museum of History in my mind. "Mindy, aren't they a hoot?" Mrs. Thompson says.

"They are. I never get tired of working with these field trippers."

We watch the teacher and her aide corral the rambunctious fifth-graders at the crosswalk and then help them safely cross over to John Jay Plaza.

"The teachers are amazing. They seem to have a never-ending reservoir of patience. I don't think I could do what they do."

"Me neither," Mrs. Thompson says. "I think of them like grandkids. I get to play with them awhile and then I send them back to school."

My cell phone rings. I pull it out and cancel the alarm. "I almost forgot. I have a meeting with my professor at three." Glancing at my watch I note 2:24. "I hope you don't mind."

"No problem. Just help me put away the field trip display carts before you go."

I follow Mrs. Thompson up the broad granite steps and through the heavy, brass-framed glass doors into the museum's foyer. The richness of the polished marble floors and the high ornate ceilings always gives me a sense of another era, a time when buildings were constructed well and lasted forever. I love working in it, and I like working with Mrs. Thompson. She hasn't turned out to be the stuffy matriarch I expected when I signed up for this semester's on-the-job training. Curator has such an old fuddy-duddy sound to it. I learned that Mrs. Thompson, though much older than I, has no fuddy-duddy in her veins.

The carts are where we left them. Closing the historic Jefferson pen set's oak box, I push my cart to the elevator, enter, and hold the door open for Mrs. Thompson.

"Thanks," she says as the door closes behind her.

"That was a really well-behaved group; they asked some good questions."

Mrs. Thompson agrees. "You can tell which classes have been studying history with a strong teacher and which are just out for a day away from school. I am constantly amazed at the difference a good teacher makes."

The elevator hums to a stop at the basement level, and as we exit I see for the hundredth time the familiar old civil defense shelter sign on the wall. Its rusty form still warns "150 max." I wonder what 150 people would eat and drink if they sheltered here now.

Walking down the hall, we turn into the old bank vault left over from the mid-1900s. I feel the vague sense of claustrophobia its massive steel door always gives me.

"Same time tomorrow?" I ask.

"Yep. And by the way, I really liked your presentation to the kids. You have a gift for this work, and I want you to know you are appreciated."

I smile. "Why, thank you." I give her a quick hug and then pick up my backpack and purse. "I'll post that comment on my 'I'm having a good day' blog."

Mrs. Thompson laughs.

Khalid Khan could see Charles grinning nervously.

Off in some faraway distance he hears Charles' voice say, "This is it, my friend; do it."

"We will pray first," Khalid says, proud of being the one chosen to strike this blow.

As he ends the prayer, a line of school buses, visible in his rearview mirror, slowly move around the fountain, the center of John Jay Plaza. As the first bus passes, the faint laughter of the children on the bus gives him pause. *I like children.*

"The children are no matter," that distant voice from across the truck's cab says. "This has to be done."

Khalid nods in agreement and feels his thumb on the red button on the small box in his hands.

With fingers caressing the device, a swell of the great honor he has been given flows through his being. His focus no longer includes buses, or children, or a square full of people. He senses nothing but an awareness of the plastic button sliding smoothly downward under the pressure of his thumb.

As I adjust my backpack and move toward the vault's door, a sudden bright light appears in the hallway outside the vault. *Someone's taking pictures?*

The vault lights go out and I find myself violently lifted and then falling in darkness. Instinctively I put my hands out to catch myself and hit hard and bounce, followed by pain from multiple impacts and a blow to the head. All this occurs amid a horrific onslaught of sound, ending with the cold, hard floor against my back. It shakes and rumbles, its convulsions dying away as the seconds tick by.

Disoriented, my ears ringing, I realize I am lying still as death in the now-gloomy vault, covered by something that turns out to be ceiling tiles, museum artifacts, books, papers, and a chair. Looking up, I can see the lights are off and partly dislodged from the ceiling and hanging by their wires. I kick the chair aside. *At least my legs are still working.*

Sitting up, I count my pains. My left knee is complaining, my ribs and my right hip ache as if bruised, and my head hurts the worst. There's an odd tickle on my right temple and cheek. A touch where the pain is centered on my head, an involuntary wipe at the tickle on my cheek, and my hand comes away wet. Holding it before my face, I see its sticky redness in the dim light coming from the one surviving bulb on an emergency light fixture, which is now hanging loose on its wires against the wall. The dampness is blood, my blood, which shocks me. As I stare at my red-soaked fingers, I feel queasy, but not just from the sight of my own blood. The emergency lamp is still swinging on its wire, making the whole room seem to sway in the play of moving shadows caused by its motion.

I become aware there is no sound now, and I remember the curator.

"Mrs. Thompson?" Worried, I call out louder, with a growing fear. "April? April! Mrs. Thompson!"

No answer comes back, so I gingerly stand up and look around the room, my mind in a fog of confusion.

What just happened?

I find Mrs. Thompson partially buried under a file cabinet and covered by papers and pieces of broken ceiling tile. With some effort, I move the cabinet off her and lean in close. She is breathing, and this comforts me a bit. When I touch her arm, her eyes open and she blinks. There is an ugly bruise on her forehead.

"What happened?" she said.

"I have no clue. An earthquake maybe? A big one though. Are you okay?"

Mr. Thompson rolls over and I help her sit up.

"My ankle hurts like hell," she says.

"Can you stand on it?"

She pushes on it and winces. "No way. I think it's broken. God it hurts, and my head too. I think I'm going to be sick."

The tears welling up in Mrs. Thompson's eyes testify to the pain she feels.

I don't know what to do, and I struggle to remember my first-aid from Girl Scout training. Her pain shakes me, and an odd sense of dread comes over me. *I need to do something!*

"I'll get an ambulance."

I pull out my cell phone and try to look at it, but my hands are shaking and that makes it hard to focus in the dim light. I get blood on the phone and this agitates me more. I feel like crying and blink tears back several times to gain control.

"No bars on my cell," I say at last. I hear my voice quavering. "I'll have to go for help." I place my hand on Mrs. Thompson's shoulder as an act of comfort, unable to think of anything else to do.

Mrs. Thompson looks pale, even in the dim, reddish emergency light, all that keeps the vault from being an ink-black cavern. She lies flat on her back. "I'll be all right. You go ahead."

I fish two granola bars and a bottle of water from my backpack and set them down next to her.

Turning to go, I can see the huge steel door of the vault has closed. *Must have swung shut during the earthquake.*

I feel a shiver of panic, which intensifies when I push on the handle and discover the door won't move.

At that point I remember lying in bed at night, fearing what it would be like to be trapped in this vault. Now this is my nightmare come true. My heart pounds, my palms are clammy, and I feel the walls closing in on me.

Hardly able to speak, I call back to Mrs. Thompson, my voice a fear-constricted squeak. "The door won't open."

Mrs. Thompson doesn't answer. I can see she is lying with her eyes closed, apparently unaware of our precarious situation.

This angers me and with the power of the anger I yell "The door is stuck!"

Mrs. Thompson opens her eyes, looks over at me, and says calmly, "Try the wheel. You have to rotate the wheel, that small red wheel. Turn it clockwise."

I do what Mrs. Thompson says. The little wheel moves only a slight bit, but this is enough, and when I push, the door slowly swings open into the hallway a little and then comes to a stop with a jarring metallic sound. I push again, even putting my shoulder against it, but the door won't budge. I try closing it slightly and then pushing hard. Each time it stops suddenly with a huge metallic clunk. It feels as if something very heavy is blocking it out in the hallway.

"It's stuck, but I think I might squeeze through." I hear the relief in my own voice.

I stick one leg through the gap and try to wiggle through. With one leg in the hallway, I realize I can't get out with my backpack on. So I shed the pack, purse, and coat, and, pushing them into the hallway ahead of me, I manage to squeeze through.

To say the hallway is a mess is an understatement. The whole floor, as far as I can see, is covered in broken pieces of marble, concrete, and shattered ornamental wood. I guess it came from the floor above, because I can see light coming through huge openings. *My God, I can see blue sky at places!*

Shafts of sunlight show how dusty the air really is. It's enough to choke on, and now I can see a huge block of marble, perhaps a piece of the floor above, lying on the basement floor where it keeps the vault door from opening fully.

A thought causes a cold chill to run down my spine. *If that block of marble had fallen just two feet farther over, I would have been trapped in that vault.*

While donning my coat and backpack, I can see the elevator is a total wreck, with the door all bashed in, so I proceed down the rubble-strewn hallway, climbing my way through debris toward the stairwell. The stairwell door is missing, and I can see that lots of those marble blocks, pieces of plasterboard, and splintered wood have fallen into the stairwell and piled onto each other. There is cold air flowing down the stairwell into my face, a constant cold breeze that smells faintly of the river.

I didn't know earthquakes could do so much damage!

The only way out involves climbing through the jumble of debris in the stairwell, which I begin to do. About halfway up, the rubble begins slipping down the stairs like a small avalanche with me perched on a block of polished marble flooring the size of an ironing board, so I just ride it down. The instant it stops I keep going and the jagged edge of some splintered wood stabs through the skin of my right thigh. It hurts so bad I can't breathe for a moment, and I cry out. When I look down at my leg, I can see the jagged piece of wood about the size of a ruler has gone through my thigh and its bloody end now sticks out of my jeans on the other side. I don't know what to do. I am scared and it hurts so much I can't stop myself from crying, and when I try to move, it hurts even worse. I can't move my leg and I can't go back to let Mrs. Thompson help me pull it out.

I hate the sight of blood, and where my pants are gashed open blood is flowing and soaking everything. My hands are covered in my own blood. *Damn blood is sticky.*

Desperate, I rip my torn pants open until I can see the place where the wood point sticks out of me. The sight of my own torn flesh and the blood makes me nauseous and I have to look away.

Preparing for the pain I know is coming, I try to pull the big wood splinter out, but every time I grab it to pull it out, the slick blood makes it hard to hold, and I just hurt myself more. What a mess. My tears make it hard to see what I'm doing.

Mrs. Thompson is depending on me and all I'm doing is sitting in my blood-soaked pants, crying. This thought makes me angry, and I steel myself for one quick, hard pull on the large splinter. After wiping my hands on a clean area of my pants, I just grab what I can of the wood piece and pull as quick and as hard as I can, as if I am ripping a bandage off so it doesn't hurt too much. This hurts like hell, but the splinter is now out of my leg, which is bleeding like crazy. After a moment or two it doesn't hurt as much and the blood flow is slackening.

I sit with my gory hands pressing my blood-soaked jeans against the wounds. The best thing is that now I can move my leg, even though it hurts with a strong ache.

I start climbing the stairwell rubble again. *I really want to get out of this place.* This time none of the wreckage on the stairway moves, and I manage to pick my way through to the top.

I stand at the top of the stairs, shocked for a minute. It hurts me to see that the beautiful old museum has been transformed from a rich masterpiece of gorgeous antiquity to just a shell of shattered granite and concrete. The ornate brass-and-glass entry is gone, and I can see out onto the plaza in one direction or turn around and look out to the river in the other. Most of the roof is missing too. All I can do is just stand here a moment in the cold wind, this bizarre view mesmerizing me as I look one direction and then the other.

Passing through the hole where the front doors used to be and out onto the top of the museum's front steps, I see the bright sunlight illuminating a very hazy, empty place. A dust devil moves across the space where the plaza used to be.

A dust devil in December? So odd.

I watch it swirl silently across a barren plain, not believing what I am seeing. Everything in John Jay Plaza has vanished: the huge oaks, the fountain, the roads, all the cars, buses, and people are gone. Only a gray-white sandlot remains, with streaks that radiate out from the middle. The surrounding skyscrapers are mostly missing, with short wrecks of buildings with pieces of what look like dark, steel beams sticking up at odd angles, out of the ground all around the plaza. And… my God! There are fires everywhere around the square, nothing moving except the smoke and little, quiet swirls of dust here and there in the wind.

Then a thought comes to me. *I know what happened! A meteorite must have struck Yorksberg! I can tell exactly where it hit because I can see a crater right where the fountain used to be.*

Working my way down the busted-up steps to the street, I look up. There is a towering gray-white cloud high above. It seems to come up from the ground somewhere north of the city. I try to connect this cloud to the scene where the plaza used to be, and I begin to feel uneasy. I can see all the smoke and dust drifting that way, to the north.

Did that cloud come from the plaza?

My heart is beginning to race as I remember a movie from science class where the teacher called a cloud like the one I see a mushroom cloud, because of its mushroom shape. The cloud I can see is not exactly a mushroom shape, but I know that mushroom clouds are caused by nuclear explosions. A bomb! Maybe someone dropped a bomb on the city. This thought scares me more than pulling that huge wooden splinter out of my leg, so I turn and run with a sort of limping run, as best I can with my sore leg, west from the square along Museum Street. I have to get away from that strange desolation. I have to get help for Mrs. Thompson.

The going is easy at first, but I soon run into a real mess. The farther I go, the more wreckage fills the street. I see overturned burning cars, a bus smashed into the side of a crumpled building, telephone poles and trees down in a tangle of wires, and chunks of concrete and bricks everywhere. There are fires in almost every building, or what remains of the buildings, and sometimes I choke and my eyes burn because of the smoke and dust in the air. I have to pick and choose my way through the rubble. Sometimes I'm forced to go very slowly. I guess I am gun-shy of loose debris after my injury in the stairwell, but I keep thinking of Mrs. Thompson lying on that cold floor in the vault, and it keeps me moving.

Looking down Washington Ave, smaller side streets, and alleys, I can see entire buildings have been laid over, smashed by their fall into impassable wreckage.

Where are all the people? Are there people buried in that rubble?

The wreckage along Museum Street begins to decrease as I move farther west, approaching Jefferson Avenue, and I start to find pieces of bodies... and then even whole bodies. Most I can't look at. They are awful, as if they are from some horror story: torn, badly burned, and many naked, just lying in the street or among the rubble.

I try to help a man who had half his clothing burned away, because I think he is alive, but he isn't. Up close I can see blood still seeping from the stubs where his legs used to be. His face is very pale and I feel nauseous at the sight. I move away as quickly as I can. Ahead I see a younger man wearing a UPS uniform, sitting in an odd position against a building. Seeing someone alive makes me feel good, so I limp over to him to see if he needs help, but he is dead too. This scares me and I recoil from him and begin crying. I don't know why I'm crying, but I'm shaking too. A few moments pass before I can go on.

Not a hundred feet away is a big oak tree lying on its side. I make up my mind not to stop again. I have to help Mrs. Thompson, but I can see this small child, just a little naked boy, hanging in the tree branches. He reminds me of my sister's kid, and seeing the body stuck up there, looking very pale and dead, makes me sob again and start retching. I cry out "Why?" to no one. Something in me wants desperately to get the boy down and rush him to the nearest hospital, but I realize he is too high up and he looks dead anyway, so what's the point?

I calm down and try my cell phone again, but still there's no signal, so I leave the little boy and continue working my way through the mess in the street.

Far down the street I can see a street light still hanging across the street, and less debris. In fact, way down the street I can now see cars moving on Railroad Avenue and that makes me feel better.

At least the whole city was not destroyed.

There seem to be lots of cars moving over there, apparently all leaving the area in a slow-moving traffic jam.

People! Real, live people. I begin to pass live people, hundreds of them. People walking as if stunned, people sitting and holding awful wounds, people with burns and torn and missing clothing, small groups of walking wounded just standing around talking. I hear crying and moaning from some of the injured, people calling to each other, and some calling to me as I walk by. Down one of the alleys I hear a woman screaming over and over again. I don't want to know why she is screaming and I feel bad about not going to help her.

A block down the street I find a taxi driver leaning against his car, just staring at nothing. His windows are all gone.

"My cell phone doesn't work," I say. "Do you have a cell phone or a cab radio I can use to call for help?"

He turns toward me, and I see a horrible, blistered, peeling burn on his left cheek and arm.

"It don't work, sweetheart," he says with an odd voice. I think the burn hurts him bad. His hands are trembling. "Cab radio don't work neither."

He doesn't really look at me. Maybe he's blind? I don't want to ask, so I run on.

Some time later I find it is more difficult to move; my legs feel weak and tired. As I pass Adams Elementary there are a lot of people out front. I can see them carrying someone from the school to a car. I want to run over to them, but they are busy and I know the fire station is just a block away, so I continue toward South Railroad Avenue.

I finally reach South Railroad Avenue and can see the fire station. I begin running as fast as I can. My leg hurts like hell.

The firemen are trying to get their trucks out of the station, which looks like it partially collapsed on their emergency vehicles.

Reaching the station and out of breath, I tell one of the firemen, who is watching the attempts to free a firetruck, about Mrs. Thompson in the museum, and then, feeling dizzy, I lie in the middle of the street and start shaking. It feels strange to lie here in the sunshine, in my nice warm coat, shaking as if I'm freezing. I close my eyes, feeling the cold wind on my face, which feels good, and notice it seems so quiet now, so very quiet here. I feel so odd….

Analysis of Chapter 1 – What you need to know from this story.

If you have read this far, you might be thinking no one could survive a nuclear explosion that close. If this is your first impression, then consider the following.

Studies of the two Japanese cities bombed in World War II revealed that within a half-mile of ground zero, blast, radiation, or burns each by themselves were often enough to kill individuals.[16] These studies also show, however, that shelter of any kind: concrete buildings, wood-frame buildings, basements, subways, and even a decorative rock wall along the edge of a garden, significantly improved a person's ability to survive.

Distance from the explosion is also important. The following data from Hiroshima shows the average distance from ground zero (in miles) for 50% of the people to survive after 20 days.[17]

Outdoors	1.3 miles
Indoors	0.45 miles
Concrete building	0.12 miles
Overall	0.8 miles

Notice that half the people in concrete buildings only 633 ft. (192 m) on average from the Hiroshima bomb survived for more than 20 days. Some may have died later due to injuries or radiation, but neither of these affected our two ladies in the vault. So the answer is yes, people could survive that close to the bomb's explosion.

The survival of the curator and her college student protégé is an accident of timing and location. They are in a strong building made of concrete, marble, and granite slabs and they are below ground with a 1000 feet of earth between them and the bomb.[18]

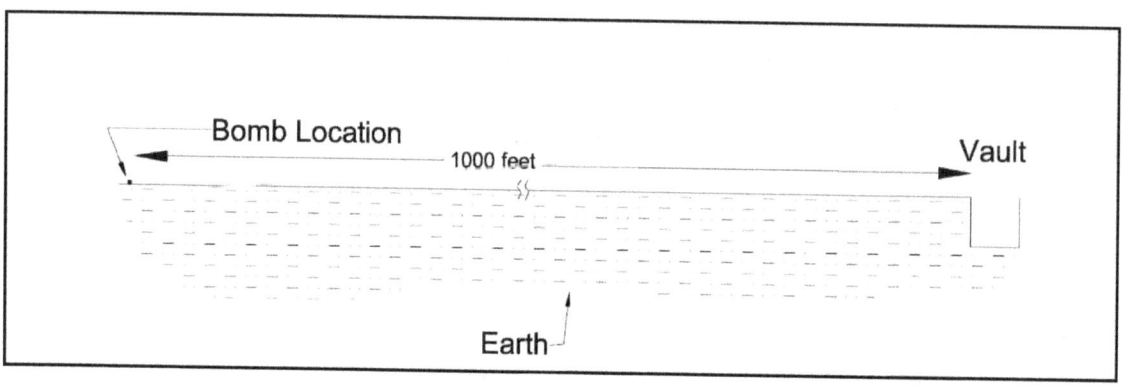

Earth Provides Shielding for the Vault

---

[16] Reference 1, 12.15.

[17] Reference 1, Table 12.17 - Note that these numbers are for the size of the weapon used on Hiroshima (or Yorksberg for this book). The distances will be larger for a weapon that yields more energy.

[18] Testing has shown that relatively small, heavy, well-designed, under-ground structures, a few crater radii from ground zero, suffered slight cracking, and severance of brittle external connections such as water and sewer piping. Reference 1, Table 6.108.

The earth shielded them from the flash of intense initial radiation that comes out the instant the bomb explodes, and it shielded them from much of the radioactive material created by the explosion. They also lived because they happened to be in an old bank vault that could withstand the bomb's blast and the collapse of the structure of the building.

The first sign Mindy sees that indicates something unusual is happening is the light in the hallway. If you are inside a structure at the instant a nuclear bomb goes off, it is possible that you will not see any light from the bomb; for example, in a basement, deep inside a building, or underground where there are no windows to allow the flash of the explosion to reach you. The first sign of trouble may be the floor shaking[19] or passage of the blast wave. The light Mindy saw is only a small part of the brilliant light created by the nuclear explosion, and it managed to reach the museum basement vault via the stairwell and reflection off the basement hallway walls.

The vault is so close to ground zero that the floor shakes hard enough to knock the two women down and topple furniture. This is the first peril Mindy survives. She is unaware that a tremendous blast of pressurized air from the explosion has passed above her and destroyed the museum.

There are many ways a nuclear explosion can harm people. We will talk about these throughout this book, but one of these is a secondary effect called entrapment, which Mindy and Mrs. Thompson narrowly escape. The blast dropped huge pieces of the building's marble floor into the basement hallway. One of these pieces prevents the vault door from opening fully. Had it blocked the door completely, the two women, although safe from the intense radiation at street level, would have died of dehydration or hyperthermia before rescuers found them.

When Mindy chooses to leave the vault, she unknowingly subjects herself to two potentially lethal dangers. One is the unstable nature of the damaged building. The risk of some debris falling on her in the hallway is significant.

The other danger is the radiation left behind by the bomb. This is such an important topic that a brief overview follows so you can appreciate the peril Mindy places herself in when she exits the vault.[20]

The nuclear reaction that gives the bomb its power causes atoms in the bomb to split. That splitting releases the energy that makes the explosion. But it also releases unstable atoms, which shoot out tiny atomic particles as these atoms continue to decay over and over until they eventually reach a stable condition. This process is called radioactive decay. As the hot mushroom cloud rises and cools, these unstable atoms coat every tiny piece of dust and rock thrown up in the cloud, and these pieces then fall onto the

---

[19] When the bomb explodes, it creates a fireball that rapidly expands in all directions. The expansion downward compresses the earth (this is called "airslap") and results in a crater and an earthquake-like wave that travels through the earth. Near ground zero the expanding fireball is faster than the ground seismic wave. As the fireball expansion slows to the speed of sound in air, it falls behind the seismic wave. Thus at significant distances from the point of the explosion (ground zero), the earth may shake before the air blast wave arrives. Reference 1, Sections 6.12 and 6.16. This shaking will likely be for a shorter time than a real earthquake.

[20] Radiation and radioactivity are discussed in greater detail throughout this book and in Appendix B1.

ground below the mushroom cloud. This dust and sand-like fallout from the cloud is highly radioactive and very dangerous right after the explosion.

When Mindy goes out into the hallway, these radioactive materials are in the air and on the floor. As the unstable atoms decay, the tiny atomic particles they shoot out rip clear through Mindy's body, causing cellular damage along their path of travel. She can't feel this damage because each particle's damage is so tiny, but it is real and **cumulative**. Cumulative means that once she gets some radiation damage, and then gets more damage, it adds up. A person will recover from this damage if there is enough time for the cells to heal, but receiving this damage too quickly can lead to enough damage to cause radiation sickness[21] and even death.

A small amount of radiation damage to Mindy's body with each hit is no problem, but the amount of unstable atoms left behind at the site of a nuclear explosion is so huge that the damage to Mindy's body quickly adds up as millions upon millions of radiation particles rip through her body tissues.

The amount of radiation damage a person receives is measured in rem.[22] Following are some numbers that will help you understand Mindy's peril and that of some of the other characters in this book:

150 rem – enough to make measurable changes in the blood of most people and make a few feel sick.

300 rem – enough to make most people sick and kill a few of the weaker individuals.

500 rem – enough to make everyone sick and kill half the people that receive this much radiation damage to their bodies if they get no medical care.

1000 rem – enough to generally kill everyone who receives this much radiation, even if they receive extraordinary medical care.

Mindy is essentially at ground zero; in other words, she is downtown, right where the bomb exploded. So how much radiation is at that location? Radiation levels measured near ground zero during atomic testing were seen to vary, depending on wind direction; method of detonation (underground, at ground level, mounted on a tower, fired from an atomic cannon, or air dropped); size of the weapon's yield (how powerful it is); and other factors. Levels as high as 3000 rem per hour shortly after the explosion have been seen following very high energy explosions (12 megaton). This would be an exposure rate of some 50 rem per minute, which would give Mindy a lethal dose (500 rem) of radiation in ten minutes.

---

[21] "Radiation sickness" shows up as a marked drop in the number of blood cells, which can weaken the immune system. It also shows up as gastrointestinal damage resulting in nausea, vomiting, loss of appetite, and abdominal pain. Radiation sickness is not a disease and cannot infect another person. It is not contagious, just as you can't get sunburn from someone who stayed out in the sun too long. Think of radiation sickness or radiation poisoning as "whole-body" sunburn, where tissue is damaged inside you.

[22] rem stands for "roentgen equivalent man." Just think of it as a number that stands for the amount of radiation damage to a human body.

> Mindy's lack of knowledge about nuclear bomb explosions can kill her, just as your lack of knowledge can lead to choices that can kill you.

Our bad guys (the PPF)[23] explode a bomb in our fictional city of Yorksberg that yields only .019 megatons of energy (19 kilotons of energy), and this should produce less radioactivity. But we will assume the bomb is a bit "dirty"[24] because it was exploded at ground level. So we assume the rate of radiation damage to Mindy's body in the museum hallway is 600 rem per hour. This is a bit arbitrary, but it will allow us to clearly present the hazard she faced and that you might face.[25]

Six hundred rem per hour is 10 rem each minute, and Mindy can thus accumulate a potentially lethal amount of radiation damage in 50 minutes. Mindy needs to get out of and away from the radiation, but she can't hear it, taste it, see it, smell it, or feel it, so she does not know she is in danger. Mindy's lack of knowledge about nuclear bomb explosions can kill her, just as your lack of knowledge can lead to choices that can kill you.

.

If you are in a city when a nuclear attack happens, you will not be able to see, smell, feel, or taste the radiation that will be around you, even though it will be there, and it will be damaging your body. If you do not have a radiation instrument to measure how much radiation you are receiving, the only thing that can warn you is your brain, which will contain the memory of what you have read in this handbook. In later chapters you will learn how to protect yourself by reducing your exposure.

Let's assume it takes Mindy eight minutes to get out of the basement, including the time she is injured and struggles on the stairs.[26] That's a total dose of 10 rem each minute times 8 minutes, or 80 rem total. We assume the radiation levels on John Jay Plaza outside the museum can be as high as 3000 rem per hour, or 50 rem per minute. So as she emerges from the museum and stands there for two minutes, trying to figure out what happened, she accumulates an additional 100 rem of tissue damage (50 rem per minute times 2 minutes). Her total exposure is now 80 plus 100 or 180 rem.

Remember that the radioactive materials fall out of the mushroom cloud, so if you travel up wind or cross wind from the explosion, your radiation exposure rate will decrease. As Mindy travels west, down Museum Avenue (cross wind), the radiation levels decrease and she gets less radiation damage per minute as she moves farther away from the plaza.

---

[23] PPF = The "People's Powerful Fist". An imaginary organization of terrorists created for this book. Appendix D1 gives a fictional account of who they are and how they obtain a bomb.

[24] Dirty bombs are ones that tend to leave behind a larger quantity of radioactive material.

[25] Most people don't know the American military leadership in World War II specifically chose to explode the two bombs dropped on Japan at altitudes above 1000 feet. This was done to greatly reduce the radioactive fallout.

[26] The wood splinter that punctured Mindy's leg probably had radioactive materials on it. If this radioactive dirt is left inside her leg, it will continue to irradiate the tissue in her leg from very close range. She needs medical help to clean out this wound and may even need surgery to remove the offending radioactive materials or the wound may never heal and will be subject to developing cancer at some future time.

The radiation intensity is still dangerous, but the only way to know how dangerous is to measure the amount of radiation using a radiation instrument (more about this later).

Mindy emerges from the museum to find a blasted wasteland. Some may doubt that the museum could survive a nuclear blast several hundred feet from it; however, photographs of the bomb damage in Japan clearly show the concrete and reinforced steel buildings remained standing after the blast. They were gutted and the roofs were gone, but the concrete structure remained.

Many of the old buildings in the downtown areas of our cities are substantially strong because of the materials used to construct them and the large mass of their walls. No one could survive outside shelter this close to a nuclear explosion.

The presence of dust after the explosion is very significant. Many of us remember the collapse of the World Trade Center after the 9/11 attacks. We need to remember the huge amount of dust stirred up by that event, how it lingered, and how harmful it was to those who breathed it, with some of the health effects appearing years later. A nuclear explosion will cause even more dust and smoke, which will have the same long-term health effects as the dust at the World Trade Center, but with the added hazard that much of that dust may be radioactive.

Test Explosion

This is a picture of a bomb being tested in the Nevada desert.[27] Note the huge amount of dust and smoke at the ground level around the base of the stem of the mushroom-shaped cloud. This weapon yielded a bit more energy than the bomb in our fictional story. The fireball may be as much as 900 feet in diameter (three football fields placed end-to-end). The deeper dust at ground level extends at least a quarter mile from ground zero, and the lesser dust farther out. This dust has been lifted scores of feet into the air, having been disturbed by the passage of the blast wave.

As a side comment, you can get an idea of how hot the center of the fireball is by considering that this picture was taken in sunlight and that the light from the center of the fireball is still able to illuminate dust and falling particles in the air surrounding the upper mushroom stem enough to make it visible. This photo was probably taken some 10 to 15 seconds after the explosion.

Avoid as much dust as you can, but you probably cannot avoid all of it if you have to move through the outdoors to a shelter or to escape from the city. If you have to breathe in a dusty area, even if it is light dust, do it through a filter. Anything will help. Several layers of wet undershirt or towel over your mouth and nose will remove some dust as you breathe. You can shake, brush, or wash particles off your hair and skin and you can leave contaminated[28] clothing outside the shelter where it won't harm anyone. You cannot get away from your lungs, however, if they become contaminated with radioactive dust.

Testing has shown the human nose can filter out almost all dust particles larger than 10 microns, and about 95% of particles exceeding 5 microns,[29] so lung accumulation of radioactive dust is limited by the body's own self-defense mechanisms.

The blast has blown the square clean, but farther down the street the debris and rubble make her travel difficult, which causes Mindy to move slower and therefore to accumulate more radiation damage. This will be a problem for folks trying to leave the bombed area, particularly if they are injured and cannot move quickly. If a good shelter is available, it might be better to shelter out of the intense radiation for a day or so before attempting to leave the downtown area. This is because radioactivity decreased with time. This technique is covered in detail in Chapter 2 ("Hiding from Zoomies"), which spotlights Yorksberg citizen Sigmund Johanson.

It is likely the debris layout will reflect the outward nature of the blast wave; unlike the collapse of the World Trade Center, falling debris from the high buildings will likely be

---

[27] Test photos are available via many World War II, national archives, or historical sites. Photo courtesy of National Nuclear Security Administration / Nevada Site Office.

[28] Anything with radiation emitting dirt on it is said to be *contaminated*.

[29] Most of the particles falling out of the mushroom cloud after a nuclear explosion within the first 24 hours will be larger than 10 microns. Reference 1, 12.167. In Mindy's case, the dust present just outside the museum is due more to the destruction of the building and the passing of the blast wave than from the fallout, because the smaller fallout particles are lofted high into the air and carried downwind before descending. Most of Mindy's exposure is due to the larger radioactive particles that immediately fall back to earth as the mushroom cloud rises over the city. They are sand-like and under her feet, not in the air.

tossed outward from the point of explosion and rain down on other parts of the city. This is another hazard for those out in the open.

Structures between the blast and your location in the downtown area of the large city may provide some light, heat, and radiation shielding, which will be advantageous to survival of people downtown.

Our scenario included a 15-mph wind blowing northward across the city. This moves the ground-level dust from the explosion a quarter mile every minute. This is why Mindy sees the cloud north of the city by the time she gets out of the damaged museum. Ten minutes after the explosion, the lower part of the mushroom cloud is ~2.5 miles from the plaza, however dust will remain in the city due to turbulence of the wind blowing around structures.

When Mindy encounters people moving about, it is a sign she has moved far enough from ground zero to where those with any shelter at all could survive. She has entered the "zone of survivable destruction," which will be discussed in more detail later.[30]

That the people are collecting in groups to talk about what happened is evidence of the abysmal civil defense training our state and local governments give to the populace. Because of the lack of knowledge, most of these people will become very sick or die in the days, weeks, and months following the blast. These people should be moving quickly to shelters or out of town. Under these circumstances, police and fire departments will be in a state of disarray and unable to immediately coordinate the mass transit of a hundred thousand people out of the downtown district. Folks will not be able to count on communications from authorities on what to do. Busses and taxis will not be running, and the subway may be non-functional.

If you are one of those who walks through some portion of the downtown area of a large city each day, your survival will be enhanced if you know where the habitable underground areas are in your city. Take time to scope out what you pass by. Check out the buildings and stores. You don't need to find an actual bank vault. How about basements? Where is the access to these basements? Are there any public buildings that have underground areas such as a public library or a utility building? Check out the subways. Even if some dust can enter a subway, the radiation levels in the subway will be much lower than on the street.

Drinking water is the most important item in a shelter. Is there water available in places where you might shelter? Keep your eyes open and your inquisitive nature active and you will be surprised at what you find underground in a big city. You may even be able to find buildings that were designated fallout shelters in the 1950s and 1960s. These may be ideal shelters even today, although you might have to coax city officials to allow food and water to be stocked there.

Keep in mind that radiation levels continually decrease after the explosion. If you can spend two days in some underground shelter, even if it is just a hellhole with little food,

---

[30] The zone of survivable destruction is where the city is destroyed but survival is possible. Closer in, survival is not usually possible. Farther out from the annular-shaped (ring-shaped) zone of survivable destruction, almost everyone survives.

water, or comfort, and then walk out[31] of the radiation zone, you will save yourself hundreds of rem of radiation damage.

The debris in a city after a nuclear explosion will be similar to the debris found near the site of the World Trade Center following the 9/11 attacks, except it will cover a larger area. The rubble, fires, and radioactivity will prevent rescue workers from entering and exiting the area efficiently and safely for some time. This means the only viable method of assuring the maximum number of people in a downtown area will survive is to prepare sheltering places that are reasonably close to where the survivors live and work. They will need to move to these shelters and stay in them for several days to allow the radiation intensity to decay (decrease) before venturing out to escape. Are the facilities in your city ready and maintained? Are the people in your city educated and knowledgeable about nuclear bomb effects and where the shelters are? Ideally the shelters will be public knowledge.[32]

The idea that a nuclear explosion is so bad that there is no reason to prepare to survive it is a self-fulfilling death wish. It is stinking thinking that has resulted in our city dwellers living without adequately prepared shelters and training, assuring that tens of thousands who could survive will not survive. This needs to change. Our city leaders should be planning for survival, not capitulation and death.

The condition of the fire station in this story makes the point that rescue and fire control equipment may be unusable due to collapsed structures and debris. A bulldozer may be as valuable to a fire department as a pumper truck under these circumstances. There will be more on this idea and about the positioning of emergency equipment and fuel supplies later in this handbook.[33]

Our heroine Mindy received quite a large dose of radiation during the time she climbed out of the museum, stood and surveyed the plaza, and then traveled out of the downtown area through much contaminated rubble that slowed her movement. What radiation is and how it damages people will be covered in more detail in later chapters and Appendix B1.

Mindy became sick from her radiation exposure within hours of reaching the fire station. She was evacuated to an out-of-county hospital and died there a few weeks later of complications related to her radiation exposure. Those who receive less radiation may see

---

[31] How far you will have to walk can be guessed. A walk of two miles would put you a good distance from the radioactive fallout for a bomb yielding the energy of the Yorksberg device, although fallout patterns can be capricious. A much larger bomb (say 5 megatons of TNT equivalent) would destroy a larger area and require a longer walk-out, but is unlikely to be used by terrorists due to its size and weight.

[32] What if 150 people run into a shelter that was designed only for 50, leaving a shelter designed for 100 mostly empty? These sorts of problems must be worked out ahead of time by communication with the public.

[33] Reference 1, Section 7.69. At Hiroshima much of the fire department's equipment was damaged in the collapse of fire houses. As a result, more than three-quarters of the fire personnel were not able to respond to alarms or visible fires. In Hiroshima, as will be true in your city, debris made many fires inaccessible. The same thing happened at Nagasaki, where one of the fire companies from a non-damaged area was not able to get any closer than 1.25 miles from the point of the explosion.

the onset of symptoms sometime later, and their chances of survival are proportionally better.

It is important to note that highly contaminated people can be dangerous to other people. People are "contaminated" if they have radioactive material on them. These people must be separated from others until they can wash off the radioactive particles or their mere proximity may damage those around them. Remember that being exposed to radiation after the explosion does not make you radioactive. It is the radioactive dust and dirt on you that gives off (emits) the radiation.

By the time Mindy reached the fire station, she had received more than 500 rem[34] of radiation, most which she got while climbing out of the museum, looking at the plaza, and then working her way through the debris within a half mile of the blast point.[35]

The museum Curator, April Thompson, was rescued by the fire department several days later, thanks to Mindy's message. Her fractured ankle kept her in place, preventing her from climbing out of the wrecked museum and getting exposed to high levels of radiation. Did she receive some radiation damage? Yes, but her location in the vault below ground prevented her from life-threatening radiation exposure and she suffered no symptoms.

By delaying the rescue for several days, her rescue personnel also did not receive life-threatening radiation exposure.

It is people like Mindy this book can save. For want of knowledge she survived the explosion of the nuclear bomb but did not survive the attack. She should have stayed in the vault with Mrs. Thompson for two or three days before venturing out.

Now check your knowledge by taking the quiz that follows. There will be a different quiz for each chapter.

Chapter 1 Quiz   (Answers are in Appendix A1)

    1.   How do radioactive materials hurt you?

    2.   What is the difference between radioactive materials and radiation?

    3.   How much radiation does it take to kill you?

    4.   A nuclear explosion produces which of the following?
   a. Tremendous heat
   b. Bright light
   c. Radioactive materials
   d. A powerful blast wave
   e. All of the above

    5.   What killed Mindy Walker? (identify two causes)

---

[34] Death from radiation damage depends on several variables, but in general acute doses above 600 rem are almost always fatal without treatment. Doses above 1000 rem are always fatal.

[35] Reference 1, Section 9.61. "A considerable quantity of radioactivity from a surface burst is contained in the fallback in the crater and in the ejecta scattered in all directions around ground zero."

In the next chapter you will visit what some would call a tough old coot with a few skills that most of us do not have. He will use his knowledge to survive an otherwise lethal amount of radiation. What's the trick? Read on and learn some things about dealing with that scary, invisible radiation from the bomb's fallout in the chapter titled "Hiding from Zoomies."

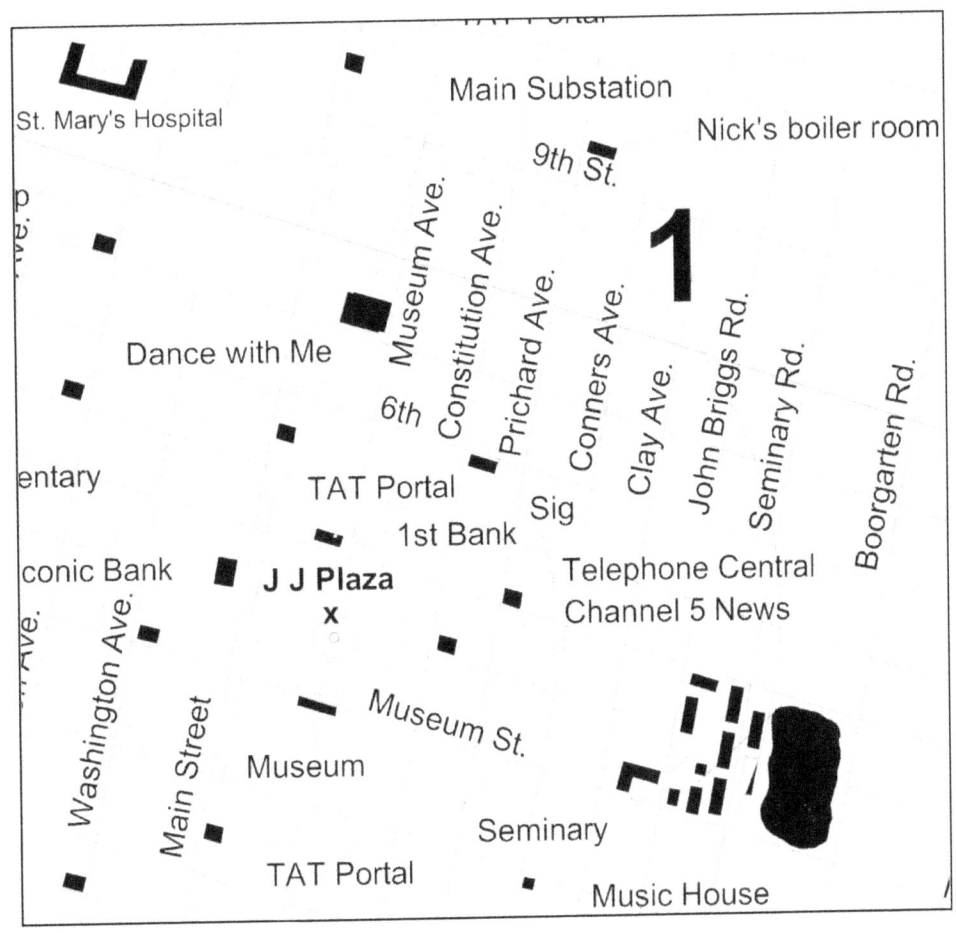

2 - Sigmund Johanson – Hiding from Zoomies (0.5 miles)

Sig enjoyed the cold, sunny December day as he approached the corner of 6th and Clay, unaware that within ten minutes a simple phone call would save his life. He shifted the bag of deli goodies in his arm and pressed the button on the side of the light pole at the corner. The small sign across the street blinked the universal sign for "Don't walk."

"W2GLS, this is W2XXR; you on frequency, Sig?"[36] Roy's voice said in Sig's ear piece. Reaching down, Sig pushed a button on the side of the small radio on his belt.

"W2XXR W2GLS, good afternoon, Roy. I thought you might call," Sig said into a tiny microphone clipped to his coat.

"Marge and I would like to invite you over for dinner and the big game. You want to have some good food and then watch my Gators trash your sorry Volunteers?"

---

[36] The call signs used in this story are just typical examples. They were picked because, at the time of this writing, they were not assigned to any radio amateur as far as the author could ascertain. As used in this story they are by no means connected to any real person, real organization, or real city.

"I wouldn't miss it," Sig said. "I'll be there, but I think we'll see a gator with a few musket balls in him by the end of the game. What time?"

"Dinner's on at six, but you come on over early and have a cold one with me."

Sig walked out onto the street as the small sign beckoned "walk."

Sig thought of the crying towel he and Roy sent back and forth each year depending on whose team won. He smiled, remembering the pleasure of giving the towel to his good friend last year.

"Deal, and you get out that crying towel; you're gonna need to wash it and hang it up on your den wall for another year."

"Hah! You hope! See you, Sig. This is W2XXR on the side for a bit."

"Later, old man. W2GLS QRT."[37]

Sig smiled again. He had been expecting this invitation and had been looking forward to it no matter which team won. He saw his neighbor Mrs. Birchfield coming toward him and stopped to talk as she approached.

"Good afternoon, Alice."

"Same to you, and Merry Christmas. Looks like you have been where I am headed. Antonio's Deli?"

"The one and only. They have the best German sausage. Are you staying in town for the holidays?"

"Oh my goodness, yes, and I am so glad you asked. I forgot a letter I intended to mail on the way to the deli. I'll walk back with you to fetch it."

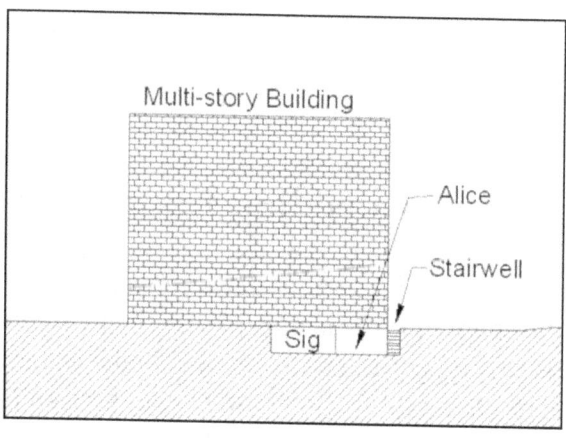

Sig's and Alice's belowground apartments are accessible from the street level via a stairwell.

Reaching their building and following her down the concrete stairs leading to their apartments' basement entrance, he entered the door she held open.

"Thanks, Alice," he said, and once inside walked past her apartment to his own. Setting his packages down on the table in the short entry hallway, he fished out his keys and

---

[37] QRT is a code sign for "I'll be off the radio for a while."

opened his door. Once inside his apartment, he put away the items he had bought and then started to go out to the mailbox when the phone rang.

Sig shut the apartment door to keep the heat in and picked up the phone.

Glancing at the caller ID he said, "Hello, Melissa," in a cheery voice.

"Hi, Dad. How are you doing?"

"Feeling well. Just got back from the deli. How is Vern?" he said, unzipping the front of his coat to get a little cool air. His apartment felt too warm after that brisk walk outside.

"We are both fine and the kids too, although Becky has the sniffles. I kept her home today, but from the energy she has I don't think she is very sick. She is wearing me out."

A quick, brilliant, blue-white light flooded Sig's apartment at the same time it jumped and shook. The world filled with horrendous noise, and Sig felt himself tumble to the floor.

A few moments later, dazed, he picked himself up on one elbow. The lights were out and he could see the signal strength indicator on his cell phone had gone to zero. He was holding a dead phone in his hand. For half a minute he distinctly heard sounds like heavy objects falling outside, and then it became very quiet, except for a car alarm sounding off somewhere outside.

Rising, and moving into the bedroom, he pulled back the partially dislodged curtain and looked up at the 12" X 24" window at the top of the wall. It was intact, so he pulled up a chair and stood on it.

Looking out, he saw an alley full of concrete and wood debris. The top part of a utility pole hung about three feet from the window, its cross-arms twisted and broken, still dangling wires, and surrounded by dust.

Sig said something under his breath.
Must have been a large airplane crash. Hit the building or in the street just outside.

He was not satisfied with this assumption. The light he had seen puzzled him. He had followed the bombing of Japan during the end of World War II with great interest, and as Secretary of the local RACES[38] organization, he remembered civil defense films he had seen.
Could this have been a nuclear explosion?
He doubted it, but held the doubt back.

Telephone pole damage 0.8 miles from Hiroshima ground zero.[39]

---

[38] The "Radio Amateur Civil Emergency Service" (RACES) is a standby radio emergency service provided by amateur radio operators. It stems from Part 97.407 of the Federal Communications Commission (FCC) rules and regulations governing amateur radio in the United States.
[39] *The Effects of Nuclear Weapons*, 1977, Glasstone and Dolan, Figure 5.98.

That bluish light, it could have been the utility pole arcing outside in the alley, but the ground had shaken. No electric arc could have done that.

Going to his front door, he had just put his hand on the doorknob when someone pounded on the door and he heard his name being called. He opened the door to find Alice. She had a distraught look on her face.

"Are you all right?" she said with concern.

"Yah. I'm okay," he assured her. "What happened?"

"My window broke," she said. "I don't know why. My vision is full of spots. That light was so bright."

He followed her into her apartment and found that indeed her window had been broken. Several fist-sized pieces of concrete lay on her floor. He could see masses of debris outside her window similar to what he had seen from his alley window. Funny though, he could not smell aviation gas, nor could he see any sign of the general fire one would expect from an airplane crash.

He did smell something odd, however, the smell of ozone in the cold winter air pouring into her apartment through the debris-filled window well and broken glass, a faint smell, but unmistakable. Whatever had happened had been a high-energy event. His doubts about this being a nuclear explosion began to fade into a hunch, and if true, he and Alice had to do something quickly.

"Alice, grab your winter coat; I will be back in a minute." He ran back into his place and got two sheets of poster board and some duct tape. Returning to her apartment, he quickly taped the poster board over the busted window. He then shut her door and took her back into his apartment.

Alice looked at him inquisitively. "Shouldn't we leave this place or at least call 911?"

"Let me check something before we go out. Calling 911 is a good idea. Please do that."

Going to his small storage closet, he pulled out the portable radiation survey meter he stored for the amateur radio club. He set it on the 0.1 R/hr scale and turned it on. The needle immediately went all the way up—off scale[40]. He switched the survey meter to the next higher scale, 1 roentgens/hr. Again it went off scale. He switched it up to the 100 roentgens scale. The needle indicated 45 R and hung there. When he moved toward the bedroom window the device quickly went off scale, so he retreated to the living room.

"The phones don't work," she said. "So much for 911, and I tried your radio to see if I could get some news, but the local stations are not there."

"That gives us some important information," he said.

"Which is?"

---

[40] The term "off scale" just means the needle on the meter goes to the top of the scale and then past the top end (i.e., off the end of the scale). This means the signal the meter is trying to display is too strong, and the instrument user must switch the instrument to a less sensitive range to try to bring the meter's needle back "on scale."

"This is not an event local to just our neighborhood. A wide area has been affected. The lack of local radio stations you found also confirms this. In fact, I think it was a nuclear explosion!" he said.

"How do you know that?"

"There is lots of radiation. Look!" He showed her the instrument's reading.

"What does that number mean?" she said, pointing at the meter.

"It's a dose rate. It's how much radiation is passing through us each hour. To understand the meaning of these numbers you have to know how much is bad."

"I'm all ears. Suddenly this radiation stuff is very important to me, and I am certainly not going anywhere."

"As a crude rule of thumb, when a large number of people get hit by 500 R (rem) of these zoomies, all will become very ill and half will die."

"Zoomies?" she said.

"It's a pet name for radiation. The guys who work with nuclear power call radiation 'zoomies' because radiation moves very fast, and it's easier to say 'zoomies' than to say 'fast-moving atomic particles and gamma rays.'"

"So if we get 500 R of these zoomies we are sick or dead?" she said.

"Five hundred is very serious. Four hundred, less serious but many sick people. Two to three hundred, sick but not as bad and few deaths. Below 200, little visible effects."

"Can doctors do anything to help?"

"Yes, the medical arts can make a big difference. Doctors know how radiation makes us sick, so they can compensate for it to some extent."

"So tell me what that thing is." She pointed at the yellow box he held. "Is that a Geiger counter, and does it count Geigers?"

Sig chuckled. "So many questions. No, it is not a Geiger counter. Geiger is the name of a man. He and another feller named Müller invented the Geiger–Müller tube, which can sense individual particles of radiation that pass through it. That's why a Geiger counter makes a clicking sound. Each click is one atomic particle passing through. Works good for prospecting for uranium, but it won't work in our situation."

"Why not?"

"Too much radiation. With hundreds of thousands of particles flying through a Geiger-Muller tube, it gets overloaded. Basically it gets hit by more radiation before it finished the click from a previous piece of radiation, so it does nothing. Scientists say it's 'saturated' when it is in that condition."

"Got it," Alice said. "A Geiger counter is no good to us after a nuclear bomb goes off. So what's that yellow box with the meter on it?"

"It's called a radiation survey meter. This device measures dose rate, which means at any given instant it shows us how much radiation we would get over a period of one hour. Like right here." He went to the inside wall of his apartment. "This is as far under the building and away from the street one can get and we have 9 rem/hr. Over by the door…" he went to the entryway door to his apartment, "it is seeing about 29 per hour."

"That's too much radiation, and I don't like that," she said. "Sig, we need to get out of here."

"I agree, but outside is much worse."

"How do you know that?"

"Where do you think the radiation is coming from? That explosion must have dropped all kinds of radioactive material on the buildings above us and in the streets around us. Here, let me prove it." He led her to his bedroom. As he approached the alley window at the top of his bedroom wall, the needle went off scale high again. He set the instrument to its highest range.

"Watch this," he said. Holding the radiation survey instrument so she could see the meter, he slowly raised it up toward the ceiling. The needle climbed and then finally went off scale.

"The dose rates are above 500 rem/hr outside. Down here in my basement apartment most of the zoomies are flying over our heads, so it is much better to stay here for a while.

She didn't say anything, and he could see the worry in her face.

"We will hide from the zoomies as best we can," he said, and led her back to the kitchen area. There he opened the storage/pantry closet and stuck the instrument in. He had to click the instrument down several scales.

"Ah, just under 5 rem/hr in here. This is the safest place in my apartment and this is where we must go. The name of the game is to catch as few zoomies as we can."

"You want me in that closet with you?" she said. "Why, Mr. Johanson, I thought you would never ask." She gave him a half smile.

He grinned.

She's worried, but a strong lady. Sense of humor at a difficult time is a good sign.

"I'll behave myself," he assured her.

"Here, take the vacuum cleaner, broom, and a mop, and just set them anywhere. I'll get the cushions, some pillows, and a blanket or two." When he returned he found her sweeping the pantry.

"Bachelors," she said, shaking her head.

He placed the cushions on the swept floor of the pantry, placed a pillow at each end, and tossed the blankets on top.

"Welcome to my humble abode," he said, offering her the seat farthest from the door. "It's tight and dark, but with a flashlight we can see well enough, and it is warmer inside."

"That's right," she said; "I forgot the heat is off. The apartment will soon be too cool for comfort."

"See if you can get any news about what happened," he said, handing her a portable, multi-band radio.

He watched her extend the antenna and turn the radio on, and he listened while he got some paper and a ruler from his desk. "I'll graph our dose rate every half hour, and our cumulative dose."

She quickly found a station on the AM dial that was broadcasting a news flash about Yorksberg.

"At approximately two-thirty this afternoon," the announcer said, "a very large explosion is reported in the downtown area of Yorksberg. Witnesses described it as a nuclear explosion similar to ones they have seen in films, with a large mushroom-shaped cloud rising high above the city. There is no word yet on casualties, but from the descriptions people are giving we expect the worst. So far we have been unable to contact any authority, police or fire, in Yorksberg. Phone lines are down, cell phones are not working, and we are too far away to pick up police radio.

Wait, one moment…. I have just been handed a message phoned in from a local amateur radio station that says ham radio operators in Yorksberg are reporting high radiation levels. If this is true, that would confirm this is a nuclear explosion."

Sig listened to the various stations Alice tuned in, and after a while he stood up and looked through the pantry shelving.

"What are you up to now?" Alice said, turning the radio down slightly.

He reached back into a rather deep shelf of the pantry and pulled out two bottles of water. "Radiation free," he said.

"Right," she said. He could see she didn't believe him. "I suppose the radiation doesn't go through water?"

"Goes right through and doesn't hurt it a bit. Zoomies go through things, and don't make them radioactive or poisonous when they pass through."

"Here, take this iodine tablet." He handed her a pill, popped one into his month, and swallowed it with a chug of water. He then placed the iodine pill bottle back into his RACES kit.

"What is this?" she said. "Why the pills?"

It's nice to have an interested student.

"Some of the radioactive material the bomb released is radioactive iodine atoms. Our bodies collect iodine from the food and water we take in and concentrate it in the thyroid gland. This is a natural, harmless process necessary for good health, but when there is radioactive iodine in the air or water and we take it in, the body concentrates the radioactive iodine in the thyroid too. Concentrated radioactive iodine in the thyroid will damage that organ and possibly cause cancer. So we take pills of normal iodine to saturate our systems with the non-radioactive iodine. The body processes will have more of the good atoms to choose from, and less of the radioactive atoms will get stored. The extra good iodine we take is harmless to us."[41]

"What's our zoomie count now?" Alice said.

Sig looked at his watch, which said 9:00 p.m.

"Well I have good news. We aren't going to die or even get sick. Look."

He showed her the graph he had been drawing. "Right after the explosion we measured a radiation dose rate of 5 R/hr in this pantry. It crept up to 50 R/hr about a half hour after the explosion."

"It went up to fifty! Why didn't you tell me?" She had a frown on her face.

"I didn't want to worry you. The fallout from the bomb continued to rain down on our neighborhood for a while until the radiation reaching this pantry built up to a peak 50 rem/hr."

---

[41] Following a radiological event like a nuclear explosion, other hazardous radioactive elements will be present. Among these are thallium and cesium-137. Prussian blue can be used to remove these radioactive elements from the body. Search for "Prussian Blue," "FDA," and "Questions and Answers" to learn about this.

"That could kill us in ten hours! I knew we should have made a run for it!" He hadn't seen her so agitated.

"Please calm down; we are okay. Look; we couldn't run for it because the radiation outside was probably 3000 R, or 50 a minute."

He let that sink in for a moment before continuing.

"If we got tangled up in debris while trying to walk to a low radiation zone, we could easily get way too much radiation exposure. If it took ten minutes to walk out, that's ten times 50 R or 500 R."

"And half the people that get that much die," she said.

"Very good," he said. "The fact is we don't know how much debris we would have to work our way through, and actually we don't yet know which way to go is safe. What if we happened to travel in the direction the fallout cloud drifted? We would never get out of it. Besides, nature has a better plan."

"A better plan? Like maybe the radiation will just go away?"

He smiled at her. "You are closer than you think. It's the old rule-of-seven. By the natural law of radioactive decay, whenever the elapsed time increases by seven times, the radiation strength will decrease to one-tenth of what it started out at. Our case is the perfect example. At three o'clock, I measured a dose rate in this closet of 50 R. That's because much of the heavy dust in the mushroom cloud fell right back down around us. The zoomies outside, I'm guessing here, were probably 3000 rem/hr."

"Oh my God," she said.

"No fear. Take a look the radiation dose rate numbers I have been collecting.

"As you can see, this trend shows the radiation decreasing back down just below 5 R/hr. Using the rule-of-seven, if we wait here for seven times seven or forty-nine hours, then the rate will be about 0.5 R/hr inside the pantry."

Time	Dose Rate R/hr
3:30	50
4:30	21.8
5:30	13.4
6:30	9.5
7:30	7.2
8:30	5.8
9:30	4.8

"Okay, smart man; convert that last idea to something useful. I really don't want to be here. Can't we just make a run for it?"

"Exactly my intention. The trick is to do it without exposing ourselves to high levels of radiation. The point is that here in this pantry the radiation levels are very low compared to outside. We can stay here many days if we need to. Now let's look at the outside."

He scribbled on his paper.

"You noticed that each time I took a reading in the pantry I also went to the bedroom window and held the meter up as close as possible. Let's assume I measured 3000 R/hr outside at the peak—like one hour after the bomb went off. Then 49 hours later the rule-of-seven shows it will be about 30 rem/hr. If we can walk out of Yorksberg through a 30 rem/hr radiation zone in less than a couple of hours, we should show no symptoms."

She smiled. "That's incredible. You mean if we panicked right after the bomb went off and tried to run out of danger we would get fried, but if we just sit here underground for two days we can walk out unharmed?"[42]

"Bingo. You win the prize," Sig said.

"Oh my God," Alice said, covering her mouth with her hand.

"What?" Sig said.

"I just thought of the thousands of people in this city who didn't know that simple rule. They probably tried to get out of the city instead of sheltering in a hole somewhere."

"I know," Sig said. "I have tried to teach this information. We held regular RACES civil defense lectures, but very few people came."

The next morning Sig woke up to a very cold pantry and looked at his watch.

"What time is it?" Alice said.

"About 8 o'clock," he said. "Time for some breakfast."

"Would you mind if I fix breakfast? I am tired of sitting around doing nothing, even if it does save my life."

"Don't mind at all. The food in here and in the fridge is yours for the picking. We could cook on my camp stove, but that is not a good idea closed up in my apartment. We could survive the bombing and kill ourselves with carbon monoxide."

"Okay, boss."

"I'll see if I can make an antenna for my radio. The one on the roof is apparently gone."

"What are the radiation levels?"

"Down. We are seeing less than 2 R an hour in our pantry. By the way, our total dose so far is about 82 R."

"How did you figure that out?"

"There is a simple formula to estimate it. The most you can get from time "t" to infinity is five times the starting dose rate times the time.[43] In our case 5 times 50 times 1 hour gives about 250 rem. But the total dose starting now with time equal 7 hours is 5 times 4.8 times 7 or 168. The difference, 250 −168 is our total dose so far, 82 R."

"And," she added, "according to what you said yesterday, that dose should not even make us sick."

"You'd probably have to go to the hospital and get some fancy blood tests to even see the effect," he said.

---

[42] *Concise Encyclopedia of Nuclear Energy*, D. E. Barnes, Interscience Publishers, A division of John Wiley & Sons, Inc., New York, 1962. p. 616, last paragraph.

[43] *Ibid,* p. 617, second paragraph.

Breakfast behind him, Sig took some tools, wire, and his trusty duct tape roll back into the pantry.

"You are always up to something, Sig," Alice said. "What is it this time?"

"I'm going to build a two-meter antenna on this broom handle. We know from the radio that the cloud drifted north, so we want to go east, south, or west when we get out. South is no good because that will take us to the center of the explosion. East runs us into the Atlantic Ocean. So the only choice is west. Before we go, I would like to know more about routes out of this area, or maybe even find someone to pick us up."

Thirty minutes later he had it done. "Here she is," he said, holding up a crude antenna mounted on the end of a broom handle. He hooked it up to his two-meter rig. Alice watched as he stood on a chair, and while she held the end of the broomstick, he opened his bedroom window at the top of the wall and worked the antenna out the window, laying it across the rubble in the alley. He wedged the base end of the stick up against the outside wall of the building above them. The antenna lay more horizontal than vertical, but when he switched on the radio it came alive.

They listened and he quickly identified several of the hams on that particular frequency as member of his RACES team.

"What's all that Morse code someone keeps sending?" Alice said.

"That's the Yorksberg Amateur Radio Club's repeater at the university. That means the bomb just got the downtown. The university across the river in south Yorksberg is still there and they have power. So they are either running an emergency generator or using batteries."

He had heard Roy and so keyed his mic. "W2ZZR, this is W2GLS. Do you copy?"

The surprised, almost ecstatic voice of Roy came back. "Sig, you old coot! We thought you were a goner. Where are you?"

"Downtown Yorksberg. In my 6th Street walk-down."

"Damn hot downtown. You got your meter on it?" Roy said seriously.

"Yep," Sig shot back. "We are seeing about 4.5 R/hr in my pantry closet right now. The building is doing a great job of shielding us."

"You got 'us' there?" Roy said.

"Yah, Alice Birchfield is alive and well in nuclear hell. Let her folks know. Now tell me how you are going to get us out of here. Have any lead-lined tanks?"

"Roger on Birchfield. We'll get that to the state's missing-person coordinator immediately. About that tank, I don't know, but I will let the National Guard know."

"Let my daughter know too," Sig added.

"If you have a Sonnetcell phone, you call her compliments of Sonnetcell. Those boys got their system back on the air in record time."

"Okay Roy, thanks. I'll call. You call too, in case I can't reach her. Thanks, buddy."

"I got other traffic to handle. We are mobile up on Copper Ridge. Break in if you need to and I'll get you that tank if I can. W2ZZR out."

"W2GLS will be off the air to conserve batteries. We'll come up on the net every half hour." They heard Roy key his mic twice in acknowledgement.

Alice handed him his cell phone. "You better call her," she said and left the room to return to the closet.

Sig followed her into the closet, ever mindful of the radiation.

He dialed and the phone rang once.

"Hello," Melissa's voice sounded tired.

"Hey, Missy, it's your dad. I'm okay," Sig teared up.

"Oh my God!" he heard her say, and then he heard her yell to others in her house. *The family must have gathered.* "It's dad! He says he is okay!" Then she said "Where are you? I gave up calling you at midnight."

Sig spent the next ten minutes explaining how her earlier phone call had saved his life.

A half hour later he turned his rig on and heard a call for him.

"W2GLS, this is RACES control, W2ZZR."

"W2ZZR, W2GLS. Howdy, Roy. What do you have for me?"

"National Guard has a couple of contaminated vehicles and they are using these to get into the area to pick up survivors while rotating drivers out to limit doses. Can you walk fast?"

"Fast as a 60-year-old retired school teacher," he shot back. Alice grinned at him.

"Right. They tell me the street level is still above 60 R/hr in places downtown. You will get less total dose if you stay put 24 more hours. Then walk to Conners and 9th. They will pick you up there. Ariel photos show lots of debris in your area, so don't try to go out on Prichard or Constitution. Conners is your best path. I'll tell them 2 p.m. Expect it to take a half hour to get to the pickup point."

"I copy, Conners to 9th Street. 2 p.m."

The next day at the appointed time Sig poured water on a couple of towels, wrapped one over Alice's nose and mouth, and tied it behind her head.

"Dust?" she said while tying a wet towel around Sig's head.

"Yep. We don't want to breathe any dust if we can. That would put the radioactive material inside us. Probably no harm would come, but why not be as safe as possible?"

"W2ZZR, W2GLS," Sig radioed.

"W2ZZR copies. Ready, Sig," said Roy.

"Let the guard know we are exiting now," Sig said.

"Will do. Best wishes, old man."

"W2GLS out," Sig signed off and held the apartment door open for Alice. It was raining outside.

Analysis of Chapter 2

Sig is what some would call a "tough old coot," but you do not have to be tough or be an amateur radio operator to survive in a big city after a nuclear explosion. Alice is evidence of that. Why did she survive?

One reason both Sig and Alice survived is because they lived in basement apartments. This provided flash, blast, and radiation protection.

In general, radiation protection is provided by three factors:

1. Time –   the less time you are exposed to the radiation, the less radiation damage you will receive.

2. Distance –   the farther you are from the radiation sources, the less damage you will receive.

3. Shielding –   the more mass (solid or liquid) between you and the radiation sources, the less damage you will receive.

Living below ground level provided Sig and Alice the distance and shielding they needed, even though neither chose their apartments with any thought of radiation shielding in mind. Consider the following sketch:

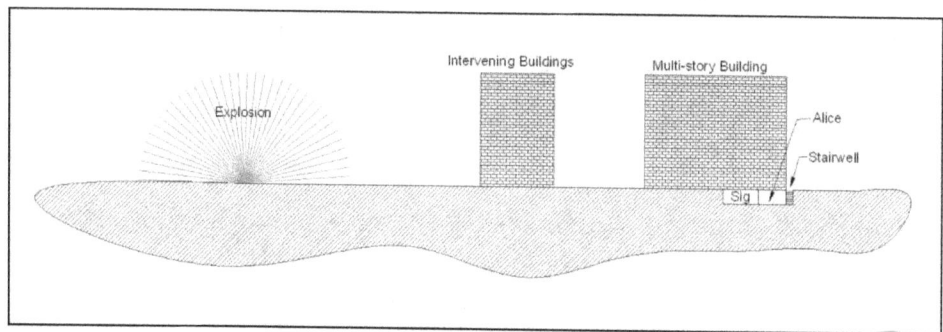

Sig's Protective Factors

The explosion occurred only a half mile away from Sig's apartment. Buildings close to the explosion would be decimated, with little chance of anyone living or working in them surviving. Intervening buildings will provide some measure of blast protection, but Sig's building is likely to receive damage and the debris field around it is probably going to be extensive.

Underground apartments may be rare, but think about your city. Are there underground parking garages? Are there department stores or other building that have below-ground facilities? Many government buildings have such facilities. Close to the explosion these places will be where you will find survivors. But will they know to lay low for two days, or will they come out after the blast to see what happened or to search for survivors, and thereby kill themselves through exposure to radiation?

How Shielding Helped Sig and Alice

Radioactive fallout sends radiation in all directions. Because Sig was below ground, the radiation from fallout on the street outside his apartment, which flew toward him, had to pass through soil to reach him. Three feet of soil is a good shield. Only a small part of the radiation directed toward him from dust on the ground ever reached him. Most was absorbed by the earth.

The floors of the building above him and the contents of the building provided multiple shields from radioactive material that fell on the building.

How Distance Helped Sig and Alice

Some radioactive fallout landed on the roof of the building above Sig. The radiation from that dust that reached Sig and Alice was reduced in intensity by the distance of the roof from Sig.

Sig's covering and sealing of Alice's broken window with tape is also an application of the "distance" rule of radiation protection. He taped up her broken window to keep out as much airborne dust as possible. He closed her door and his for the same reason. Inside his apartment, Sig stayed away from his bedroom and the wall separating her apartment from his. He located the place with the lowest dose rate (the pantry) and they spent most of their time in it.

Note that while poster board and duct tape cannot shield you from gamma rays, it can keep the gamma ray emitters (dust particles) from getting closer to you or being breathed in.

How Time Helped Sig and Alice

Sig chose to stay in radiation (5 rem/hr), which before the bombing would be considered extreme and to be avoided at all costs. He and Alice stayed in a lower radiation field rather than emerge into a much higher one (1000 to 3000 rem/hr) outside. He used time to allow the stronger radiation to decay down to a level that would allow them to move quickly through the higher intensity radiation with minimum additional exposure.[44]

Keep in mind that it is the total accumulated radiation dose that is important because it represents the total damage done to the human body.[45] Some might argue that Sig should have sheltered longer, and indeed he probably could have calculated a "perfect" time for he and Alice to run for safety, but there are other factors not discussed in the story such as a lack of food, especially water; a lack of sanitary conditions (restroom facilities);

---

[44] Radiation effects include the short-term and the long-term effects. Young people are more sensitive to the long-term effects of radiation because they have more years of life left and therefore will be more divisions of the cells in their bodies. Radiation damage to DNA in their cells has a higher probability of being expressed in their lifetimes. Children, especially the very young, need to be protected as much as possible from exposure to damaging radiation.

[45] The numbers for the radiation dose rate in this story is an assumption based on the maximum dose rates seen near ground zero after nuclear tests of much larger weapons. No claim is made that this is what you will see in your city. It is likely that the dose rates from the fallout from a 19 kt weapon will be significantly less than 3000 R, but it will be deadly for several days nonetheless, and it is to be avoided for months after the explosion.

and the need to get treatment for injuries. All these could drive people to leave a shelter sooner than is best for their health.

If cities do not plan, train citizens, designate shelters, and provide at least two days' worth of stored water, they are setting up their citizen survivors of a terrorist's nuclear attack for more death and damage than is necessary.

Sig and Alice's total dose will include more each hour they stay in the shelter and then a bigger dose when they escape to be picked up by the National Guard, probably in the neighborhood of a total of 230 rem. Compared to the allowed[46] radiation total accumulated doses, what Sig and Alice received is huge, but considering Sig lived one-half mile from the blast point and downwind, he and Alice are lucky to be alive at all. Besides, at their age they should not expect long-term radiation concerns (cancer). The most serious health effect they will most likely see over the eight weeks following the explosion is severe leucopenia (an abnormally low white blood cell count) and purpura (the appearance of red or purple discolorations on the skin cause by bleeding underneath the skin). They may need blood transfusions to combat a tendency toward infections because of the low white blood cell counts.

Do not miss the point that Alice's survival depended on Sig's knowledge. Without him she would have survived the blast and then exited her apartment and walked out of the blast-damaged area. While doing so she would have accumulated so much radiation damage that she would have eventually died.

Knowledge is power to survive, but it is not enough. City planners would do well to work with neighborhoods to educate the people and to set up shelter areas that provide the three keys to effective sheltering: time (close to the people who need to shelter and set up for a stay of several days), distance (to keep radioactive fallout as far from the sheltering people as possible), and shielding (to block and absorb most of the radiation).

The vast majority of inner-city dwellers live above ground in high-rise apartments. These provide grand views in some cases but little shelter from blast or radioactive dust. In general, the better the view, the more exposed the apartment is to the flash, heat, and blast effects of a terrorist's nuclear bomb.

Should we all live underground? Of course not, but those living in a big city's downtown area need to be aware of the effects of a terrorist's bomb and what they need to do if one is set off far enough from them that they survive the initial flash and blast. Many hundreds of thousands of people will survive the explosion. The question is will they survive the radiation it leaves behind?

Some general guidelines as a response to an actual nuclear explosion would include:

1. Not running to the window to see what is causing that bright light outside. Move toward the core of the building and stay low (below window sills) until the blast wave passes.

---

[46] NRC = Nuclear Regulatory Commission allows nuclear plant workers 5 rem a year.

2. Not staying to fight a fire in your apartment started by the nuclear fireball; there are probably 30 other fires all over your building that you can't see. Also, remember you will more likely die from the smoke than from the fire.

3. Note that a blast wave with the power to hurt you will most likely arrive within 10 seconds of the initial flash. Beyond 2 miles (10 seconds) a blast wave from a bomb the size of the one described in this book will probably not kill you. If you survive the blast wave, always take the stairwell down to leave the building. The elevator could be a death trap, and, since power will likely be off, it won't work.

4. Go to your shelter. Do not try to get to your car and drive out. Why not? Because that is what hundreds of thousands of others will be doing and they will be caught in a massive traffic snarl. They will sit there and, depending on the wind and fate, may be rained on with radioactive fission products from the mushroom cloud. This is not a place you want to be. Most of them will die several days after they drive out.

5. Wait for the authorities to get you out, assuming the shelter was planned and that adequate food and water is available. If it is not, then you and all your sheltering friends should stay in the shelter at least two or three days and then walk out of the blast area as quickly as possible.

6. A portable radio and a radiation survey meter would take away much of the unknown. You could assess your own radiation situation and learn which routes out are the best.

Some large cities have subway systems. These are touted as underground radiation shelters and they can provide that shelter, but there are several serious problems. These include airborne radioactive dust getting into the subway, the contamination people will carry in, and the absence of stocked food, water, medical supplies, blankets, cots, and functioning restrooms.

These problems can be mitigated with proper planning and preparation. A method of sealing the entrances from dust should be ready to deploy or built into the entrance. This could be some kind of large plastic curtain that can be erected and sealed within a few minutes at the narrowest entry passage. City planners should consider what contribution subway ventilation systems might play in pulling radioactive fallout into the subway.

Unless public officials stock subway terminals with adequate food and water for the thousands of folks who may attempt to use them, thirst and hunger will drive those seeking shelter to exit too early. Medical supplies also need to be stocked and maintained.

Finally, and key to the subway working as a shelter, are trained responders who will report to the subway station with the authority to erect dust shields, to scan folks entering the subway (to control incoming contamination), to ration food and water, and to organize a medical team out of those seeking shelter to care for the injured brought there. Ideally, such persons should be identified ahead of time and be given some kind of symbol of authority (think of the air raid warden in London England in World War II.)[47] Just saying the subway terminals will be used as shelters is not sufficient. They, and trained people, must be ready. Remember Sig and that it only takes a few with knowledge to organize the masses to survive.

Some may wonder why the museum (section 5.1) shook so violently and Sig's apartment shook less. We could say Sig lived a bit farther away, and indeed that is true, but there is more to it than that. Studies of the effects of earthquakes have shown that waves of ground disturbance propagate through different types of soils in different ways. Change in soil density, such as from sand to rock, can actually cause the earthquake waves to refract, concentrating them in some areas and lessening them in others. Thus a ground-level nuclear blast may not cause damage via its propagating ground wave a mile away and yet may cause a building's foundation to be damaged a mile and a half away.

The light given off by the bomb at the moment of detonation is often commented on in these stories. That is because of what it can do (blind, injure, burn, alert) and because it is unique.

There are two components to the light given off by a nuclear explosion in your city: the flash and the fireball.[48]

When the bomb explodes, there is an intense, short (< 1/10-second) pulse of heat (and light) followed by a second broader pulse of energy. This second pulse includes the expanding and rising fireball. Due to the extremely high temperature in the initial energy release (early growth of the fireball), much of the visible light is in the ultra-violet region of the light spectrum. This may give the first light (the flash) a bluish-purple hue in some cases. Only about 1% of the bomb's released energy appears in this initial pulse of light. Ninety-nine percent of the total thermal radiation energy is emitted in the second, longer pulse. Because the temperatures in the fireball are lower in the second pulse than in the first pulse, most of the light given off in the second pulse consists of visible and infrared light (radiant heat).[49]

Alice suffered temporary flash blindness (she saw spots after the flash). This is typical of people in the vicinity of a nuclear explosion (i.e., Japan). This effect usually diminished after a few minutes, but may last as long as a few hours. This is not the same as flash blindness, which can occur many miles away and is actual damage to the eyes, occurring when someone is looking directly at the point of the explosion.

The smell of ozone is a possibility. This has often been reported after high-energy events such as electric arcs or intense gamma radiation releases. It is included in this story to demonstrate the clues that lead Sig to take prompt action.

---

[47] Search the internet for "Air Raid Wardens" and "London World War II.".
[48] *The Effects of Nuclear Weapons*, Samuel Glasstone and Philip J. Dolan, United States Department of Defense, 1977, Figure 2.39.
[49] Ibid, Sections 2.39 and 2.40

Alice's window was broken by debris from the blast. The front door to the street was below ground level in the walk-down stairwell. It faced away from the blast at J. J. Plaza, and was therefore shielded by the multi-story building above Sig's apartment and by other intervening buildings. That it was not broken in by the reflection of the blast wave off the building across the street, or by flying debris, is pure chance.

Sig asked Alice to get her coat because he knew that without power their apartments would eventually cool down. Why didn't he tell her to grab all her food too and bring it to his apartment? The answer is he knew that even in the stronger radiation fields in Alice's apartment they would still be able to make quick forays into it to get what they needed. He also knew that all the food in her fridge, sealed in cans or boxes, or in unbroken plastic bags, would remain okay to consume. Gamma radiation does not make anything radioactive, and as long as radioactive dust does not get on the food, Sig and Alice could eat it.

What About Zoomies? (a brief review)

Any moving particle of nuclear radiation can be considered a "zoomie," but the gamma rays are a primary concern because of their penetrating ability. Radiation travels in a straight line from the emitting particles of dust and damages your body's tissues as it passes through you (visualize a microscopic-sized bullet crashing through your tissue.) The rate at which these little bullets strike you is called your dose rate. The total damage to your body is your accumulated total dose. You can get 50 rem of damage by standing in a 3000 rem/hr radiation field for one minute (3000/60), or you can get 50 rem of damage by remaining in a 10 rem/hr radiation field for 5 hours. The damage is the same. Your total dose rate will be the dose rate multiplied by the time of exposure.

Once the radiation damage is done, your body needs time to heal. So the trick is to limit the total damage. A general rule of thumb is that 500 rem over a few minutes or days is sufficient to kill or severely incapacitate most people, especially with no medical care. Prompt and constant medical care can improve the odds of survival.

Sig knew he and Alice would receive a certain amount of radiation exposure when they exited and left Yorksberg. He also knew if they stayed put awhile longer, they would also receive some radiation exposure, so at some point it becomes better for him and Alice to get out of the shelter and make a run for the uncontaminated areas, even if it means being in a higher-dose-rate field of radiation for a short time. One thing to consider in this situation is that debris and fires may make egress from the area a bit more difficult than anticipated. Any delays, such as blocked streets, while moving to a non-contaminated zone, will result in additional radiation exposure.

Sig made good use of his radiation meter. The meter cost about $175 and can be found on the internet[50]. So what do you do if your preparation and planning is poor and you find yourself in a shelter with no radiation meter? This is a tough spot to be in. Do you make a run for it or stay? If you stay, here are some things you might consider.

Look at the geometry of the shelter in relation to outside walls and the structure above. Are you well shielded? Move to the best spot. Make some intelligent guesses as to where the contamination that is falling out of the sky will land. Move to where it is farthest from you and with as much intervening mass as possible.

Remember that the intervening material should be heavy. Cinderblock walls are better than sheetrock. Earth is better than cinderblock. Think massive and heavy. Move to put the heavy stuff between you and where the zoomie-emitting dust has fallen.

Move materials around in the shelter to provide more shielding. If there are full 5-gallon water containers, use these. Water is a good shield because it is heavy. You can drink it too, but empty water containers will be worthless as shields.

A battery-powered radio is a life saver. From it you can learn what is going on around you, where the safe zones are, where the best egress routes are, and where the rescue parties will be moving in the destroyed area. Without it you will be blind and just have to operate by guessing.

If you are shielded well, allow time to pass before you exit. Once you exit, move away from the blast zone and upwind or across wind from the direction the mushroom cloud traveled after the explosion. Never go in the direction the mushroom cloud went. You will just be walking in a narrow zone of high radiation.

Iodine

Post-exposure cancers are statistical events. Cancer is very real to those who get it and we do not mean to diminish this fact, but most people exposed to radiation do not get cancer. Some do. Whether it shows up at all and the type of cancer you might get has to do with your genes and exposure to more than just radiation.

We know that some biological processes concentrate radioactive emitters, such as iodine in the thyroid or calcium in the bones. Thus after a nuclear terror attack our public servants should make iodine and calcium supplements available to the general population at large. This could have a significant impact on thyroid- and bone-cancer rates, which tend to increase statistically years to decades after the exposure event.

Note that it was raining when Sig and Alice egressed from the shelter. Natural phenomena can also increase or decrease the concentration of contamination. Rain, for example, can wash off roofs but will concentrate the radioactive dust in places wherever the runoff carries these materials. It has been reported, for example, that the roads outside the Chernobyl nuclear accident site in Russia have been washed by rain, so the radiation

---

[50] The author is not recommending any particular survey meter; he is simply using it as an example to tell Sig's story. You will need to research these devices to find one that meets your needs and finances.

levels are less at the center of the road and increase toward the edges where the radioactive material was deposited by rain runoff.[51]

Radioactive Decay

How did Sig predict when the radiation level would drop to a certain value? He did it using a particular mathematical curve that describes radioactive decay.[52] This curve follows the laws of nature and results in the rule-of-seven (i.e., if you pick a time after the explosion, say one hour, then when seven times that amount of time has passed, the radiation will decrease to one tenth of what it was at one hour). Look at this table which shows Sig's situation.

Yorksberg Time	Time in Hours after the event	Dose rate inside R/hr.	Dose rate outside R/hr.
3:30 PM	1.0	50.0	3000.0
4:00 PM	1.5	30.7	1844.2
4:30 PM	2.0	21.8	1305.8
5:00 PM	2.5	16.7	999.1
5:30 PM	3.0	13.4	802.7
6:00 PM	3.5	11.1	667.2
6:30 PM	4.0	9.5	568.4
7:00 PM	4.5	8.2	493.5
7:30 PM	5.0	7.2	434.9
8:00 PM	5.5	6.5	387.9
8:30 PM	6.0	5.8	349.4
9:00 PM	6.5	5.3	317.4
9:30 PM	7.0	4.8	290.4
10:00 PM	7.5	4.5	267.3
10:30 PM	8.0	4.1	247.4
...	...	...	...
~ 1.7 Days Later			
1:30 PM	47.0	0.493	29.6
2:00 PM	47.5	0.486	29.2
2:30 PM	48.0	0.480	28.8
3:00 PM	48.5	0.474	28.5
3:30 PM	49.0	0.469	28.1
4:00 PM	49.5	0.463	27.8
4:30 PM	50.0	0.457	27.4
5:00 PM	50.5	0.452	27.1
5:30 PM	51.0	0.447	26.8

Using the table, note that at 3:30, one hour after the explosion, the dose rate in Sig's pantry was 50 R/hr. Seven hours after the event it is 9:30 and you can see the dose rate is close to 5 R/hr.

Now look forward in time starting 7 hours after the explosion; then increase time sevenfold. Seven times seven is 49, and note the dose rate has dropped to a tenth of what it was at 7 hours after the event, or .469 R/hr. And this continues whenever time grows by a factor of seven (i.e., the dose rate drops to 1/10 of what it was before).

You can apply the same rule to the radiation outside in the city. You might be interested to know that, assuming 3000 R/hr an hour after the explosion, the following are the predicted dose rates:

One month	1.1 R/hr
One year	0.056 R/hr (56 millirem/hr)
Five years	0.0081 R/hr (8.1 millirem/hr)
35 years	0.0008 R/hr (0.8 millirem/hr)

---

[51] You may search for http://www.kiddofspeed.com/chapter1.html and http://www.kiddofspeed.com/chapter2.html for an interesting motorbike trip into the contaminated area around the Russian Chernobyl-4 power plant.

[52] Each radioactive atom decays at a different rate. The decay follows a type of curve called an exponential curve. But a nuclear bomb creates thousands of different types of radioactive atoms. The decrease of the radiation from many different radioactive atoms all combined follows the rule-of-seven, which can be written as $D = D_1 t^{-1.2}$ where D is the dose rate at time t and D_1 is the dose rate at unit time after the burst.

After many years these "hot spots" would be safe to spend time in, but would give you a larger dose rate than that from naturally occurring minerals and cosmic rays. These dose rates could be further reduced by burying or hauling away the soil from more contaminated areas.

Below is Sig's pantry radiation rate decay graph. You can clearly see the rule-of-seven at work. Locate the 7-hour mark along the bottom of the chart. Go straight up from the 7 mark

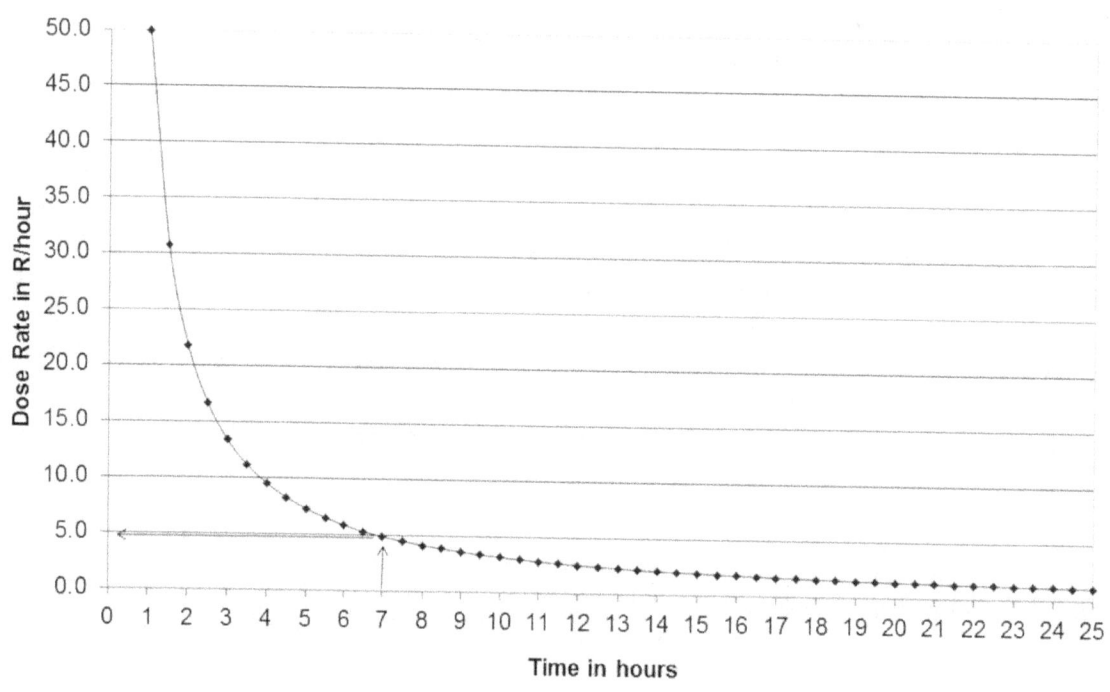

Sig's Pantry Radiation Rate

at the bottom until you cross the curve, and then look at the left side to see what value the curve has at that point (5 R/hr). In seven time periods the dose rate is 1/10 of its original value.

Amateur Radio

Amateur radio operators often take on the job of connecting "found" persons with their loved ones after a disaster. Undoubtedly this will occur following a nuclear terror attack. This is typically done in conjunction with the city, county, and state authorities. Two of the differences between a nuclear terror attack and the common hurricane, tornado, or earthquake will be the larger number of casualties, wounded, and missing; the contamination of persons fleeing the city; and the inaccessibility of the area due to contamination.

The reestablishment of cell phone service will be a boon to law enforcement, EMT personnel, fire services, and the population in general. Prior to cell technology, areas hit hardest by a natural disaster were often the "silent" areas. These are areas from which no reports are heard following the disaster. These would be zones in a city where the devastation was so terrific that either no one survived or no one could call for help. Emergency response plans sometimes send aerial reconnaissance into the silent zones as soon as possible to assess the conditions there.

With cell phones being common, many with photographic capability, areas that would have previously been silent will likely have an immediate voice, providing that cell communication is not lost. Rescue personnel should be prepared to get requests for help from even the most devastated areas if cell phone communication is active. This will put an increased work load on responders and involve some tough choices. Do you send rescue teams into dangerously contaminated areas? There are ways to do this as safely as possible if adequate planning is done ahead of time.

Cell communication will decrease some of the emergency communications traffic. People whose land lines are disabled by the attack, for example, may be able to use their cell phones to report in to loved ones.

When Sig and Alice emerged from Sig's apartment, there was a light, cold rain falling and the streets were slick. The first block was the most difficult. It required climbing through a lot of rubble and both Sig and Alice had some difficulty. But they made steady progress and within an hour had reached Conners and 9th where a National Guard driver wearing a white contamination suit spotted them and picked them up. Two hours later they were in a hospital showering and preparing for a medical evaluation.

The next day a cold front passed through the area, dropping temperatures into the upper twenties. By nightfall there was an inch and a half of new snow on the ground in Yorksberg, where it lay like a mantle across the rubble-covered grave of more than 286,000 people.

Would it surprise you to know that Sig died of pneumonia about three years after his egress from his apartment? Doctors dismissed the idea that his radiation exposure at Yorksberg had anything to do with his passing, since the pneumonia occurred during a flu outbreak.

Alice never returned to her apartment and lived to be 91 before passing on from old age. She never forgot Sig, and often told tales to her grandchildren of their two days together.

Please take the quiz that follows.

Quiz on Chapter 2
(Answers are in Appendix A1)

1. Can your body heal itself from radiation damage?
2. Why should people exposed to nuclear bomb radiation take iodine tablets?
3. Briefly state the rule-of-seven pertaining to the decay of radioactivity.
4. What does the acronym RACES stand for?
5. Radiation protection is provided by what three factors?

Next we will see how the bomb affected Yorksberg's port. We will also discuss the affects you might expect if the bomb is placed in the river or ocean near a port. Read on and discover a Port in Peril and the value of a helping hand.

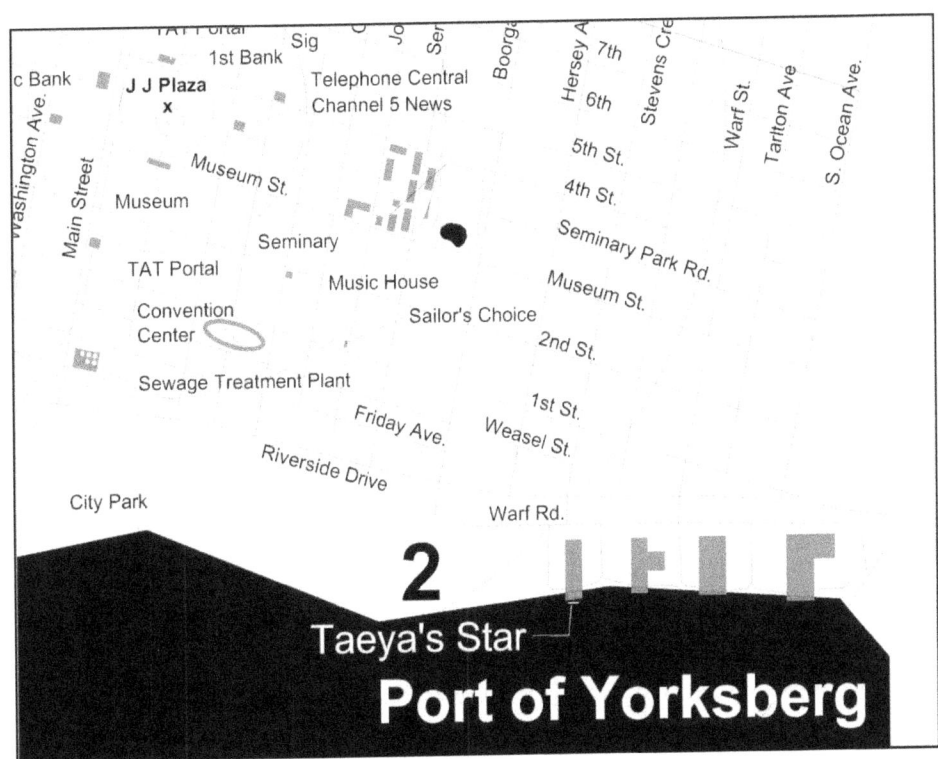

The ship MV Taeya's Star Docked at the Port

3 – Fletcher Evans – Peril near the Port (1 mile)

Fletcher Evans stood at the bow of the ship *MV Taeya's Star*, tip-toe on a coiled cable, leaning forward with thighs against the gunwale, arms outstretched in the fashion of Jack Dawson in the movie *Titanic*, and as he leaned into the wind his foot slipped. At that moment his senses were immersed in the cold air rushing past him, the sparkling sunlight on the water, the blue sky above, the smell of the nearby sea, and... he had Niki on his mind. Only his youthful-quick reflexes kept him from tumbling over the gunwale into the Taconic River, where the ship would have run right over him. Heart racing, he looked down at the light chop on the cold river rushing by the *Star*, glistening in the sun as the prow of the ship rhythmically sent a crashing cascade of spray right and left, creating a rainbow in the air. *This is why I work on a ship!*

The distant rumble of the *Star*'s powerful engines changed slightly as the ship approached the interstate highway bridge northwest of Yorksberg. Fletch knew the bridge as a way-point for the ship, and he knew that for this 220-foot-long container ship to slow to a stop off the port she had to start bleeding off her way now. He felt the ship begin that just-perceptible slowing that always marked the beginning of the end of a voyage.

He looked down at the prow cutting through the water and remembered what the First Mate had told him: "The prow is where way becomes spray."

The word *inertia* came to his mind and Fletcher smiled. He remembered Niki telling him that a ship's way was just the inertia of its moving mass driving it forward.

53

She is so pretty and so smart. How could a college girl be interested in me?

He took a deep breath and strained to see Sailor's Choice where Niki worked, but the ship was still too far up river. No matter, he knew *Taeya's Star* was bound into the Yorksberg port and that with any leave at all he might see her. His spirit lifted and his heart warmed at the thought of her bright eyes and long black hair.

Life is good!

For a second or two he gave in to the fantasy that he and Niki might marry someday and have children. This dream was broken, however, when he thought of Niki as a mom.

I promised Mom I would call!

He pulled out his phone and dialed his parents' home.

"Hello," his mom answered as she always did. "Evan's residence."

"Hi, Mom," he said.

"Fletch! Good to hear from you, son. Another port I suppose?"

"We are approaching Yorksberg. Should be docked within the hour and I will be really busy for a while. Just wanted you guys to know I am okay and I've shaken off that cold."

"I'm glad to hear it. Have you been at sea, or up the river?"

"Up the Taconic River. We made two stops inland and have a good load of containers on deck. We drop some here, pick up a few, and then I believe we'll sail for New York."

The ship's PA system came active. "All hands prepare to receive the pilot."

Fletcher could see the tug, just a spot ahead now, beginning its run out to meet the *Star*.

"Got to go, Mom, I'll call you later if I can."

"Okay, son, but you can't get away that easy. Are you going to see Niki?"

"If I can get to shore, I will."

"Well don't jump ship for her. Dad says no girl in any port is worth that trouble."

He heard his dad laugh in the background.

That's how they met.

"You worry too much, Mom."

"I love you, son, and Dad says love to you too."

"Thanks, Mom, love you too, bye."

An hour later the ship was docked at the end of Pier One, and Fletcher wondered why the offloading did not start. The answer came a moment later when the First Mate walked up to him.

"Our Kyoto aft hoist has electrical problems. The crane is down for good until we get the part we need, and that will take about two hours. So the Captain has granted shore leave while we wait, but he wants everybody back on board at five. We should be able to start moving cargo then."

"Hot damn!" Fletcher said.

The First Mate grinned. "I knew that would just break your heart, lover boy."

"Thanks, Mac. I gotta go get cleaned up a bit."

"Well hug her for me, and doggone-it, bring us a picture. You talk about her so much the crew has a pool going as to how pretty she is. Help me out here; on a 1-to-10 scale how would you rate her?"

Fletcher didn't hesitate. "A ten, of course."

"A ten? You wish," said Mac.

Now Fletcher grinned. "You're on, Mac. I will get a picture if I can."

Dressed in clean clothes and looking sharp, Fletcher could hardly wait to reach the Sailor's Choice Sports Bar on 1st street. As he crossed John Briggs Road he spotted Niki's car in the parking lot, and he quickened his pace.

She's there!

In no time he was pushing the glass door open and hearing the tinkle of the small bell hung on it. He swiped his orange and blue ski cap from his head and felt his long blond locks fall along the side of his head.

"Well, look what the cat drug in," Barb heard Ruby say as she placed the last of the dishes on the stack. "Blond head, rugged face, and muscles; if that isn't a chick magnet, I've never seen one!"

Barb looked toward the door.

"Down girl," she said. "That Niki's fellow, Fletch." She pushed the kitchen door open slightly and said, "Hey, Niki, looks like your lucky day. Some handsome stranger just walked in."

Barb saw Niki's eyes light up and a big smile break out on her face.

"I'll go seat him if you want to fresh up," Barb said.

"Thanks, I will," Niki said.

Fletcher saw Barb approaching and smiled.

"Hello, sailor. Have you come for our hot chili special or for something else hot?"

Fletcher laughed. "I'll take the something else, please. Would you please tell Niki I'm here?"

"Already done. She'll be out in a moment. Why don't you sit down here and I'll bring you a cup of something warm. Chocolate, tea, coffee?"

"Coffee would be great," Fletcher said.

"Coming up. Niki's been looking forward to your next visit."

"What's the deal?" Ruby said as Barb walked back into the kitchen..

"This is a sweet one," Barb said, "a real storybook romance. Niki says that for all his rugged looks, he is a mild-mannered man that treats her like a princess. We've been watching this relationship grow for many months now."

She filled a cup with coffee, set it on a saucer, and added a spoon to its side with a clink.

"He drops in every time his ship is in port."

"Probably got a fish on the line in every port," Ruby said.

"Well aren't you cynical. I don't read him that way. Seems to be too young and straightforward for that."

"I wish I'd spotted him first. I could use a good man."

"Ruby, you are too old for this one." With that, she carried the coffee out to serve Fletcher, leaving behind Ruby's "Who's old?" response.

His hands were starting to warm up from holding the coffee cup and he was bouncing one knee in nervous anticipation when he spotted Niki coming out of the kitchen.

She was dressed in the usual Sailor's Choice waitress outfit and had combed her hair back on one side. Fletcher immediately spotted the necklace he had given her, the one with the leaping dolphin on it.

"Are you cold, sailor?" she said with a warm smile.

Fletcher grinned back. "Yah, but the temperature just went up ten degrees."

"Let me take your coat off."

He stood and she helped him remove his coat, tossing it into the booth seat. A big hug followed.

"I'm working, but it's quiet right now. Barb gave me five or ten minutes. She is such a sweet person," Niki said.

"Howya been, Niki?" Fletcher said. "I missed you."

"Doing well, and I missed you too. What brings you in? I thought you were going to be away until next weekend." Niki pulled her long black hair back over her shoulders. She did this every minute or so and Fletcher found it cute.

"Our hoist has problems. First Mate tossed us on shore for a couple of hours while he gets some electricians to fix it. I was hoping I would find you here."

"Well, I have some news for you. I made an A in chemistry." Niki grinned.

"You sure are smart," Fletcher said sincerely.

She's probably going to try again to get me to start college.

"I remember all that chemistry stuff you showed me. You gotta be smart to learn that."

"No," she said. "You are smart enough too. What it takes is work. You work at it, just like you work at your work on ship."

"We have had this conversation before, Niki. Let's talk about something else."

"Okay. Will you be on shore a week from Saturday?"

He thought for a moment. "Well, that is still on the schedule, but this down time will put us several hours behind. No telling what that will do to us at future ports of call. We might miss a time slot for unloading and that could mess us up further down the line. I'll let you know later in the week."

He sipped the still-too-hot coffee. She looked at her hands.

"I'm free that Saturday."

Fletcher grinned and said, "I like it when you hint." He smiled at her. "Well, as a matter of fact I know this sailor who, if he is in town two weeks from Saturday, would like to take you to dinner and a movie."

Niki reached across the table and took his hand. "I'd love to go. I was hoping you would ask."

Fletcher felt warm all over.

I've never felt like this about a girl before.

He stared at her eyes and the thoughts of marrying her and raising a family came back. The idea of having a wife was comfortable when he thought of Niki.

She smiled shyly. "What are you thinking? Your eyes kinda glassed over for a moment."

"About you and me, and Saturday," he said, unable to tell her the whole truth.

"I mentioned that Saturday because we can go to a musical if you'd like to," she said.

"A play?" Fletcher raised his eyebrows as he sipped.

"No, a musical. The characters sing songs. The college is putting on *Fiddler on the Roof*. Have you heard of it?"

"Can't say I have. This is not an opera; is it?"

"It's not an opera; it's a musical, and you will love it. You have heard some of the music; surely you have."

"Like what?"

Niki thought for a moment and then gave him as much of "If I Were a Rich Man" as she could remember.

"Haven't heard that one."

She tried a couple of other tunes that she remembered. It was not until she sang a piece of "Matchmaker" that a light came on.

"Yah, I remember hearing that one somewhere. So that's in the musical?"

"Yep. Please come with me. I'll get tickets as soon as we know when you'll be in town again."

"Okay, a musical and dinner. Sounds like a good evening."

"I've got to get back to work. Barb will last only so long. I'm off at five," she added hopefully, rising from her seat.

"The Mate said to be back on ship at five," Fletcher said.

Niki stood up. "Let me talk to Barb. Maybe I can take an hour or two." As she started to walk away, something white caught her eye, and by habit she stooped to pick up the napkin lying under the table. Fletcher watched her bend down and lean slightly under the table to get it.

The lights went out. There was a momentary silence as the music system died and the light coming in the front windows waxed brilliant and blue white. Then the floor jumped violently and the world went wild. It was as if a giant fist hammered the building with one great blow. He heard glass shattering and saw the building move, and as he looked up, he watched the building fall over them in what seemed like slow motion. One of the inverted U-shaped, pre-stressed concrete panels that made up the roof of Sailor's Choice fell directly across them. He ended up flat on the floor, his legs partly on top of Niki's legs, and it was soon clear that they were both trapped underneath the beam's protective inverted U-shape.

Fletcher could see that by the grace of God he and Niki were safely in a concrete tunnel, in the dark. Stunned by what had happened, he listen to the cacophony of crashes and impacts on the floor around them, some so loud his ears rang, until all that remained was the sound of multiple car alarms sounding in the parking lot.

After peace returned, he heard Niki coughing repeatedly.

"Niki! Are you okay?" he said.

He could hear that she was having trouble speaking. "I'm bleeding." He heard her say this with what sounded like fear in her voice. "Are you hurt?" she added.

"Amazingly, no."

Fletcher surveyed their situation as best he could. Niki lay facing toward the back of what had been the restaurant, and their legs were partially entwined. He too was prone, but facing the front, where he could see some light entering the end of their protective concrete tunnel through what he guessed was the remains of the wall it had fallen across.

"We have to try to get out," he said.

After a moment he heard her voice again. "How?"

"Look this way. We are in some kind of tunnel. I see daylight."

He felt her try to rise.

"I can't get up. My back hit something. But I did see some light. I can't turn around," she said, voice shaking. "There's not enough room."

"I can slide forward. Can you slide backward? Just push yourself backward with your hands." He wiggled toward the light.

There was a moment while she tried.

"My uniform is caught on something. I can't move."

"Can you rip off the piece that is caught?"

There was a grunt from Niki, still coughing. "No."

Fletcher struggled in the tight space until he got his right hand down to his pocket. He had his pocket knife out a moment later.

"Niki, I am going to toss my knife to you. Use it to cut the uniform off where it is stuck."

He tossed the knife and it managed to get part way to Niki.

"Not far enough," Niki said.

"Shhhh. Listen," he said.

They both rested and listened.

"Fire," he finally said. "That sounds like fire." Fear and foreboding came over him like a wave. *The smell of smoke is getting stronger.* "I'll try to push the knife to you with my foot. Hurry."

"I can't see anything. It's so dark in here." Niki's voice was a cry.

Fletcher pushed one shoe off with the other and felt with his toes for the stubborn knife. Finally he located it.

"Move your legs over to your right. No, your other right."

When he felt her legs move he pushed the knife with his foot. He estimated it must have stopped somewhere around her knees and told her so. A moment later he heard her say, "I got it."

He heard the distant sound of the *Star's* horn sound three short blasts, repeated three times. This was the ship's distress signal. The Captain was recalling all hands.

He desperately wanted to start sliding toward the light, but did not want to leave Niki. There was motion at his feet and he could hear her breathing hard and the sound of the knife cutting fabric.

"I'm free. Go go go! I'll be right behind you." Niki's voice sounded stronger, more confident.

Fletcher slid himself about 15 feet through the tunnel until he came to its end, which was partially blocked by what looked like shattered cinder blocks. He was able to move some of the block debris but not enough to get out.

"Help!" he yelled. "Anyone out there? Come to my voice. Help! Get us out of here."

It took several minutes before someone responded to his calls for help. A voice outside said, "Where are you?"

The *Star* sounded her crew emergency recall signal again.

"Here!" Fletcher said and waved his hand out of the hole. A moment later he could hear shattered concrete block being pulled away. There was a period of silence and then the rescuer returned with some kind of metal bar or pipe. Progress was rapid with this aid and a few minutes later the voice said, "Reach out and I'll pull you out."

He followed the voice's direction and was pulled out by a dark-haired teenage boy. Fletcher stood there, one shoe on, staring at the kid for a moment. The youth's clothing was torn and tattered, his face burnt red on one side, and his eyes held a dazed look.

"I heard your voice from the street," the kid started to explain.

"My girlfriend is still in there. Help me get her out," Fletcher said. He then encouraged Niki to continue sliding herself backward until he could see her feet. When they finally could, he and the boy grasped her feet and pulled her free. She held his missing shoe in her hand.

Niki's face and arms were streaked with blood, as was the blood-sticky knife she handed back to him. She was pale and had to sit down. Fletcher wished he had paid more attention to the first aid classes he had attended when he was a Boy Scout, and he set about trying to determine where she was bleeding from.

"I've got to go," the youth said weakly.

"Hey, thanks," Fletcher said, rising and extending his hand, which he quickly withdrew and wiped on his jeans. His hand was wet with Niki's blood.

"It's okay, mister," the youth said. "You take care of her now." Fletcher watched his good Samaritan walk east through the jumble that was the parking lot. Then he noticed the cars in the parking lot were blasted, smashed, and overturned everywhere. Several were on fire, some just smoking ruins, others fully engaged in flames. There were several bodies strewn around. Fletcher turned back to Niki and looked at her face and arms streaked in blood.

Taeya's Star's horn gave the same three short blasts, repeated three times. Fletcher looked toward the port, while putting on his shoe, and could not see the ship, but he could see fires in the wharf area. Torn between duty and Niki, he made a quick decision. Lifting Niki into his arms, he took one last glance at the ruins of the Sailor's Choice restaurant, now with smoke billowing from what used to be the kitchen area, and began walking toward the port.

Arriving at Pier One, he could see some damage. One of the warehouses was leaning at an angle. Refuse along the wall of another was burning. Several men were bucket-brigading river water to the scene and had the fire pretty much under control.

The ship seemed untouched. The metal shipping containers also seemed untouched until one looked closer. Plastic and paper tags and labels on the city side of the containers were charred, or in some cases burned away.

The First Mate hailed him from the *Star* as soon as he saw him.

"Dammed good to see you, Fletch. Who is that?"

"My girl, Niki," he said and then added, "She's bleeding."

"Bring her to the infirmary. I'll call Jose."

Fatigue came over him as the adrenaline wore off and he set Niki down. He helped her walk onto the ship.

"Captain wants to get to sea before any more radioactivity falls on deck. As soon as you get her settled, go forward and help Carl hose down the deck."

"Radioactivity?" Fletcher raised his eyes and looked over the city to the enormous dark cloud off to the north and east.

(Note to the reader: This book is not rated to print what Fletcher said at this point. Just call it sailor talk.)

Analysis of Chapter 3

Fletcher has come though this experience with only a bruise on his head and one on his back. Niki is a survivor too. She lost some blood and had a mild concussion, but she will heal from both. Before you think Fletcher and Niki's excellent condition unrealistic, keep in mind that these stories are, for the most part, about the survivors. These are the less injured. In fact, all the other people in Sailor's Choice died.

Some people call it "luck," some will just say it "wasn't their time," but for every survivor in the big city after a nuclear explosion there will be a story, a tale of overlapping circumstances, of choices made, that resulted in survival. If Barb had seated Fletcher and Niki in any other booth, for example, they would have died. This was pure chance. Had Niki been in the booth seat or one step toward the kitchen when the building structure came down, she would have been crushed and would have died instantly. This was not chance. This occurred because of a combination of timing and her stooping to pick up a napkin. You could argue that her dedication to her job saved her, because a more slothful worker would not have tried to pick up the napkin and would be dead.

Even if you could collect a hundred such stories and unravel each of them into thousands of circumstances, choices, and events, you still could not put together a workable plan to guarantee your survival. You can, however, increase the probability of remaining a survivor if you make it through the initial explosion. You can become Nuclear Terror Street-smart. Know where the shelters are, formal and informal. Know what needs to be stocked in a shelter. Know about the effects of radiation on food. Know the physics of a nuclear explosion so that you recognize it early on in the event. Duck under your desk instead of running to the window to see the pretty light. Whenever you begin to believe the lie that surviving a nuclear bomb is hopeless, remind yourself that at Hiroshima more than 100,000 survived. It is never hopeless for the survivors.

Many structures are built with reinforced concrete. We have all seen these panels. Sometimes they are flat, but often you will look up and see the ceiling is made of side-by-side, upside-down concrete "U"s. These are common in parking garages and motels.

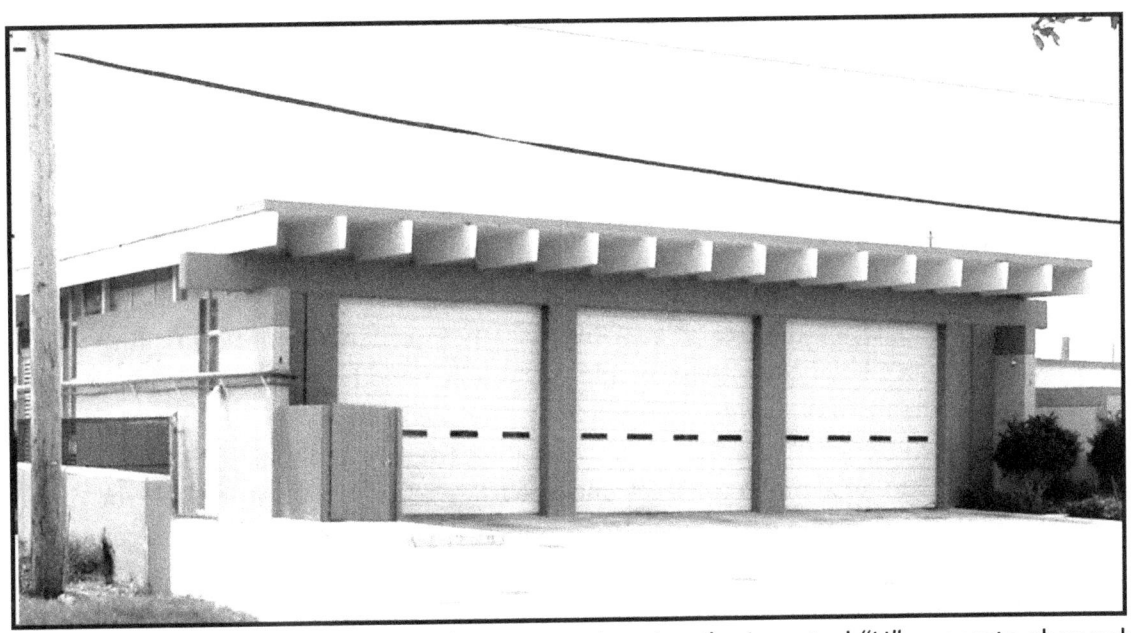

An Example of Sailor's Choice's Roof Structure showing the inverted "U" concrete channels.

This is what was above Fletch and Niki. Sailor's Choice was a concrete block structure with a concrete ceiling, which was given a terrific push to one side by the blast wave and dynamic pressure from the terrorist's bomb. Weaknesses in the side wall structure, and the heavy roof made of the concrete panels, caused it to pancake on top of those inside. Most occupants died instantly.

Fletcher and Niki were trapped by block wall material at the end of their "U"-shaped protective concrete tunnel, and Niki was held in place by part of her uniform, which had become caught under the ceiling beam when it fell.

Many survivors will be trapped following a nuclear explosion. Their ability to get out of the trap will make a difference in their survivability. Several of the scenarios in this book involve trapped people. Personal resourcefulness (Fletch's knife) will extricate some, and human help such as that provided by Jetta Goldberg, the dance instructor in upcoming Chapter 6, will save others. You as a survivor will have the difficulty of balancing the desire to rescue against the lethality of time and radiation.

The teenager who helped Fletch and Niki out of their trap had the time and resources to help and thus saved their lives. He did not survive, however, due to the radiation dose he accumulated at the instant of detonation and due to his failure to get out of the area afterward. He actually could have survived if he had been trained better.

Fletcher made a decision to take Niki to the port. He did not do this because he was nuclear smart. He was comfortable with the port, and he was only concerned about her safety. He was actually thinking someone at the port could get her to a hospital. That would have been a bad decision since the path to the hospital would have taken them under the main drop zone for fallout. Had Fletcher left her and gone to the port alone, Niki, not being nuclear street-smart, may have died from radiation exposure.

We often run to the comfortable (places, people, and material things we know) when our world becomes stressful, even if those comfortable places are more dangerous. Take care that you follow wisdom and careful preparation when the big flash happens. Take care that you do not run to comfort. You might, for example, be tempted to run into and hold up in your undamaged, but unshielded, apartment instead of walking or hitching a ride with a stranger to get out of town. This is especially true when you have nowhere to go out of town.[53]

The Captain had the right idea. Obviously the port would not be shipping any cargo for a while. In fact, the berths there would eventually need to be open for a lot of heavy equipment to be moved in, perhaps even a hospital ship.

Aware of the problem of radioactive fallout, the Captain took the ship to sea and tasked his crew to hose down the deck and deck-side cargo with water. This would prevent the accumulation of radioactive dust and greatly reduce the exposure of his crew. In fact, due to the prevailing wind, he had only to pull 10 miles off shore to the east to be clear of any further contamination.

The Effects of a Nuclear Explosion on a Port
There are basically four possible scenarios for a nuclear bomb affecting a port.

1. The nuclear bomb explodes in the port.

In this case there will be little left of the port. It will resemble the scene of the downtown district of Yorksberg — a crater (perhaps underwater) and a barren, blasted landscape. A few concrete pilings might survive and the hulls of sunken and broken ships may be recognizable, but little else. Warehouses will be gone but their contents may be found scattered away from the explosion point. Immediately after the blast small fires may be present, but as time passes, depending on the amount of flammable materials in the area, huge fires may develop. Large, smoky fires may immediately result if large quantities of petroleum fuels are stored in the port area.

For obvious reasons, port workers should not worry about being at work at the port when a nuclear bomb goes off there. They should, however, plan for the possible explosion of a bomb near, but not in the port.

---

[53] You have heard it is a good idea for all the family members to know to call a certain phone number if a cataclysmic event causes disaster and separates them. If you live in a big city, a possible target, it would also be a good idea to read this book with out-of-town friends and make an agreement with them that you can head for their place if the city becomes unlivable. Alternately, you can just rely on civic authorities in another city to have a school gym for you to live in for a short time. Plan. Plan. Plan.

2. The bomb explodes near the port (the Fletcher Evans story).

    In our story the bomb was about 2.1 miles from the port. This is far enough away from a 19 kt explosion that much of the port will survive the heat and blast. Fires can be started in susceptible materials, and the blast overpressure, below 1 psi[54], will likely only damage some windows or large walls facing broadside to the oncoming blast wave. Individuals inside most structures and virtually all ships will survive the initial heat and blast. People standing outside have a high probability of not sustaining injuries caused by such factors as being hit by blast-propelled flying objects, falling walls, infrared radiation heat burns to exposed skin, and eye damage for those not looking in the direction of the explosion when the bomb explodes. If one is looking at the site of the bomb's explosion the instant it explodes, the light is so intense and its onset so quick eye damage can occur faster than the human-protective blink reflex.

    Fallout is a problem this close to the blast. It will come soon and will still be highly radioactive. Personnel who continue to work outdoors or in areas of inadequate sheltering will likely receive a lethal dose of radiation within an hour. If they retreat into a shelter, however, their survival is almost certain, provided they know the dos and don'ts of dealing with radioactive fallout. A concrete bunker-type warehouse, particularly one with several feet of soil on top, may provide excellent attenuation of the radiation. The holds of large metal ships, particularly if one can descend below the water line, may provide adequate protection. The ability of ships to run pumps to wash the decks adds another level of protection.

3. The bomb explodes far from the port.

    An explosion far from the port only exposes port workers to eye-flash damage, which can occur out to 20 miles or so on a clear day, and to radioactive fallout if the mushroom cloud drifts toward the port. There are two advantages to being far from the explosion. The first is the port's measure of fallout will arrive after some time has passed. This will allow the intensity of the radiation to decrease before the fallout arrives. The second is that workers will have time to leave the area and move a minimum of 20 miles cross wind of the oncoming cloud. If far enough away, ships may even be able to get out of port to sea and thus escape the fallout.

    If the wind carries the fallout in another direction, the explosion will not directly have an impact on the port.

4. Terrorists drop a weapon from an offshore ship, causing a nuclear explosion deep underwater.

    This type of nuclear attack is not part of the Yorksberg scenario, but it still needs to be mentioned. This is where a terrorist drops a bomb from an offshore ship. The bomb is then set off deep underwater, causing a huge bubble of white-hot steam to form. This bubble rapidly rises to the surface where it explodes into a cloud of water and steam.

---

[54] The abbreviation for "pounds per square inch" is psi. The psi is the pressure of air pushing on each square inch of a surface. At sea level the normal air pressure is 14.7 psi.

During the process of expanding and rising, it lifts a huge quantity of water, initiating a tsunami-like wave. If the bomb is dropped offshore of a city or port, the result may be a huge wave delivering the bomb's energy in the form of a wall of fast-moving water. This wave will top existing barriers and may impinge on buildings and streets at the port and into the city.

This wave will not be radioactive if the detonation site is miles away. A wave is an energy-transport phenomenon, so the radioactivity in the water remains at the site of the explosion. It will not be carried by the wave.[55] Radioactivity spewed into the air above the sea when the explosion reaches the surface will move with the wind. Radioactivity in the water will drift with the current and may present a danger to beaches quite some distance away at some later time.

<u>All more those thank you on Chapter 3</u>   (Answers are in Appendix A1)

1. What does it mean to be nuclear terror "street-smart"?
2. Would Niki and Fletcher have survived if the teen had not stopped to help?
3. Does exploding a nuclear bomb underwater render it harmless?
4. Is the huge wave from an underwater nuclear explosion radioactive?
5. The mushroom cloud moved away from the port at Yorksberg. Why then did the Captain have to wash the decks?

In the next chapter we will visit a girl whose life is filled with music, until the evil men do their evil deed. Read on to see why "Tomorrow Brings Calm."

---

[55] You can see this yourself. Find a body of water with good waves and toss in something that will float, such as a cork. Notice the waves pass under the cork (representing radioactive debris), lifting it up or down, but the cork does not travel with the wave. Wind may push the cork, but the waves just lift and drop it.

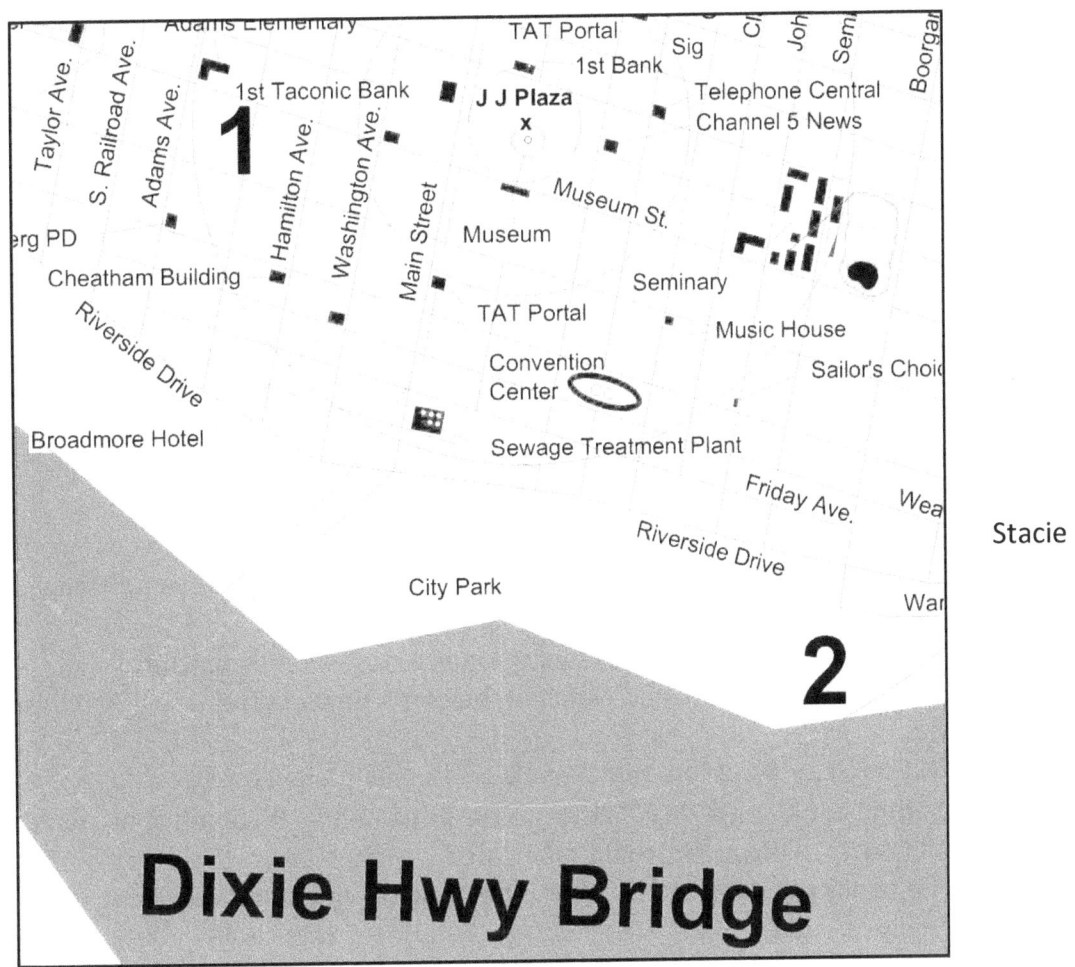

Taylor Ave.
S. Railroad Ave.
Adams Ave.
Adams Elementary
1st Taconic Bank
Hamilton Ave.
Washington Ave.
Main Street
erg PD
Cheatham Building
Riverside Drive
Broadmore Hotel

TAT Portal
1st Bank
Sig
Cl
Joh
Sem
Boorga
J J Plaza
x
Telephone Central
Channel 5 News
Museum St.
Museum
Seminary
TAT Portal
Convention Center
Music House
Sailor's Choi
Sewage Treatment Plant
Friday Ave.
Wea
Riverside Drive
City Park
War
Stacie
1
2

Dixie Hwy Bridge

Fredericks Music House Cityscape

4 - Stacie Fredericks – Tomorrow Brings Calm (0.7 miles)

The family car had just reached the high point on the Dixie Highway Bridge when the right front tire blew out. Stacie's mother struggled to keep the car from veering right, but was not strong enough, and the car rammed the right guard rail. The rail buckled, and before Stacie really knew what was happening the car was through the rail and flying out into the empty space far above the cold, dark water of the Taconic River. Falling, falling, falling so fast now, Stacie could hear the wind roaring through the partially open windows. Then they impacted in one gigantic splash.

Will our car float? Stacie broke out of her daydream about running off the bridge, something she often thought about as they made the weekly traverse across it. She remembered seeing a television show where a car floated after driving into water, so she decided to ask her mother if their car would float, but before she could get the first word out of her mouth, Carl's voice came from the back seat: "Mom, where do fish go when it is cold?"

"What fish?" Stacie said before her mother could answer.

"The fish in the river, down there."

65

She looked back at Carl. He had his hand up with one finger pointing at the dark water below.

"They just put their little fish coats on when it gets cold," she said. She remembered her dad teasing her the same way when she was younger, and smiled at her own clever comment.

"No they don't!" Carl sounded a little miffed. "Fish don't have coats."

"How do you know they don't have coats?" she said.

"Mom!" Carl's voice pleaded for help.

"You two are priceless. You are right, Carl; fish don't have coats. They don't have warm bodies like us, so the cold doesn't bother them. I think they just move slower when it's cold."

That seemed to satisfy Carl for a moment before another question came.

"Mom, what is priceless?"

By the time Mom had explained the idea of priceless, they were coming off the bridge and Stacie could see Riverside Drive. She followed its curvy sweep along the north bank of the Taconic River with her eyes.

"Pew. Pinch your nose," Carl said through a nose already pinched.

Stacie held her breath and watched the stinky Sewage Treatment Plant as they drove by.

"No smell today," Mom said. "You won't smell it when it's this cold."

As they turned right on 2nd Street, Stacie saw her mother look at her watch. "Five minutes 'til two. I told you we wouldn't be late."

The family cell phone rang in her mom's purse, and Stacie dug it out.

"Hello."

"Hi, Stacie. This is Lynn; may I speak to your mom?"

"She's driving right now. We are almost to the Music House. Can you hold on a minute?"

"Who is it?" Mom said.

"It's Lynn."

"Sure I can hold a bit. What is a Music House?" Lynn said.

Stacie could see the Music House sign up the street a block away.

"It's this neat old house owned by the Seminary. It's used by their Music and Arts Department for voice and instrument teaching. I take lessons there every week. Mrs. Bell is my coach."

"Is that the Colleen Bell who sang on Broadway?" Lynn's voice revealed surprise and interest.

Stacie smiled. "Yes, she's sort of famous."

"She sure is. How do you like her?"

"A lot. She sings to me to show what she wants me to do, and her voice is beautiful."

Mom pulled the car into a parking spot and held out her hand for the phone.

"Thanks, Stacie; you go ahead in. I'll be right behind you," she said.

"What are you looking at, Ms. Bell?" one of her voice students said.

"My two o'clock appointment, John. She's coming up the walk now."

"Who is that redhead?" he said while peeking out of the blinds.

"Stacie Anne Fredericks. She's a 12-year-old with an unusual gift of a Broadway-quality voice."

"Broadway?"

"This girl has a powerful, pitch-perfect voice. She has been chosen to play Annie in the upcoming production of the musical."

"That good, huh?"

"Stops adults in their tracks whenever she opens her mouth to sing. And not only that, she is a natural redhead with freckles, the quintessential Annie if there ever was one."

As she entered the door to the Music House, Stacie heard the sound of violin music coming down the stairs from the second floor, the sound of a piano being played in one of the rear music rooms, and some kind of wind instrument struggling with a melody down the hall. She loved the warm, happy feeling this musical background of instrumental dissonance gave the house. She looked forward to adding her own voice.

"Hello, Stacie. I see you are wearing your neck scarf," Ms. Bell said. "You are wise to keep those vocal cords warm. This cold, dry weather can cause a raspy voice in no time."

"Pick up at the usual time?" Mom said as she came in the door with Carl. As Stacie took her coat off, she saw her mom hand Ms. Bell a check for December's lessons.

"Yes, thank you for the check. We will be done promptly at 3 p.m."

Stacie gave her mother a goodbye hug.

As Mom and Carl started out the door, Carl said, "Can we go see the ducks?"

"That's a great idea!" his mother said, looking back at Ms. Bell. "We can walk around in the cold for an hour. They might have their little duck coats on too!"

"Mom, ducks don't wear coats."

"Yes and your mom isn't going to walk in the cold for an hour. We'll go by the Plaza and look for your ducks, but I think we will find a little warm coffee shop. Bye," she added, smiling at Ms. Bell, who smiled back and shut the door behind them.

Turning to Stacie, Ms. Bell said with a smile, "I want you to warm up with the scales for ten minutes, then pick a song or two and just let me hear you sing. Then we will work on some Annie songs."

"You heard, didn't you?" Stacie said, smiling up at Ms. Bell.

"Sure did, and I think you are the perfect choice to play Annie. God knows you even look the part!"

Stacie warmed up and then sang a few songs before her first read of the song "Tomorrow." By her third time into it, she really started to like the song and noticed that Ms. Bell seemed to like what she was hearing. Two other music students had ceased their practice to stand at the door and watch.

After a while, Stacie asked Ms. Bell if she could be excused to go to the restroom.

Inside she saw that someone had added a violin-shaped clock to the wall. Its little bow pointed to 2:29.

After washing her hands, she began primping in the mirror. Suddenly the restroom light went off, plunging the small room into darkness. As she turned to feel for the nearby door knob, there came an insane inferno of cacophonous sound and violent shaking that flung her to the floor.

The next thing she knew, it was mostly dark and it was cold. Looking up she had to blink something out of her eyes and realized she was lying on her back. A cold wind was puffing up her left pant leg every now and then, and when she moved her leg to try to seal off the cold wind's access to it, she felt as if she was on a pile of broken sticks. Aware that she hurt all over, she just lay there staring upward until the cold became too much of an irritant. She tried to move her neck and arms, and in the process realized something was pinching her left arm. Turning her head, she could see she was lying amid broken wood, plaster, and shards of glass. The violin clock was smashed and lying on the floor next to her.

She could see light creeping in through the jumbled ruin that moments before had been the restroom. Its neatly painted, smooth walls are now very close to her on the floor, and they appear shattered, with pieces hanging down and sharp, broken sticks jutting into the small space to the left of her.

She became aware of a growing pain in her arm and looked down the length of her body. There a shattered piece of the restroom cabinet lay against her. A jagged piece of splintered wood poked into her arm, and there she saw blood. The sight of this repulsed her and she wriggled her right side away from the pointy wood.

An overwhelming urge to escape from this wreckage came over her, and she wriggled and squirmed to get free of the debris that lay on her. Trying to stand was out of the question because of the shattered wood over her.

Looking around for a way out, she could see a light coming from a hole in the debris, and she immediately thought she might squeeze out through the hole. The cold wind apparently entered there. She could feel it blow against her face as she crawled toward it. Through the opening, she could see what looked like a bare piece of concrete. This puzzled her because there was no bare concrete floor in the Music House.

She held her breath and listened. A small bell rang, and after a moment it rang twice more. The bell sounded clear and quite distinct in the silence: "ting, ting," a pause, and another "ting." It sounds more like a wind chime with one note than something someone played.

"Help me!" she said. "I am in here. Help!"

No one answered; there remained just the sound of gusts of wind and the intermittent "ting" of that strange small bell. She began to crawl out through the hole in the wreckage. Tight and scratchy, it resisted her, but with some effort, and stopping once to remove a glass fragment from her hand, she came free.

Gingerly she stood up and looked around a bit confused. *Where is Music House?* A shattered skeleton-like frame of a house stood over her, with pieces hanging down and what was left of the upper floor teetering in a crazy arch that looked like it might fall at any moment. She slowly turned around, surveying the scene until her eyes rested on the remains of the restroom, which had trapped her for a while. The little space she had crawled from appeared to be closely covered by the half-collapsed stairs that now went up to nowhere. The sight made her afraid, and she felt a strong desire to be home, safe, in her daddy's lap with a warm blanket snuggled all around her. Tears came.

The Music House after the Explosion.[56] Survival was possible only in the space under the stairs.

Shivering, she thought of her coat, and called out "Ms. Bell, Ms. Bell," but there was no reply.

Where did they all go?

Her stomach felt queasy, and she began wandering through the rubble, shivering, looking for her coat. Following the small bell's "ting," she found two coat hangers swinging in the wind in the remains of a closet. For a moment she watched as the wind swung the coat hangers back and forth. Whenever they collided, their metallic touch sounded a small "ting."

The wind is playing music.

Her shivering continued, and she found it difficult to see where the front room of the old house had been. She remembered laying her coat on the couch there.

Turning to where the kitchen should be, she spotted a wad of cloth entangled in the water pipes sticking up out of the floor. The sink, now fractured, sat on these bent pipes and struck her as looking like an old, broken birdbath.

---

[56] *The Effects of Nuclear Weapons*, Samuel Glasstone and Philip J. Dolan, United States Department of Defense, 1977. Figure 5.67. This house experienced a peak overpressure of 5 psi.

Pulling the wad of cloth out and straightening it, she realized it's someone else's coat. It's a bit torn and too large, but she put it on anyway, and felt grateful for the instant warmth it brought.

Desiring to find her mom, who will be here soon and make everything better, she worked her way out to the street by climbing over and through scattered wreckage. No traffic in sight.

"Mom," she called softly, not knowing what else to do. *Mom should be here soon.*

Looking right and left, she saw that all the houses along the street look like copies of the ruined Music House. They are splinters and sticks and pipes and remind her of pictures she has seen of a neighborhood hit by a tornado.

She can't see anyone at all to get help from at first, but then she spots someone sitting on the curb some distance away. It looks like a woman praying, so Stacie walks rapidly over and then, suddenly, stops short. In spite of the cold, the woman is raggedly dressed and has no shoes on her feet. The woman is sitting with the stub of a missing arm held tightly to her breast. There is much blood on what is left of her clothing and she is rocking and crying, and when their eyes meet she says what Stacie was about to say.

"Oh god! Little girl. Help me, please!"

She doesn't know what to say. A flashback memory to Girl Scouts where she learned first-aid comes, and she really wants to help, but a cold panic sets in.

They never told me about this.

"I'll go get some help for you," is all she can say. Not knowing what else to do, she backs away slowly and then runs from the broken, crying woman.

"Mom, where are you!" she cries out through tears.

Looking down a side street, she spots the red-blue flashing lights of a police car, and forgetting her own injuries and gaining strength with the thought of helping the woman, she runs through the debris scattered along the street, until she reaches a large parking lot. There is a sign that says "Convention Center." Beyond the sign, she sees the bodies. There are quite a few strewn around the lot. Although she can see one of them moving, as if trying to get up, she does not approach any of them, fearful she will encounter another armless or legless person needing help.

The police car's front windshield is gone, the door is standing open, and the front seat is smoking as if a fire is burning inside the seat. She spots the policeman sitting on the ground on the other side of the car.

"Who's there?" the policeman says.

"Stacie," she answers. "I need help. There is a woman with no arm." She points back the way she came as she speaks.

"I need your help too," the officer says. "I can't see."

As he stands up, using the car for support, Stacie sees his face. It is cut up and his eyes are bloody. She draws back in fear.

"Wait; don't go, Stacie. I have a little girl too. She is nine. Her name is Ann. Just lead me to some adults. They will help me and the woman. Please?"

At the sound of the name of the policeman's little girl, Ann, a melody comes into Stacie's mind. Calmed as she steps forward to take the policeman's blood-encrusted hand, she begins singing softly as much as she can remember of the lyrics to the melody playing in her mind.

"Sun, please come out; tomorrow, hang on; hang on, tomorrow; tomorrow clears away the sorrow."

She can see the convention center is on fire and many people are coming out, so she, policeman in tow, walks carefully toward the people, warning the officer of trip hazards and steering clear of the bodies. All the while she continues to get the lyrics wrong, but sings without ceasing, the uncontrollable shaking of her body giving her voice a strange, uneven vibrato.

Analysis of Chapter 4

"She will make the perfect little orphan Annie!" Ms. Bell said, not realizing that in a few minutes Stacie will be an orphan. Her father works for the telephone company at the central switching exchange at 4th Street and Prichard, 1900 feet from the ducks on John Jay Plaza, where her mother and brother were standing. The terrorist's bomb got them all.

The flash is so bright in the Music House that all the melodies cease by surprise. The restroom is windowless and located under the stairway leading to the second floor, so Stacie does not see the light.

The Music House is not set at random on the map of Yorksberg. It is set at a distance from the nuclear explosion point of three-quarters of a mile, or about 3900 feet from the center of the blast. Why? Because for the explosive yield of the Yorksberg bomb, three quarters of a mile is the distance from the explosion where the blast wave overpressure falls to about 5 pounds per square inch (psi).

The Music House is a wood-frame structure with not a lot of tall buildings between it and John Jay Plaza. Thus it receives a blast wave unencumbered by impact with previous structures.

For well-built, wood-frame houses, a blast of 5 psi overpressure causes serious damage to the building. Structures closer than three quarters of a mile experience almost complete destruction and for them there is little chance of the building protecting those inside. Beyond three quarters of a mile and less than 5 psi overpressure, the structural damage of a wood-frame house decreases significantly the farther the structure is from ground zero. Thus our music student is just about as close as she can get while inside a house and survive.

For a short time after the flash, while the last piano note still sounds, the paint on the north and west side of the Music House blisters and bubbles; black smoke wafts off the entire surface of the exterior walls. During the first second, the intense heat causes the synthetic fabric in the curtains hanging at the front windows to crackle, shrink, and shrivel up into hot, sticky, smoking clumps.

The three components of the blast wave are... 1. The blast wave overpressure, 2. The dynamic pressure (load due to the burst of wind flowing by) and 3. A weaker suction wind flowing back toward ground zero. The blast wave reaches the Music House in about three seconds with an overpressure of approximately 5 psi. How can 5 pounds per square inch turn a strong wood-frame house into matchsticks? Well, remember that the 5 pounds pressure is on each square inch of the house at the instant the blast strikes. Suppose the front of the house was 40 feet wide and 20 feet high (two stories). The number of square feet on the front of the house is 40 times 20 or 800 square feet. Now change that to square inches; 800 square feet times 144 square inches per square foot and we have 115,200 square inches. Multiply that by 5 (the force on each square inch) and we see that the Music House feels a sudden impact of 576,000 pounds. That is 288 tons, which is enough to break all the seams, disjoint the roof from the house frame, break the house frame from the foundation, buckle in the walls, and fracture lumber and concrete throughout the house. And don't forget that immediately following that huge impact that basically breaks all the house's strength, the dynamic pressure of the blast follows. At three quarters of a mile from the Yorksberg bomb, the wind is approximately 163 mph. Since the house has no strength left, this wind disburses the pieces, leaving only a shell behind. All this happens within 5 seconds. Boom! Whoosh! The house is ruined. Chances are it may burn afterward, although in our case this does not happen.

Why did Stacie survive? Here are the reasons she survived each of the hazards threatening her:

Light and heat.	She was inside a room inside a house.
Blast wave.	She was under the stairs, which deflected the blast and falling debris, and hung over her like a protective cap.
Entrapment.	She was just lucky.
Fire.	Luck of the draw, although not far from reality.[57]
Initial Gamma Radiation.	She did not escape this (see the additional text on gamma radiation below)
Fallout.	Stacie was upwind of the bomb and left the area promptly. She did receive some radiation damage from the fallout in the area of the Music House and convention center.
The cold.	Stacie was resourceful in getting herself free and finding and putting on someone else's coat.
Her injuries.	Luck again that nothing vital was cut or broken.

The initial gamma radiation that is emitted from the exploding bomb at the instant of detonation is worth discussing. Had Stacie been standing out front of the Music House (1300 yards from ground zero), and had the bomb been set off 1000 feet above downtown Yorksberg, she would have instantly received a lethal dose of gamma radiation.[58] Since the Yorksberg bomb was set off at ground level, much of the initial radiation was shielded from the Music House by intervening buildings and houses. Add to this that Stacie was inside the house, which itself provided some shielding, and that she was under the stairs. We conclude

---

[57] Ibid., Sections 5.55 through 5.70. During nuclear testing on wood houses, often the blast wave extinguishes fires set by the thermal heat from the rising mushroom cloud, and the cooling air flow in the following wind helps depress material temperatures below the flash point. Wood houses set in the desert near nuclear tests were scorched but did not burn.

[58] Ibid., Figure 8.33a. Note that had she been out front, the blast would have killed her, making her radiation dose irrelevant.

that the dose of radiation she received probably fell into the serious but not immediately life-threatening range.

Stacie did become an orphan. Her mother and brother were in a shop on the Plaza and killed instantly. Her father died shortly after the explosion due to injuries suffered in the collapse of the telephone exchange building a few blocks away.

She was able to lead the policeman to help, and to send help to the armless woman via some brave men from the convention center. They improvised a stretcher and carried the woman to medical help.

Stacie's voice was so clear and pure in the cold December air that the policeman, who never did find out who his helper was, insisted he was led to help by an angel with a beautiful voice.

Stacie walked the bridge to south Yorksberg with thousands of others, where she was carried out of the county to be decontaminated and to receive medical treatment for her many cuts and contusions.

After a period of depression and sorrow, Stacie was taken in by her aunt on her mother's side. She completed school and was successful at state voice competitions; little theatre; and, eventually, as a pharmacist. At age 29 she contracted leukemia, which she defeated using bone marrow transplant technology and the help of many skilled physicians. She has been cancer free for many years now.

The doctors told her that her radiation exposure during the attack on Yorksberg might have been responsible for the disease, but since a distant cousin in her family line, far from Yorksberg, died from leukemia, there was also the chance that she was genetically disposed.

Oh, did we mention that Stacie eventually married, had three children, and never returned to Yorksberg?

No one else at the Music House survived the Yorksberg nuclear terror attack for more than 5 seconds.

Quiz on Chapter 4   (Answers are in Appendix A1)

1. A well-built, wood-frame house, hit by a nuclear bomb's blast wave of 4 to 5 psi would receive what kind of damage: light, moderate, or serious?

2. Most well-built, wood-frame houses can withstand a 160-mph wind for a short time. Why is the dynamic pulse of a 165-mph wind from a nuclear explosion able to shatter a house? What are the three components of a blast wave?

3. Why wasn't Stacie threatened by fire after being trapped in the shattered Music House?

4. For a Yorksberg-sized bomb, three quarters of a mile from ground zero is the outer edge of the no-survival zone. Few at this distance will live. Is it realistic then, that Stacie survived?

5.   At three quarters of a mile from ground zero, the initial flash of intense nuclear radiation at the instant of explosion is deadly. Why didn't this kill Stacie?

It might be more difficult for a stranger in a city to survive, since that person would lack knowledge of the city's layout and shelters. In our next chapter let's look at a stranger's struggle to survive.

We will ask the question, how could a runaway teenager, lost in a large city, survive the terrorist's attack? She will survive the same way you will survive, partly by chance and partly by the actions she takes. To make it more interesting, we will throw in a nasty pimp who captures her for his own purposes. Read the next chapter to see how Janie McAskin survives to live another day.

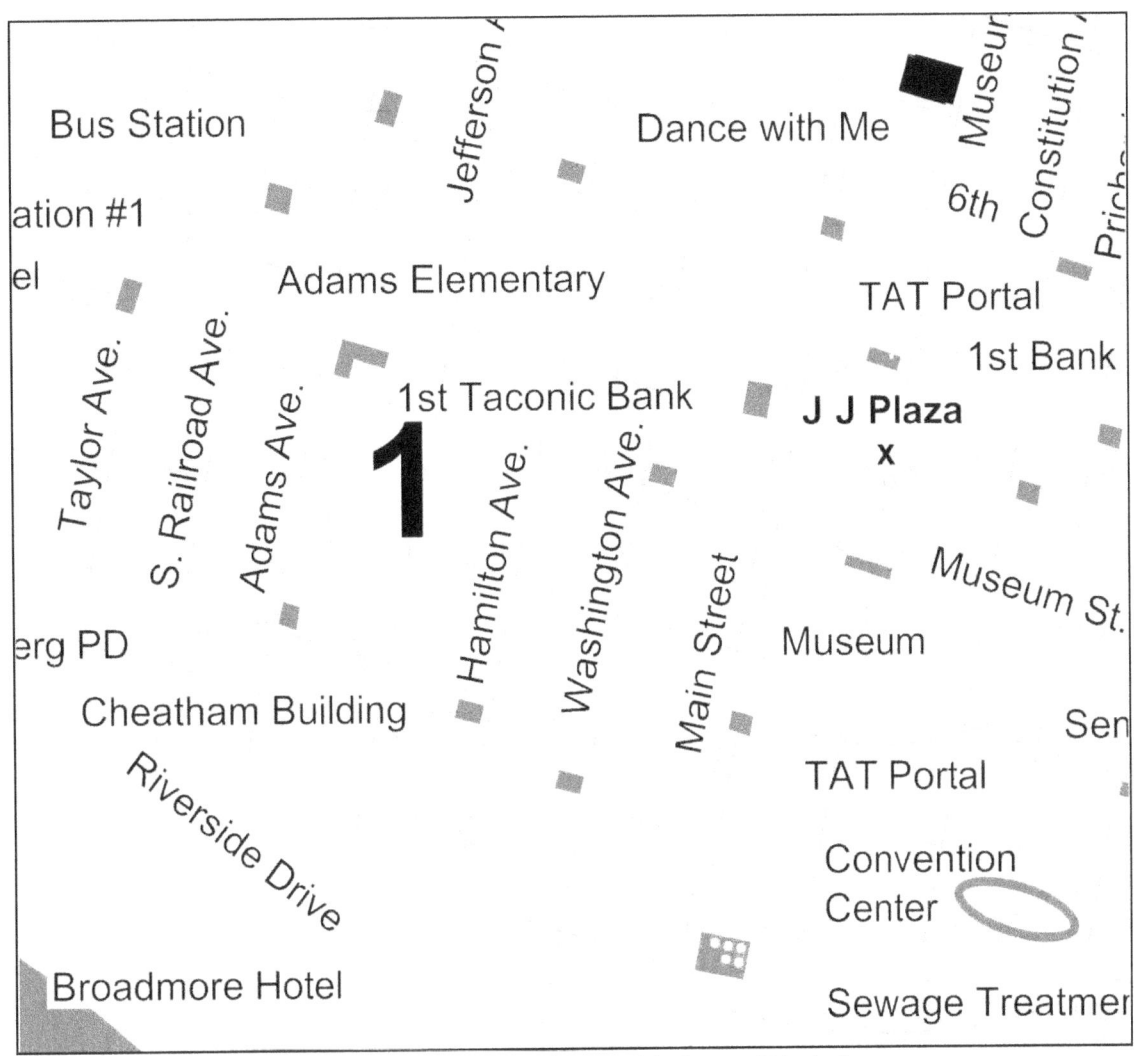

A Young Girl Finds Trouble in this Part of Yorksberg

5 - Janie McAskin - Running to Trouble (0.75 miles)

Janie Lynn McAskin was out of money and scared as she stepped off the 11:15 a.m. bus from D.C. and walked into the warmth of the bus station vestibule. As the door closed off the cold wind behind her, she stopped and looked around. The space had high ceilings, polished floors, an odd smell, and was virtually empty. The lady in the ticket office looked up at her and Janie turned away, her eyes falling on the only other living person in the area, a solitary man reading a newspaper at the far side of the room.

Wondering what to do and with hunger making her feel a bit light headed, she walked to a bench some distance from the door, slid her backpack off, and not wanting to sit after hours riding the bus, sat anyway.

Tired, she put her head down on her arms in her lap and tried once again to stir up the intense anger that had caused her to run away the day before. The argument with her mother was a dim memory now.

As she thought over the last 24 hours, however, she remembered running out of money and an awful run-in with a drunk at the D.C. station. Thinking of that event caused fear to come back, and she sat up and quickly looked around.

He smelled awful! And why is it cold, so blasted cold?

She looked around the station. No one seemed to be aware of her except the ticket lady.

The oak benches caught her eye. They looked like pews displaced from a church somewhere, and they reminded her of the one happy time in her life, when her father took her to church.

Why did he have to leave us?

Tears welled up and she blinked them back.

Sometime later a sharp hissing sound startled her, and she looked out the window to see a bus pulling away. Her hunger was worse now, and she was thirsty. She pulled out her pocket-purse and looked in again, hoping she had missed some change.

In the window's reflection she could see the ticket lady coming over.

Oh God, she's going to ask questions and will probably call the police.

Janie pretended to be looking out the window, which was damp with condensation on the inside. She did not like where she was, but did not want to go back, at least not now, not this soon. In the reflection the lady walked up behind her.

"Excuse me," the ticket lady said; "Is there anything I can do for you?"

"Nope, I'm good," Janie answered not looking around.

"You have been hanging around here for quite a while. I just thought you might need some help."

"Naw, I said I was good. Thanks anyway. My aunt was supposed to pick me up. She said she might be late," Janie said. Her heart was racing and her palms cold with the lie she was telling. She wanted help, yet resented the fact that she needed it.

"I see," the ticket lady said. "It is always an aunt or a sister. Why don't you kids ever say father, or brother, or uncle?" And then she paused, as if another thought was coming. "Perhaps a man is the problem? Well honey, I hope she does not keep you long. You know the station closes after the 7 p.m. bus departs. You can't wait longer than that in here."

Crap!

"Thank you," Janie said.

"My name is Joy. Come talk to me if you change your mind and I can help you."

She watched the lady walk back to the ticket office.

Thinking she should look as if she was expecting someone, she went outside and looked up and down the street. The cold wind was biting, lancing through her hooded sweatshirt and sweater.

I should have brought my winter coat.

Turning around, she walked back to the station front doors and pushed in. The brief excursion into the cold followed by the warmth only intensified her hunger.

Tommy Jenkins watched her come out of the bus station, look around, and then turn and go back in.

Damned if that don't look like a runner.

He pulled out his jewel-encrusted switchblade and snapped it open, enjoying the "Thack!" sound the metal smacking metal made, and began using its wicked-sharp tip to clean under his fingernails. The Cadillac's pricy sound system was low, and rich, and playing some slow, cool jazz.

Nobody is going to come rescue that little bird, or my name isn't Jade the pimp!

He smiled at his acute discernment, closed the knife, and placed it at the ready in his pocket.

He flipped down the visor's lighted mirror and checked appearances. Tie straight, hair in place, expensive suit clean, and shirt pressed.

You do look fine, Mr. Gun, even if I say so myself!

Tommy briefly buffed his shoes with a handkerchief, shut off the caddy, and stepped out. As he walked to the station entrance, he deftly avoided the piles of slush ice mashed up by parking-lot traffic.

Janie saw him come into the station and was immediately attracted to him simply because he dressed so well. The shoes, the fur-lined winter long-coat, and a confidence that practically said "important man."

He's got to be a banker or rich real estate dude.

When he walked right up to her this surprised her.

"Excuse me," Tommy said; "I am looking for my sister. A petite lady, about 30, probably with a black purse on a long strap. Have you seen her?"

"No" Janie said, noting the smile and kind look of his eyes.

He looked at his watch. "Well, she should have been here by now. Are you waiting too?"

She answered in the affirmative. He had a way of engaging her eyes as he talked that she found interesting. It was hard to look away from him.

He smells good.

"I'm Tommy, Tommy Jenkins," he said offering his hand.

She accepted the hand limply. "I'm Janie." His hand was warm, and when he put his left hand on hers as they shook, she noticed he was wearing a beautiful, expensive wedding band. Everything about him shouted that he had money.

After a half hour of polite conversation about the weather, the city, and his fictitious wife and kids, Tommy changed the subject.

"I am really getting hungry; I think I'll go get a burger across the street," he said, pointing to the fast-food restaurant visible through the window. He turned and started to walk off, and then, in a calculated move that he knew would look like a second thought, he turned back.

"Janie, I'm sorry; I should have asked. Would you like to come over? My treat." He saw her eyes light up even before she replied, and he marveled at how easy this was.

It's always easy with these little running birds.

Janie thought of food as they walked across the street.

Luck has finally broken my way.

She could smell the delicious aroma of hamburger cooking and her stomach was growling.

Tommy Gun, you are going to enjoy this evening, he thought as they walked across the street. He remembered the last girl several months ago, cowering before his fist and his "training tool," a piece of rubber hose, until she was submissive, under his control, and willing to take the tricks he found for her.

He held the door open for Janie to show his kindness and to increase her trust, and they walked into the thick, warm smell of onions and grease.

As they seated themselves, Tommy looked Janie over.

This one has a pretty face and a good figure.

He did some mental calculations as to how much money he could ask for her. Actually she was so pretty he toyed with the idea of calling Ramon, who was always looking for pretty prizes to "disappear." This was tempting since he owed Ramon some money, but he pushed the idea out of his mind for the time being.

He watched her open the menu.

This little bird will earn me enough money in a month to pay Ramon and then some and I can sell her to him anytime when it comes time to get rid of her.

He watched her choke down a hamburger, a large order of fries, and a hot chocolate as if she were a starving person. He ate lightly, and then bought her a second burger when she finished the first. It was quickly gone.

Damn! That girl is hungry.

Janie felt a glow of warmth and relaxation when the food hit her bloodstream. The feeling was wonderful, and the man across from her was so kind. In the ensuing conversation between them, he had even offered her the chance to stay at his sister's apartment. This, she knew, solved the next problem she faced.

"She won't mind," he said; "Deloris has been through some tough times too, and she loves to help. You wouldn't be the first, and you can stay a few days and then be on your way. She can probably find you a job if you want one."

Tommy paused while she finished off her fries, to give her time to think. A moment later, to encourage her to make up her mind, he placed a cell call right in front of her.

"Hey, Mac, it's Tommy. Did Deloris call? She was not at the bus stop."

"Hi, Tommy," Mac answered. "We both know you ain't got a sister. You got a live one?"

"Yep," Tommy replied, and then added for Janie's benefit, "Tell her to call me if she calls you. Also tell her she will have a guest for a day or so. Yah, she does not mind. She likes to help when she can."

Mac laughed. "You are so smooth, Mr. Gun. No wonder they call you 'Smooth J.' I'll be ready."

"Later then," Tommy said and closed the slick, thin phone, knowing that Mac would be ready when they got to the Broadmore Hotel.

"Mac is my younger brother. He said he has not heard from Deloris, but that she did say she might arrive early. I wish that girl would communicate better."

He redialed the phone and a moment later he heard a woman's voice on his answering machine.

"Well look at you," Tommy said, "all snug and warm at home while your poor brother is walking around a cold bus station waiting for you."

Tommy grinned at Janie, and pointed at his phone. He paused as if listening and then said, "It's okay, sis; Mac forgot to tell me. How was your trip?" Again he paused as if listening to his sister. Eventually he got around to the real purpose of his call.

"Say, Deloris, I have a friend from out of town whose ride never showed up at the station. Her name is Janie. Would you mind if she spent the night with you?" As he fake-listened, he smiled as if receiving good news. "You are fantastic, girl. Mama would be proud of you; I'll let her know. Thanks, love you too. Bye." He closed the instrument of his deception.

"Well, you're in for tonight, and even a few days if you need them she said. That girl has a heart of gold. I go right by her apartment on the way to mine, so I can give you a lift if you'd like."

Janie hesitated. She recalled the awful stories she'd heard about girls getting raped or sold into sexual slavery and knew that those things happened. But this seemed different. Tommy was obviously a decent man who had a brother and a sister he loved. Janie knew such a person could never harm her. She glanced at a clock on the wall.

2 p.m.

Besides, the bus station closed after the 7 p.m. bus, and she had nowhere to go after that. The idea of being on the cold streets after dark made her shiver.

Tommy sipped his coffee and watched the wheels turning in Janie's pretty head. Instinctively, as a wolf going for the jugular, he knew how to close this deal.

"I know; you really shouldn't go with me. I mean, you hardly know me, so here is what I will do." He got out a card on which he wrote as he was talking. "Here is the address of my sister's apartment. You can walk there in an hour or so. If you hustle, you can get there before it gets dark. And I know the area. It is a fairly good part of this city; no one will bother you. Just tell her Tommy sent you."

As he handed the card over, Janie was thinking about how cold it was outside.
An hour walking in that cold!

On a warm summer day she might have gone for it, but it was freezing outside, and for the first time since she got off the bus she was actually warm and comfortable. She did not want to go back to being cold.

She looked at the card. He had written "Broadmore, Washington and Weasel, Apt. 312." The other side of the card said "Tommy Jenkins, Manager, Interpersonal Relations, Inc."

"Interpersonal Relations?" Janie said.

"Counseling. Marriage, divorce, that sort of thing," he said, and smiled at his card's clever description of his business.

"No, that's okay," Janie said, handing the card back. "I'll let you take me over to your sister's place, and thanks. You are a very kind man."

On the way to the Broadmore, Janie found she could hardly keep her eyes open. The caddy was toasty warm, smelled of Tommy's wonderful cologne, and the two hamburgers weighed heavy on her eyelids. The next thing she knew they were parking in a parking garage.

Janie felt a little nervous about walking through the garage with Tommy, but she was still sleepy and just wanted to find a couch to crash on. She was comforted by the fact that a janitor with a push bucket and mop entered the elevator just ahead of them. He was a very large man.

If this Tommy tries anything in the elevator, at least this janitor will be there to stop him.

Tommy smiled at Mac in the janitor outfit.

"Good afternoon," Tommy said, playing the game.

"Good day to you too, sir," Mac said, stifling a grin.

As soon as Tommy had entered the elevator with Janie, and his little bird turned to face the front, Mac's arm suddenly came around her neck, choking her wind and lifting her off the floor.

They always claw at the arm.

Tommy stopped the elevator door with his foot and watched her kick and thrash while Mac held her. It was a brief, silent struggle. Then, as expected, she went limp.

"She's a strong one," Mac said.

Tommy led him out the elevator door back into the parking garage, and then through a door only five yards from the elevator. They passed through a short hallway where he unlocked an inner door to his "training room." He stepped in and turned on the light, a single, bare bulb in the ceiling. It illuminated a ten-by-ten room, which had a single bed, a doorway to a small bathroom with a shower, and a few pieces of furniture.

"Toss her on the bed," Tommy said. He watched as Mac laid her down, briefly massaged her neck, and made sure she was breathing.

"She's a pretty one," Mac said, and then added "Ka-ching ka-ching."

"You'll get your usual go at her," Tommy said. "A little thank you for your help."

As they left the little room and locked the two doors behind them, Mac hung a "Danger, High Voltage" sign on the outer door.

"Smooth as ever, Tommy," Mac said.

"Damn fine merchandise. Not much like that lately. They tend to run more when it ain't so cold," Tommy said.

"Did you get it for me?" Mac said, burly eyebrows raised in expectation.

"Does Tommy ever fail you, man? Of course. Come on up to my place."

They entered Tommy's penthouse suite. He casually tossed his keys on a table and glanced at the clock on his wall. It was 2:29 p.m.

Mac walked across the plush, immaculate carpet, stood at the large glass window, and looked down at the square four blocks away.

"Fine view," Mac said.

"You're looking right down on the heart of Yorksberg," Tommy said. "My favorite view is the south window, though. I love the boats, especially the sailboats in the summer."

"Here, my good man," Tommy added, handing Mac a small medicine bottle.

Mac took the bottle and shook it. He smiled at the satisfying rattle. "Man, I am going to have a blast tonight." The antique chiming clock on the wall began the Westminster chime for the half hour.

Instantly the room was filled with an incredible light, as if God had suddenly stepped into the room in all His glory to deliver to its occupants everything they deserved. Tommy recoiled from it in uncomprehending blindness. He did not have time to even begin to scream in pain as the skin on his face burned, when the blast wave drove the inch-thick glass window out of its frame, through the room and then out the other side of the reeling building.

Janie's first thoughts were confused and mixed with a pounding headache. She lay there, trying to get her breath back. Her neck hurt and she was nauseous. It was very quiet and pitch black.

She felt fear as she remembered what had happened. She lay on the bed, heart pounding, very afraid.

Someone choked me.

There didn't seem to be anyone in the room, so after a few minutes she got up, slipped her backpack off, and felt along the walls, trying to find a way out. She eventually located the light switch and turned it on. Janie looked around the room and felt sick. She sensed she was in deep trouble and felt like a fool for being taken.

She realized she did not know where she was, her parents and friends did not know where she was, and the two men who did know were obviously up to no good. She began crying. She suspected the worst and felt a growing anxiety that drove her almost to desperation to get out of this cell.

She continued exploring, checking out the only connecting room, a small bathroom. Peeking behind the shower curtain into the tiny 3' x 3' molded shower stall, she found nothing except a used bar of soap. As she stepped back and closed the curtain, the light went out, and a second or two later the bathroom shook with one violent lurch. There was a terrible deep rumbling sound for a full minute. In the room it sounded like distant thunder, or a train passing for several moments, and then all was quiet again.

She remembered her backpack and located it by feel in the pitch-black room. She opened it and took out her tiny penlight. With it she found her cell phone. Hands shaking, she tried to call her mother, but the cell phone did not work at all. It showed no signal strength.

Using the pen light, she explored the small, beat-up dresser against one wall and found a pair of handcuffs and a short piece of rubber hose in the top drawer. She could only imagine why they were in this room, and it terrified her. She began crying again, afraid that Tommy would be back at any time. The small pen light rolled out of her hand and she watched it lying on the floor, its tiny spot of light shining under the dresser in the darkness.

After a few moments she realized she'd better not waste the batteries and turned off the small light. She used it sparingly to check the bottom drawer of the dresser and found paper plates, a can opener, and plastic ware. Looking at the shelf above the dresser she saw several cans of soup; some chili; three cans of various vegetables; and a large jar of peanuts, the salted kind.

At least I can eat.

She switched the small light off, laid back down on the bed in the dark, and prayed. She was not religious, but it seemed to her the thing to do. Eventually she fell into a deep fatigue-induced sleep.

Many hours later Janie awoke, and lying very still, tried to remember where she was. It was as quiet as a tomb and so dark she could not see her hand in front of her face. She remembered Tommy, and the bus station, and being choked in the elevator, and sat bolt upright, suddenly fearful that he would return.

Nature called, and Janie fumbled for her small penlight. Finding it, she located the bathroom and took care of her needs. She even tried to lock the door in fear of Tommy, but found the door did not have a lock on the inside. When she flushed the commode, she noticed it did not refill.

Water's off?

Having helped her uncle fix his commode, Janie reached under the commode's water tank and tried to turn on the water. She found the isolation valve, but it was already on. Then she tried to turn on the water in the sink and confirmed there was no water.

Janie cursed Tommy for putting her in this situation and began searching the room for a knife, or any weapon she might use to get out of this place when Tommy came back.

Several times she tried the door, but always found it locked tight. Eventually she got hungry and opened a can of chicken-noodle soup. Unable to heat it, she ate it cold right from the can. The only positive aspect of this meal was that behind the cans of soup she found a small transistor radio.

She was surprised to find that it worked! But there was no music, just news, and as she listed she was stunned to hear reports about what had happened. Although she did not know exactly what a nuclear bomb was, or exactly where she was in relation to it, a bit of hope came back to her.

Tommy might not come back! I hope the bastard was killed.

Then the cold realization hit her.

If he is dead, no one in the world knows I am trapped in this hole. I have been buried alive.

A great, aching emptiness came over her, and she began sobbing in the hopelessness of her situation.

"Oh, God, help me; help me. Please let someone find me."

Many hours later she woke up feeling very thirsty. There was nothing to drink and the water still did not work. She spent many hours in the darkness in despair and an increasing thirst. It was the thirst that finally drove her to pull the lid off the toilet tank and scoop what water remained there into a paper cup. It tasted odd, but it really helped her thirst. She wished she had not flushed the tank. The water stored there could have lasted many days.

Bored out of her mind in the dark, cold silence, Janie played the radio for comfort, sang to herself, and repeated her explorations. It was then that she discovered a small hot water heater mounted behind a curtain in the cramped bathroom. She had seen it earlier, but at that time it meant nothing to her. Now she looked it over, thinking it might still be full of water. Where could the water go? No one was taking showers. At the bottom of the tank was a small spigot. Fetching her paper cup, she opened the spigot and found that clean water came out. She drank her fill.

Janie continued to use the penlight sparingly after the radio battery died. She realized she had played the radio too much. It had been a companion with her in the dark and the news had been interesting to follow. She ached for human companionship and wanted more than anything to go home to her mother and brothers. She regretted deeply the hard, means words she had spoken to her mother before running away.

After what must have been several days, the little penlight died, leaving her in darkness. From then on, she managed by feeling her way around the room. The penlight had given her just enough knowledge to be able to find the food, water, and commode, which by now smelled so foul that she had to keep the bathroom door shut.

The room was too cold for comfort, so she wrapped herself with the bed cover and walked back and forth in the dark for some time. She felt nauseous and lay down on the bed, curled up into a fetal position, and stared into the blackness of her prison room, her exhausted mind filled with anxiety.

How long will it take me to die? I wish I had never had that stupid argument with mom. Will dying of starvation hurt? I don't want to die, I don't want to die.

She imagined someone, perhaps months later, opening the room and finding her shriveled cadaver, wrapped in these bed coverings, lying in this dark sarcophagus, and a long, deep, pain-filled moan escaped her half open mouth.

Analysis of Chapter 5

This section is not about runaway children. The chain of events in Janie's young life provides us with a framework of people, locations, and survival around which we can let you once again see what it takes to survive a terrorist's nuclear attack in your city. The two villains had retired to a penthouse apartment exposed to the plaza less than a mile away in direct line-of-sight to the explosion. The intense light and heat will start fires in places like these, and then the blast wave will blow through the buildings, much like the 9/11 aircraft came through the World Trade Center towers, only with far more power behind it.

City dwellers in high-rise apartments should keep in mind that if there are many large, substantial buildings between them and the point of the explosion, some protection may be provided. Most tall office buildings, such as the museum described in an earlier story as constructed of granite, marble blocks, and concrete, are not what would be termed "substantial." Most modern buildings are skeletal steel frames covered with architectural siding and as such will not provide a substantial shielding effect for buildings behind them. Note that depending on the blast's relative location to a given building, certain floors in that building may remain virtually unscathed and others completely gutted.

Our two villains were about 0.8 miles from ground zero. The blast wave reached their building within four seconds and both were killed. They were close enough that the overpressure from the blast wave was greater than 4 psi, severely damaging the upper parts of the Broadmore Hotel that were not shielded by intervening buildings.

Janie had been placed by their evil intentions in a place of great safety. She was below ground level, and near the center of the building. There were 15 floors above her, and she had enough food and water. That her shelter was dark, unheated, and stuffy was survivable.

Janie was far enough away from ground zero that the ground wave effects were not strong enough to bring the building down on her. There were no windows in her prison, so the light and heat of the blast could not reach her. Because she was below the ground level she was largely shielded from the direct radiation from the explosion. Finally, the fallout from the explosion tended to fall away from the Broadmore due to prevailing winds, and the fallout that did rain down on the hotel was kept at least 100 feet above her and behind many floors of poured concrete, each of which acted as a shield. Most of the apartments and offices near the top of the building ended up as blown-out shells, with no windows and with their floors covered in a fine layer of radioactive dust.

The majority of the fallout that rained down from the rising mushroom cloud remained on what was left of the roof, and on the once-plush carpet in Tommy's penthouse below where the blast had removed a portion of the roof. Gamma radiation from the street-level fallout could not reach Janie in dangerous amounts since it had to pass through many feet of earth to reach her.

So our protagonist, Janie, survives the explosion and has only to face her human basic needs: water, food, and air. City dwellers who intend to survive will do well to remember that shelter areas need these basics. In Janie's situation, Tommy, the villain, left small quantities of canned food for his victims. Food in unopened cans will always be good to eat after a nuclear explosion even if the can is covered in radioactive dust. One only needs to carefully wash contamination off the can before opening it. The focus here is not to eat the dust.

There are three types of nuclear radiation: beta rays, alpha rays, and gamma rays. The first two are solid particles and they are very tiny. The third, gamma, is not a solid particle; instead it is a light wave, just like red or blue light, or x-rays, just a lot more powerful.

Beta and alpha rays are not a problem when we are talking about avoiding whole-body radiation exposure, because they are stopped easily. A piece of tissue paper will stop beta rays, and a thin piece of card stock will stop alpha rays. Alpha and beta rays are generally only dangerous when the emitter gets inside the human body. This is why you will want to keep everything involving eating and drinking very clean if you are in a fallout zone. If alpha or beta radioactive emitters can't get inside you, they can't hurt you.

Gamma rays are a different story. Like x-rays, they can pass through you. In fact if a container is too thick to take an x-ray of what is inside, gamma rays can be used to reveal the contents. They have a greater penetrating power and can do more damage to tissue than x-rays.[59]

Alpha and beta rays from the radioactive dust cannot penetrate a metal can, or plastic bottles, or cardboard boxes, or even the waxed bag holding cereal in a box. And even if alpha and beta radiation could reach the food, like gamma radiation can, none of this radiation can make the food either radioactive or bad. Be sure to catch this distinction: radiation does not make food dangerous or harm it in any way, but radioactive materials are dangerous and can harm you if they get into food or drink that you consume.

The radioactive materials in fallout are dangerous. Use time, distance, and shielding to protect you from gamma rays coming from fallout, and do not get contaminated dirt or dust inside you. The idea is to protect your insides from the materials that emit all three forms of radiation: alpha, beta, and gamma.

Water will be a problem for a shelter, particularly for an unprepared shelter or one with more people in it than the stored water can support. Rainwater or water collected from streams may be contaminated with radioactive dust, so in general it should not be used. Water should be obtained only from sealed containers.

You cannot kill the radioactive dust by boiling it, like you can kill bacteria. You might get away with distilling water if you are careful not to carryover any of the radioactive dust into the distillate. Likewise, filtration may work too, but you would do well to have a radiation survey meter to scan the filtered water to assure no radioactive materials get through the filter. Three feet of pure sand will filter out many of the impurities in water.

Rainwater caught directly as it falls will be good to drink after local dust is removed from the air by the rain. It should be caught only on clean surfaces such as a plastic tarp that has been stored and sealed away from dust and contamination.

Think of bottled water, toilet tanks, and water heaters; all these can store and supply drinkable water.

Survivors attempting to get drinkable water from their hot water tanks may need to open the hot or cold water valve in a nearby sink to let air into the hot water heater. As a side note, and not applicable to Janie's situation, remember that a commode can be flushed with dirty, non-potable water, such as ditch water, river water, or standing water in puddles

---

[59] Gamma rays are quanta of electromagnetic radiation, which are emitted by atomic nuclei when these nuclei undergo transitions from a higher energy state to a lower energy state. The energies of gamma rays may vary between a few Kev (Kilo electron volts) to 20 Mev (Million electron volts). *Concise Encyclopedia of Nuclear Energy*, D. E. Barnes, 1962, p. 282.

after a rain. Just scoop up a bucket full and pour it quickly into the toilet bowl. Alternatively, you can fill the toilet tank.

Janie did not have the problem of people entering her shelter and bringing contamination in. This is a problem that requires some forethought and planning and is not dealt with in this section. Contamination in a shelter must be minimized and controlled.

Conserving emergency batteries is important because those sheltering need to maintain communication with the outside world, and to have light in the enclosed shelter area. Persons in a community shelter may try to duplicate the comforts they knew before being driven into the shelter. This is one reason it is an advantage to have a system of trained shelter leaders in place with recognized authority prior to the attack to control the rationing of food, water, light, radios, medical resources, and contamination.

Janie did not die in that dark room. We pick up where we left off, with Janie on her fifth day in the room.

Janie woke up and sat up. She had been dreaming that her cell phone worked and that she was using its light to see. Hungry, she got out of the warm bed and scrounged around the floor, trying to find her backpack. She could not find it and searched with increasing anxiety. The phone might not allow her to call, but it would light up. Frustrated, she finally gave up, and then decided to check the bathroom.

I don't remember taking it in there, but what the hell. God it smells in there.

She tripped over the backpack just inside the bathroom, and quickly took it to the bed. When she turned the cell phone on, there was indeed light. Then she noticed the signal-strength bar. The phone was getting a signal! She dialed and the phone at the other end rang.

"Hello," said her mother. Her voice sounded so good.

"Mom, it's me, Janie."

"Janie, oh my goodness!" Her mother's voice sounded concerned. "Where are you?"

"I'm in Yorksberg," she replied.

There was a pause. "You can't be," her mom finally said. "That place was destroyed five days ago."

"Mom, I want to come home. Please help me," she began crying.

"Okay, okay baby. Your dad is here. We will help you."

"Dad's there?" *I haven't seen him in five years.*

"He came to help search for you."

At this news, Janie brightened up.

His voice came on the phone. "Janie, are you really in Yorksberg?"

"Yes, Dad. I got grabbed by some guy named Tommy – it is a long story," Janie said. "He locked me in this room – I think it must be somewhere under the Broadmore Hotel parking garage. Please come get me out."

"Okay, honey. We will get you out. We miss you very much. Now calm down. I want you to tell me what happened, what you remember seeing so I can tell the police."

When she finished, he said, "Now turn your cell phone off for about thirty minutes to save the battery. Call us again and we'll let you know what is happening."

By this time the radiation levels had dropped enough that rescue teams could be sent in on short forays, wearing protective gear. Many of these men and women were National Guard soldiers who were given dosimeters and sent in on search and rescue missions when leads like Janie's surfaced. Within a few hours of receiving Janie's father's call, they had contacted Janie and were making a detailed search of the lower floors of the hotel and parking garage. They recovered several bodies, but could not locate Janie. On their way out they noticed a room near the elevator marked "Danger High Voltage." It was locked. One of the men hit it three times with the back of an axe he was carrying and called out but there was no response. Nearing the end of their allowed radiation exposure time, the team members began retreating out of the parking garage to their vehicles.

Janie heard the three heavy thumps.

"I am in here!" she said. She found she could not make much noise with her hand, so she got a can of soup and used it to pound on the door.

When no one came, she got on her cell phone and called the number they had given her.

"This is team four leader," the voice said.

"Hi, this is Janie. I heard you guys."

"Hold it!" The team leader said to his team. He then spoke in the phone. "What did you hear?"

"Three bangs or thumps. I yelled but no one heard me."

"Did any of you hit something three times?" she heard him ask someone.

"I did, chief," one of the men said. "That electrical door near the elevator."

"She's in there. Go take that door down and make it quick. We have five minutes."

Janie heard them breaking through both doors to get in. When the inner door swung open, Janie was surprised to see three space-suited figures. One of them spoke.

"Hello, Janie. I'm Carl. Let's get you out of here." He fitted a funny-looking mask over her face, while a second man went through the room with a flashlight and a little yellow box.

As they left, Janie heard the man with the box say, "It's really clean in there. Most of my readings were from our feet. She should be okay."

Janie had survived the nuclear attack.

She had not tried her cell phone for days, thinking it did not work. Is it reasonable for a teenage girl not to try her cell phone for days? Probably not; however, the author maintains this peculiarity by noting the severe stress and fear she was under, given her situation. The reader is urged to consider her fate had Tommy removed her cell phone from the room.

Once Janie's situation was known to the local emergency response authority, help was quickly sent. Radiation outside her prison shelter had dropped significantly by the 5th day so that rescue crews in protective gear could enter and attempt to locate her. They almost did not find her. It is likely that in the weeks following the nuclear attack, search and rescue will be done by teams of men and women working in the radiation zone for carefully controlled amounts of time. As these men and women are "burnt out" (meaning they reach the allowable radiation exposure limits), they will be retired from the search and rescue effort and fresh (unexposed) persons will replace them. In this manner, the search and rescue can continue, and the exposure is spread over a large number of rescuers so that each person receives as little radiation as possible.

The windows on the plaza side of Tommy's penthouse were blown clear through the building, throwing everything inside the suite out the south windows. Mac and Tommy's glass riddled, burned bodies were flung out of the building and, after a fall of nine stories, landed on the roof of the buildings on the south side of Weasel Street.

The crumpled, decaying bodies of Tommy and Mac were picked up on aerial surveillance and some weeks later were removed for hazardous (radioactive) waste burial. Curiously, those removing the decayed body of the once egotistical and proud Tommy "the Gun" Jenkins found a burnt and twisted street sign lying next to his body. The sign was from the corner of Main and Weasel and it still said, through its charred green and white paint, "Weasel." The ironic humor of this message was missed by the body recovery crew.

What happened to Janie? After some national media exposure of Janie and her story she returned home to her mother and brothers. No, her experience did not bring her dad home for good. His alcoholism and anger were not cured by this event. But Janie never ran away again, and with some counseling turned out to be a pretty nice person, wiser and willing to face her problems rather than running from them. Janie went on to graduate from high school and attend a junior college for her AA degree. She ended up with a four-year degree and a good job as an RN at a hospital in New York State. Years later she actually treated burn victims from the PPF's second and last bomb attack on a great city that shall remain unnamed.

Oh, and one more thing. Janie's story prompted the opening of an investigation into Mac's phone, internet, and cell phone records. After much investigative work, and surveillance, several top dogs in the clandestine and illegal sex slavery industry in San Francisco, Mexico, and as far away as Columbia were uncovered and eventually incarcerated, and four girls who had disappeared were recovered from a brothel in Mexico.

Please take the quiz that follows....

Quiz on Chapter 5   (Answers are in Appendix A1)

1.   When sheltering for some length of time, what one commodity should you be sure to have in the shelter in sufficient quantity?
2.   What are the three types of nuclear radiation that will hit your body that comes from fallout after the explosion?
3.   What types of nuclear radiation can only seriously harm you if the radioactive material gets inside your body?
4.   Apartments in high-rise buildings make good shelters from the effects of a terrorist's nuclear bomb. True or False. Why?
5.   Name two sources of water in most homes that is available after the city water system fails. Also, how can contaminated or dirty water be useful in a shelter?

Being trapped is no fun, especially when a nuclear explosion causes the entrapment. In the next story you will be with a dance instructor named Jetta Goldberg, at her *Dance with Me* studio in downtown Yorksberg, who is trapped by the explosion. Will she get out alive? Will she survive or die? You will have to read on to see.

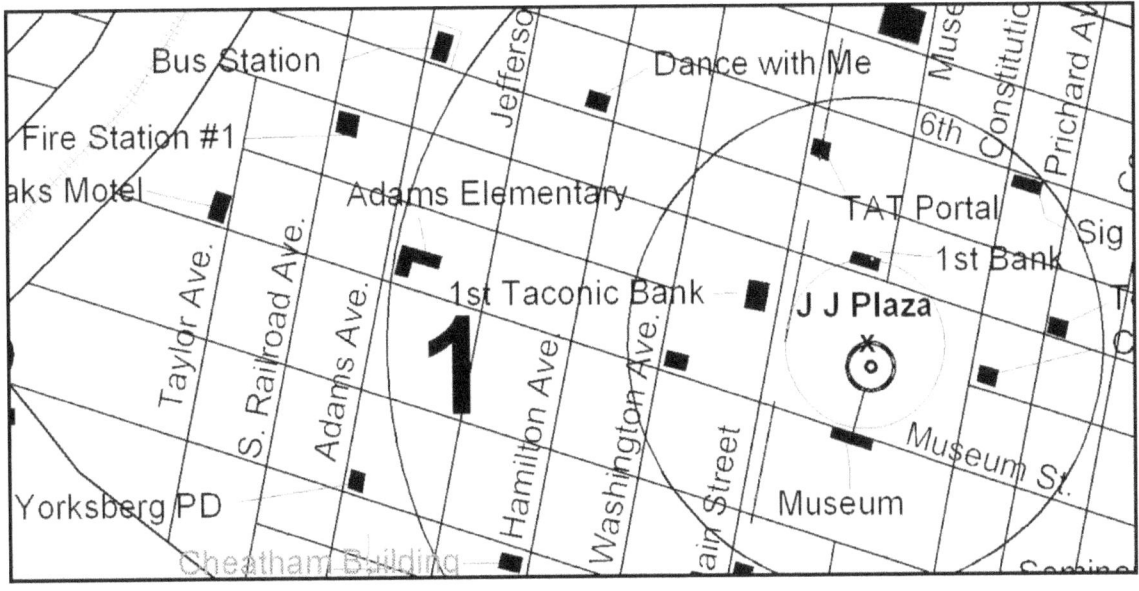

6 – Jetta Goldberg - Dance with Me (0.75 miles)

Jetta stared straight ahead, her eyes glazed over with fatigue and the cold, and thought of nothing except her nine beautiful, young dancers, all dead. She wiped the tears from her eyes and shivered.

The bus's transmission howled through a gear change as it accelerated up some unnamed hill in the dark, and then a voice came on the PA system: "This trip to Ackersville will take about two hours. There you will find sleeping accommodations in a church gymnasium, and the local people will provide meals for you. Phones will be available so you can contact loved ones and get other help, and FEMA will have a representative in the area within the next few days. Be sure to fill out the paperwork if you need assistance. My name is Margie and I will be up here in the front if you have any other questions. Oh, the bus's heater is on full blast. I'm sorry, but the heat we have in here is as warm as it gets."

The metal wall of the bus felt ice cold, and the windows leaked little puffs of winter air as the bus moved down the road. Jetta could feel every little breeze through the paper smock she wore, so she slid away from the window, thankful no one was sitting next to her.

She wanted to sleep, but when she put her head back, it leaned against the shiny steel rail at the top of the seat. The bouncing of the bus kept the back of her head thumping against it.

It's only two hours, if I can just hold on.

Catching snatches of sleep, she awoke to find the bus still barreling down some dark highway. There seemed to be no other traffic, and now she had a cramp in her neck. She was hungry too.

Thoughts of the previous day did not bring tears this time, but filled her with an aching despair.

An atomic bomb. Who would do such a thing? I hope mom is okay. God, I had no idea what was about to happen when she called.

As the old bus ran through the darkness, Jetta remembered the last conversation with her mother.

"Mom, the color lavender would look better," Jetta said.

"You must speak louder, dear. You have a habit of mumbling." Mother sounded peeved. She always sounded peeved.

Jetta visualized the Taconic River Assisted Living Center and her mother's room. She bit her lip and then spoke with more energy. "Okay, Mom. Is this better?"

"That's fine, dear. Did I ask you to pick up some of those hair scrunchies, you know, the ones all those little teenage girls wear?"

"Yes, you did. Is there anything else I can get for you?" Jetta looked at her watch. *2:15.*

"The girl is here to help me with my bath. I have to go now. When are you going to come see me?"

"I already told you, Mother; I will be over to see you after my last class this evening. Probably about 8:30."

"Okay, dearie. Love ya."

"I love you too, Mom," Jetta said, and then realized her mother had already hung up. She shook her head and smiled as she set the phone on the desk. She grabbed a note pad and jotted down her mother's list.

As she put the sticky note in her purse, a flash of light from passing traffic caught her eye. Looking out the window she noticed two ladies walking up to the studio. The tall lady looked familiar, even though she could not say she recognized her. She knew she had never seen the shorter woman or the young girl with her. They had dark hair and rich olive-colored skin. Jetta noted the beauty of both and that the girl had her mother's face to a detail. She heard them enter the dance studio, so she left the front office to greet them.

"Jetta!" the tall woman said as if expecting recognition.

Jetta hesitated, starting to be embarrassed that she didn't recognize this person, and then something about her bearing brought up a memory.

"Listy?"

"It must be my hairdo," Listy said, patting her hair on one side.

"It has been years, lady. What has Listy Mitchell been up to and what brings you back to Yorksberg?" They embraced in a tight hug.

"Listy Duginski now. Mr. Mitchell abandoned ship years ago."

"Well, times change," was all Jetta could think to say.

"Jetta, this is Susan and her daughter Kate." Turning to Susan, Listy said, "Jetta and her husband were neighbors of mine for years until my ex decided to move to Alaska. I haven't seen Jetta for, well, probably 15 years."

"Nice to meet you." Susan extended her hand.

"Me too," Kate said, extending her hand. "Are you the dance teacher?"

"I am," Jetta said with a smile. "Actually, one of several instructors. Are you interested in taking dance lessons?"

"Uh huh. Mom says I can."

"What type of dancing do you want to learn?" This brought a pause, and Kate looked at her mom.

"She saw the Nutcracker on TV at Thanksgiving. I think the ballet interested her, but why don't you tell her what there is to learn?"

"Better than that, she can come and see. We have ballet, jazz, tap, hip-hop, inspirational, interpretive, and gymnastic dance. Right now we have a hip-hop class in the back room for high school girls," she pointed to the room at the rear, "and at 3:30 we will have second year ballet in this front room with all the mirrors."

Kate tried a few improvised dance moves while watching herself in multiple reflections.

"What is hip-hop?" Susan said.

"Oh, Mom, you know what that is," Kate said, and spun and did some popping and locking, still watching herself perform.

"Let's go take a look," Jetta offered. "There are seniors here working on their winter recital pieces. They get out of school for a couple of hours one day a week to come here." Jetta walked them to the back room and they stepped inside.

Kate saw nine girls in a mixture of shorts and leotards being led by a girl in purple. They were dancing to a loud, rhythmic beat.

"I've heard that song on the radio," Kate said, smiling.

It was a long piece, and when the music finally ended she applauded the girls, who sat down on benches around the room, apparently a little out of breath.

"Looking good, Andrea," Jetta encouraged.

"Thanks, Ms. Goldberg," the girl in purple shorts said, and then added, "Mom sent back the costumes. She washed them." She pointed to a small pile stacked on a table in the corner by the sound system.

"Tell her that is much appreciated," Jetta said, and then turned to Listy, Susan, and Kate. "It always helps when the parents clean things."

They walked back to the front.

"Is it still ballet?" Susan said to her daughter.

"Ya. I already know how to hip-hop."

The women exchanged knowing glances.

"Okay, we have a class suitable for you, starting in two weeks. Let me give you a pamphlet with classes, times, and prices. We would love to have you join our dancers, and I know you will have a lot of fun," Jetta said.

After talking with Susan and Kate a bit longer, Jetta walked them to the door and watched as the group started toward the downtown parking garage.

Jetta glanced at her watch.

2:25. I have just enough time to put the costumes up and maybe balance the checkbook before my ballet students begin arriving.

She walked back through the hip-hopping teens, picked up the bundle of clean costumes, and then walked to the rear wall where an old staircase led to the basement.

At the bottom of the stairs she pulled the string hanging from a bare bulb, and the light came on. A quick snap of a second pull-string part way across the basement turned on another bulb, revealing a room full hanging dance costumes on racks on rollers. She set her bundle down and began hanging each costume according to its theme and size.

The lights went out. The basement shook violently and a tremendous crashing and banging began, which subsided after several seconds. Jetta momentarily felt herself flying backward.

She awoke in great pain. Lifting her aching head, she could see her leg buried under debris. She looked up and could see daylight and a badly splintered and collapsed floor above her. It looked like a smashed pile of lumber, with wood, sheet metal, flooring, and insulation hanging precariously. There was total silence except for the steady drip of water off to the side somewhere.

"Help! Help me!" Jetta said. "Andrea!"

She found herself unable to move from under a costume rack, which had been smashed by debris from above, because its clothing bar was pinning her leg to the floor. She struggled to sit up, called out until she was hoarse, and then just listened and prayed, calling only when she thought she heard something.

Moving was painful, and it was growing very cold, so finally, in desperation, she rolled herself over as far as the pain in her pinned leg would let her see what she could see. There, under the debris next to her, was a patch of purple fabric and a hand sticking out.

Andrea? Oh my God!

"Andrea, Andrea," she said, and reached out. She could barely reach the hand and found it cold. This shocked her and she turned away, began praying, and crying.

Where are the rescue people? That blast must have been heard all over town.

Then she remembered something she saw when she turned toward Andrea. Lying next to her was a short piece of metal pipe. Reaching around again, she grabbed it even though the pain in her leg increased every time she struggled.

She wedged the pipe under the smashed clothing rack and pried. It moved a bit as her leverage slightly lifted the crushed rack and the broken lumber piled on it. The pain was excruciating, but it had moved, so she pried again, sending a shower of dust and smashed plaster down on her face. She cried, but tried again and again, until she finally worked her leg free.

She hurt all over: her back, her head, her leg, and both knees, but she was free, yet trapped in her own little enclave of smashed flooring and debris. She stood up and shivered in the waning light of the day. She could smell wood smoke and the faint smell of natural gas.

"Hello? Is anyone up there?" she said over and over again. She heard the sound of a helicopter and the distant sound of what she thought might be a car or a truck. So she yelled again, and finally she heard a voice.

"Where are you? Keep yelling," a man's voice said.

She could hear him moving on what remained of the broken floor above her. Finally she could see him. It was a Yorksberg fireman, and she could just make out "Station 1" on the front of his hat.

"I'm going to go get some help," he said, and disappeared.

The rope under her armpits bit into her flesh and she gritted her teeth against the pain as her rescuers pulled her up. She was surprised how fast they pulled her up, a rate that sent her scrambling over the debris and caused several cuts and bruises on her legs and arms, but she didn't care because at last she was free.

They put her on the "hot" bus as the firemen called it, and she and a few other survivors made a quick trip south. There, in some parking lot in the dark, she was made to strip and shower under the cold spray from a fire hose, while standing in a plastic swimming pool surrounded by temporary curtains of some kind, which glowed in the light pouring from several portable light units. After Jetta finished washing, someone in a protective white suit with a bubble helmet waved an instrument over her and sent her back to the cold shower. She could see a line of others waiting for the shower.

"If you want to get out of the shower, scrub well, or you'll go in again," an impatient voice said. She worked hard at cleaning and passed the instrument's second check.

Then she put on the paper smock someone gave her. They hadn't even given her underwear back, and then she was put onto the "clean bus," cold, tired, shaken, and hungry

Finished with her reminiscing, one thought remained. *I am alive, and I am clean.*

As she looked out the window, she noted the bus was passing through some small town and then stopped at a red light. It was quiet for a moment and then the bus was on its way again.

Looking down she noticed a folded piece of paper that was apparently on the seat when she first sat down. It was a school's music program. A portion leapt out at her. It said...

"I danced on a Friday when the sky turned black
It's hard to dance with the devil on your back
They buried my body & they thought I'd gone
But I am the Dance & I still go on!"

She mulled that last line over in her head. *I am the Dance & I still go on. What does that mean? Is that a message for me?*

Closing her eyes, she thought about what had happened. *I am the Dance, and someday I will have another dance studio, and I will go on.* And that, she realized, was the biggest mistake the bastards who had bombed Yorksberg had made, thinking a hard sucker-punch would make a dance instructor, or a nation, roll over and die. The Japanese had tried that stinking thinking at Pearl Harbor, and it had taken their nation into devastation and ruin. *The nation will rise up and hunt down these evil people, and I will be glad when that is done.*

95

Must have dozed off for a while. She could feel the bus slowing and turning into a large parking lot in front of a brightly lit church. Jetta could see people standing outside waiting for them, though it was well past midnight. They had what looked like coats and blankets in their arms.

"All right, folks, we're here," Margie said from the front. "Step off carefully and grab something warm. And God bless you all. Have a nice warm night of rest."

Analysis of Chapter 6

The building where Jetta's dance studio was located is typical of older structures found in some neighborhoods in our large cities. The high end businesses have, over the years, moved to other areas of town, and a new genre of retail has sprung up in the vacated buildings. Unique art stores, tattoo shops, guns shops, leather shops, hobby and craft shops, delis, martial arts centers, and dance studios gravitate to these now lower-cost parts of town. So Jetta's dance studio is where an expensive dress shop once stood. She is ¾ of a mile from John Jay Plaza.

Jetta does not see the flash of the nuclear explosion at all. It is really a very bright light, but she is deep in her building and below ground and does not see anything except the lights going out when the electrical distribution fails.

At ¾ mile from ground zero the dance studio experiences 5 psi overpressure and a wind gust of above 165 mph. To get an idea of what that is like, take a look at the following pictures. First, a frame Construction House at 1.2 Miles from Ground Zero from Nevada testing. [60]

This wood-framed house has been hit by a 1.7 psi overpressure blast wave. Note the windows and the door have been blasted in, but the frame, siding, and lower chimney are basically intact. This corresponds to a distance of approximately 1.2 miles from the Yorksberg bomb. It does not matter what yield in tons of TNT the

[60] *The Effects of Nuclear Weapons*, Samuel Glasstone and Philip J. Dolan, United States Department of Defense, 1977, Figure 5.59.

bomb releases because at some distance from any atomic bomb explosion the blast wave weakens as it goes and reaches 1.7 psi overpressure, and this is the damage it can do.

Frame Construction House at 3/4 Mile from Ground Zero from Nevada testing.[61]

Second, this is a wood-frame house that experienced a 5 psi overpressure blast wave, as did Jetta's dance studio. Note the difference in damage between 1.7 and 5 psi overpressure. For our bad guy's bomb, that is the difference between being 1.2 miles or ¾ of a mile from ground zero. That 0.7 miles additional distance from the explosion makes a lot of difference. As a general rule of thumb for a 19 kt explosion, total devastation will rule out to about ¾ of a mile, serious damage out to a mile, and substantial but reduced damage out to a mile and a half. Most of the survivors will be found ¾ of a mile and farther out from the point of explosion. Those beyond a mile will largely be walking wounded. Those inside a mile or so will be more seriously injured, trapped, or dead. For the Yorksberg bomb, ¾ of a mile to 1.2 miles is the zone of survivable destruction.

Jetta's building after the blast looked like the 5 psi house in the picture on the previous page (i.e., reduced to blasted sticks with only portions of the oak flooring surviving). Flying heavy debris from other buildings was particularly damaging to the dance studio. Jetta would not have survived if she had been on the ground floor where the students were practicing.

Broken gas and water lines will be a problem. In this story, Jetta is aware of them but they do not directly affect her.

---

[61] Ibid., Figure 5.57.

The cold is serious. One of Jetta's teenage hip-hoppers actually survived the blast. She ended up tangled in the debris, unconscious somewhere above Jetta. Had she received prompt medical care she would have survived. Silent and not seen by the firemen, she died early the next morning from her injuries and hypothermia.

Jetta's spirit and resourcefulness with the piece of pipe freed her from the clothing rack. Many who are trapped following a terrorist's nuclear attack will not be able to free themselves. They may experience a lack of emergency response rescue efforts because of the nagging presence of deadly radiation. How do authorities justify killing five rescue workers to try to save a trapped individual? Those trapped in a high radiation zone are essentially dead, and depending on the radiation levels, rescue should not be attempted.[62]

Cold, thirst, hunger, and lack of medical aid will be the cause of death for many trapped in the debris in the city in winter. As for Jetta, none of these took her life because of the gallant efforts of Fire Station 1, a group of men who volunteered to take high radiation exposures to rescue as many as possible.

For many of you, like Jetta, the cold bus ride in the dark to places unknown will be your reality after the terrorist's strike. To control the spread of contamination the authorities may take your clothes, perhaps even shave your head to get rid of the radioactive materials lodged there, make you shower in primitive conditions, and give you whatever is available to cover yourself. Those who have to go through this discomfort are the lucky ones, the survivors, so just cooperate and don't give your benefactors grief.

Consider this. If one tiny radioactive piece of material gets into your body and lodges there, it will continuously irradiate the cells of the nearby tissue. This may lead to cancer. Why would you want to carry this danger to cities far from your Yorksberg to endanger the rescuers and families who will open their communities to you in your time of need? So do all you can to protect them and yourself.

You may be taken to a church, or a school, or a city building. Some of you may even be staying in complete strangers' homes. The giving of Americans is unbounded when a common enemy strikes a hard blow. Use that time to contact loved ones and to begin getting your life back together. This may be hard, but as you move on, always remember the hundreds of thousands who just died.

The rubble that is Jetta's dance studio burned the next day from small fires gone wild. If she had remained trapped in her basement, she probably would have died of smoke inhalation before the fire ever reached her.

From history we find a similar story, that of Shige Hiratsuka, whose house was brought down upon her and her family. She managed to extricate herself and her husband.

"I began searching for my children. As I was calling their names, a voice emerged from a spot two or three meters away. 'Help, Mummy, help.' It was my six-year-old daughter Kazuko. Hurrying to the spot, I found her tightly wedged from the chest down by

---

[62] The epitome of this sort of heroism has to be the gallant effort of the Russian firefighters who were ordered to put out the fire in the burning radioactive core at the Chernobyl reactor after its accident. Many of those men were dead a few hours later. They are true heroes of the first order.

fallen plaster and timber."[63] Unable to free her daughter, she was forced to retreat from the flames. This couple lost two trapped children and a neighbor.

Quiz on Chapter 6
(Answers are in Appendix A1)

1.   Is there a difference between the explosion of a bomb on a city in a nuclear war, and the explosion of a terrorist's nuclear bomb? Explain.
2.   Why didn't the radiation kill Jetta?
3.   Why is fire such a danger to trapped individuals?
4.   Why didn't Jetta just walk up the stairs once she got herself free?
5.   Why will some survivors from areas near the location of the bomb explosion have to get rid of their clothes before being evacuated?

In our next chapter, we will look at the life of a nice guy. He has given his whole life to caring for others, and because that is why he traveled to Yorksberg one fateful December day, we name the chapter after his life's work. Read on, and survive with Sonny Sommers, who is "Caring for Others."

---

[63] *Hibakusha. Survivors of Hiroshima and Nagasaki*, in the chapter called "A Voice from the Flames," by Shige Hiratsuka. Translated by Gaynor Sekimori. Kōsei Publishing Co., Tokyo.

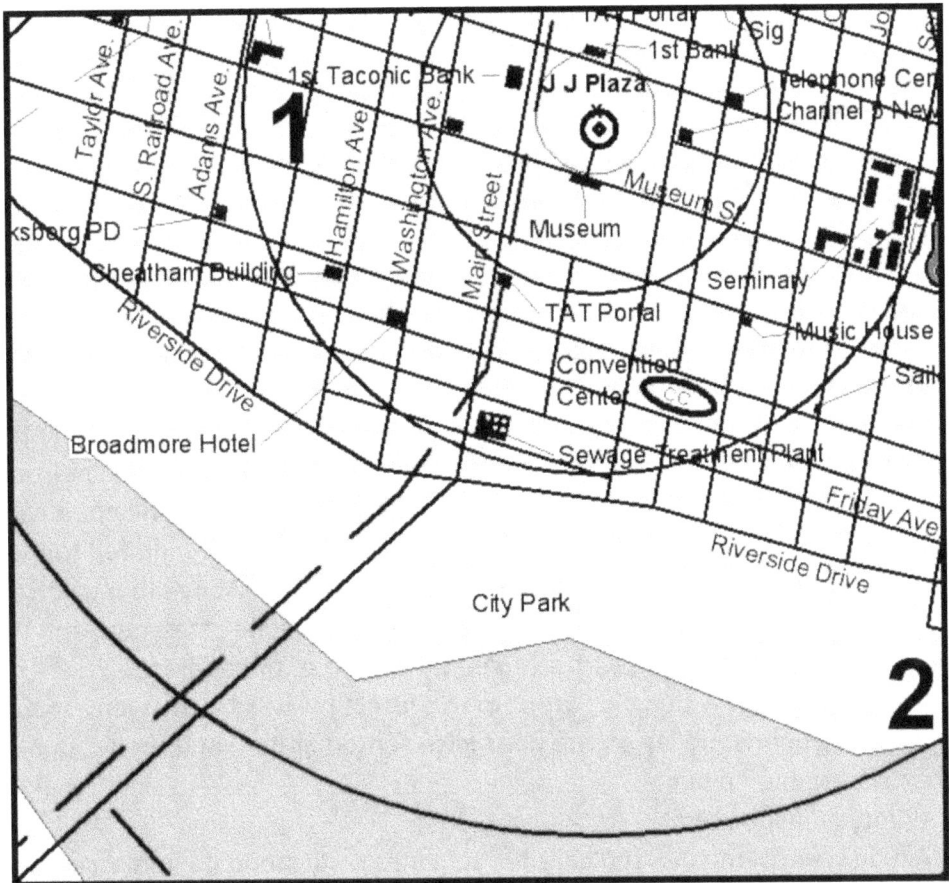

7 – Sonny Summers – Caring for Others (0.9 miles)

Sonny Sommers has heard of other people having a close call, but he had never experienced this himself, that is, until today. Sonny was not thinking of survival when he said, "I'm going to sit up front. The Yorksberg College Choir will be singing and I want the full effect. Join me?" He flashed an encouraging smile at his friend and fellow pastor Bob Harrisil.

"Sure. Let me find Brooke and we'll join you. She loves a good choir," Bob said.

"I think she's in the book sales room," Sonny said.

"That would be my Brooke. Loves shopping and books," Bob said. "Save us two seats, please?"

For a moment he watched Bob walk down the long, curved hallway that circled Yorksberg's Kennedy Convention Center's main auditorium, and then he entered the nearest portal and walked to the front of the large auditorium. He picked a row about 25 feet from the stage and, before entering it, turned and looked at the gathering crowd.

Not too bad for a single mother's conference on a Monday afternoon. There must be nearly a thousand people here.

Sonny approached a man already seated.

"Are these taken?"

"No, help yourself," the man said and stood up and held out his hand. "I'm Pastor Marvin Compton from Concorde. Christ's Episcopal Church."

Sonny shook his hand warmly. "Sonny Summers, Atlanta, Beacon Hill Baptist."

They talked awhile and watched the choir members assembling on the stage. They were all young and dressed in black robes that gave them an austere formality that seemed out of place for a single mother's conference. Sonny looked at his watch.

2:28. Where are Bob and Brooke?

The conference coordinator took the stage and the audience quieted down. He introduced the afternoon's session and then the choir.

A moment later, with the crowd hushed, the choir began an a cappella rendition of the American classic "Shenandoah."

The wonderful choral work made Sonny wish his wife could have come to the conference. The choir began the third stanza, singing "Oh, Shenandoah, I'm bound to leave you; Away, you rolling river" when suddenly all the lights went out. The choir continued singing in the dark, and then Sonny heard a tremendous explosion and fell to the floor, violently shaken. The world seemed to shift into slow motion. Above him came a cacophony of screeching metal, the choir stopped in mid phrase, someone screamed, and then something came crashing down with a huge roar on top of the audience.

Instinctively Sonny flung his arms up to protect his head as he went down amid a shower of falling debris. He lay on the floor, disoriented at first, and then found a steel girder had barely missed him.

What just happened?

Amid screams, moans, and calls for help he slowly stood up and assessed his condition. His arm hurt where something had struck it, but other than that, he seemed to have survived whatever had caused the roof to fall..

Looking around he took stock of the situation. Steel girders boxed him in, one of which landed directly on Pastor Compton. The sight of the poor man crushed to the point where bloody bones were protruding from his broken body sickened him, and he turned away. No one could have survived that impact.

The metal folding chairs he had reserved for Bob and Brooke were also crushed flat. No one else near him got to their feet. Most were buried, unmoving in the twisted debris that had fallen on them from above.

A loud, baritone voice called out across the disheveled hall, bringing Sonny's thoughts into focus. "Everyone stay calm and listen to me. If you can walk out, help someone who cannot walk. Take those who cannot walk to the parking lot. Do not move anyone who appears severely injured."

The voice had a comforting effect on the crowd. Sonny looked around and could see the collapse of the convention center roof seemed worse toward the rear of the room, and he could see uninjured attendees converging there to help others. Shafts of dusty sunlight were beaming in like floodlights through what remained of the ceiling, and he could feel the cold winter air quickly filling the convention hall.

Out of the many sounds of human pain and calls for help surrounding him, one seemed to stand out.

"Help me. Someone help me!"

He turned toward the voice of a young woman on the stage. She waved at him and pointed down at her feet. Sonny climbed through the surrounding debris and on to the stage, noting many crushed and broken bodies under the fallen roof structure.

Upon the stage he could see a long, triangular truss containing stage lights, as well as portions of the ceiling had fallen directly across the choir and there were bodies down everywhere.

"Can you help me?" the young woman said, an agonized pleading in her voice.

He helped her lift part of the broken light truss off a young man, who cried out in pain when they lifted.

"I think my leg is broken."

"Fire!" called a voice from the wreckage at the back of the auditorium. The alarm came again with the edge of panic in the voice. "Fire!"

In the rear of the audience he could see an already-large fire spreading through the debris on the floor. The acrid smell of burning plastic reached him.

"Can you walk okay?" he said to the young woman. She had a bloody gash behind the ripped sleeve of her left arm.

"Yes," she nodded, fear in her eyes, her face drawn.

They lifted the lad up onto his good leg and he winced with pain and cried out as his injured leg dangled. Carrying him into the circular hallway, they gently set him down on the floor. He appeared white as a sheet, and the girl, shaken and looking down at him, had tears streaming down her face.

"We need to get some help," he said to her.

He looked both directions down the curved hallway. Men and women were quickly moving out of the hall, most carrying or assisting someone. One or two looked as if they could help, but when he called to them they continued on their way out of the convention center.

He suspected the fire must be growing rapidly because its orange-colored, flickering light illuminated the hallway through the meeting room portals. Smoke pouring out of these openings had already begun to fill the top of the hallway. He could see the hovering gray wall of it creeping down the hallway toward them. The smell of it in the air nauseated him.

"He is my fiancé. Please don't let him die!" the girl pleaded.

Desperate to get the injured singer to safety, he looked around. The hallway appeared not to have suffered much damage. There were just a few ceiling tiles scattered on the floor. About 100 feet down the hall he spotted a load of cold drinks on an abandoned dolly next to a soft drink machine, its door hanging wide open.

The vendor must have been restocking it when the roof came down.

"Stay with him," Sonny said, "I'll be right back."

He ran down the hall to the vending machine and indiscreetly dumped the cases of drinks onto the floor with a crash; placed the cardboard boxes and plastic strapping back on the dolly; and then rolled it back, positioning the dolly on the floor next to the injured youth.

"Quick, help me break these boxes down and lay them out on the dolly like this. Something for him to lie on." Sonny took the first box and busted its edges out flat, and then laid the flattened box on the dolly.

"I see," the girl said, and began breaking down another box. They repeated this many times until Sonny, satisfied that their work would support the young man, removed his jacket, folded it, and placed it on the dolly.

"That's for his leg," he said. "Now we need to quickly put something around the leg to support it."

The girl took a flat piece of cardboard and rolled it into a "U" shape.

"That's the idea," Sonny said. "Only get that longer piece. If we can, we need to circle his whole leg, from above the knee to the ankle." The piece did not quite provide complete support, but as the smoke was becoming unbearable, Sonny knew they had to move, and soon. So he commandeered a man who passed by.

Sonny took one arm, the man the other arm, and while they lifted the injured fellow, the girl carefully lifted the leg onto Sonny's folded jacket. This process caused the young man a great deal of pain, and Sonny found it heart wrenching to watch him suffer.

"Use your sash to secure his leg," he said. He then began to use the dolly's straps to tightly strap the young man down. He removed the young man's belt, and his own, and used them to further immobilize the leg.

He then carefully lifted the dolly, and with all of them coughing from the acrid smoke, he wheeled the dolly and its human load out an exit into the cold December air. He found the bright sunlight and clean air to be refreshing, but very cold.

In the parking lot he could see hundreds and hundreds of people scattered across it, some alone, and some gathered in groups where injured were sitting and lying.

Looks like only about 10 percent got out.

Sonny considered going back in to help someone else out, but changed his mind. Nobody else could be seen coming out, and he could see fire with smoke pouring out the exits.

It's too late.

He noted a police car with its front windshield and one headlight busted out parked nearby, and then spotted two officers moving through the crowd. One walked up and pointed to the Old Dixie Highway Bridge about a half mile away.

"You will have to leave this area quickly. All the roads are blocked by debris. The only way out is the bridge. Walk to the bridge and then go across to South Yorksberg." He pointed across the broad Taconic.

"Officer, this boy has a broken leg. I think he may be bleeding. Why can't we wait here until an ambulance comes?"

The officer patiently pointed up behind Sonny, where he saw high above the city a huge gray and black cloud reaching into the stratosphere above them. It had risen so high that its top had a strange cap of white cloud over it.

"We are pretty sure that was a nuke. There will be radiation falling out of that cloud. You can't stay here. Besides, if we can't drive you out, how would an ambulance get here?" The officer did not wait for an answer, but went on to the next group with his grim news.

Sonny felt weak and a little dizzy, finding it hard to comprehend that someone could have done this to the city. He looked at the cloud and then at the convention center with smoke and flames pouring out the doors. For the first time, he really looked around and felt astonishment at the scene of destruction. Whole buildings were smashed, light poles were down, fires were burning in several other buildings, and many cars in the parking lot had been rolled here and there. Strangely, many of the cars in the parking lot were on fire, as if some capricious arsonist had run through the parking lot, setting the insides of cars on fire at random.

The cop must be right. It must have been a bomb. My God!

Groups were rising and beginning the walk to the bridge as the officers reached them and explained the situation. Sonny joined them with the dolly and the girl followed. She had removed her black blouse cape with a rose still pinned to it and had draped it over the pale young man.

Soon there were several hundred people strung out for a mile from the convention center, walking, limping, or being carried toward the foot of the bridge. As they got closer to the bridge Sonny noticed other injured walking out from other parts of the city to the bridge. Only a few cars seemed to be moving. Several of the roads he could see seemed to be full of stopped cars, as if traffic had been somehow frozen.

"Why are the cars stopped? People are just walking," the girl said.

As he looked he could see she was right; people were getting out of their cars and walking, and he realized they were witnessing a huge traffic jam.

"Someone probably abandoned their car. Perhaps it broke down or ran out of gas, but in their haste to leave they just left their car stuck in the lane."

"And everyone behind them is just stuck. No wonder they are all walking."

Sonny's arms ached, and he turned his attention to plodding on. A steady southerly wind blew off the river from the south, and he found its damp cold went right through his shirt. It had been refreshing at first after being in the smoke-filled convention center, but soon became bone-chilling cold. He did not look forward to the cold, windy walk across that bridge.

Looks like more than a mile across.

As he and the girl walked, with him pulling the dolly along, they passed several people who could not continue without help, but he could not help them. Another black-robed choir member joined them, and this young man helped them by taking turns with Sonny in hauling the injured singer.

At the foot of the bridge they came upon a young girl. She appeared to be about eight years old. Sonny could see burns on her face and from her right heel up to her right ear. The shirt and pants she had been wearing were melted against her skin along her right side and she had little clothing left. She seemed dazed and did not respond to questions asked her. She just stared ahead in silence, visibly shaking. Sonny picked her up. She laid her head on his shoulder, and making no sound, shivered continuously.

Sonny looked back at the fiery, smoking city, the long line of wounded walking out, and the convention center now fully engaged in fire.

He said a prayer for their safety.

As they reached the far end of the bridge, half frozen and shaking with exhaustion, cold, and shock, some bystander took a picture of the exodus. Sonny wished he had the man's warm coat, and then remembered the shivering girl in his arms, and walked up to the photographer.

"Give this girl your coat, please. She is badly injured."

The man hesitated.

"Come with us to the hospital – you'll get your coat back."

Sonny thought he might to have to take the coat by force, but the man only hesitated a moment. He not only gave up his coat, but took the girl from his cold and aching arms and carried her to his car, and then to the hospital.

Analysis of Chapter 7

Auditoriums, convention centers, gymnasiums, churches, malls, theaters, and other large structures may be particularly vulnerable to collapse during the passing of a blast wave from a nuclear explosion. Since these are places where a large number of people gather, they are potential sites of mass casualties at distances from the explosion, which would not otherwise result in a large number of injured people.

The reason for this vulnerability has to do with the effective cross-sectional area of these structures in relation to the construction material strength. Remember that the blast wave is just an air pressure wave traveling at the speed of sound. As it passes, it effectively raises the air pressure on one side of a structure virtually instantly. This creates large sideways forces on the structure, which is usually designed to resist vertical forces, not horizontal pushes. The total force felt by the building increases proportional to the area of the side of the building.

In the case of the Yorksberg convention center the blast overpressure was sufficient to break parts of the facility's structural strong points and drop part of the convention center auditorium roof onto the assembled crowd. Most of the initial casualties were due to falling building structure and debris.

The presence of fire following a nuclear explosion is always a strong possibility given the intense heat radiation emitted by the bomb. In this case, we imagine the fracturing and collapse of the roof exposed some fire-susceptible materials, which were ignited by the heat radiating from the rising fireball. Small at first, this fire eventually consumed much of the auditorium and caused the deaths of those too injured to leave.

Sonny is like most folks hit by a sudden disaster. His first thought is to extricate himself and get to safety. Some people panic and run out, leaving the injured behind. In Sonny's case he began to care for others by checking the man next to him.

The man with the baritone voice, giving directions, is an example of leadership spontaneously arising when needed. His intent is to marshal those who are able to help others, and to some extent this worked.

The young man Sonny helped was saved by chance, by the fact that the light fixture did not kill him, and because his fiancé refused to leave him when most of the other surviving choir members bolted for the exits. Others in the choir who were on the stage and survived the falling debris, but were immobilized by injuries or debris, died in the smoke from the fire. Fires can spread and grow very rapidly among wreckage, and the attendees in the convention center did not have much time to get everyone out.

The use of the dolly is a classic case of improvising and allowed the badly hurt young man to be quickly removed to the far side of the river.

What about the fallout? Like in real estate, location is very important. The convention center is upwind of the explosion by about ¾ of a mile. The prevailing wind at the ground was 15 mph. At 5 to 10,000 feet the wind was closer to 40 mph in a northeast direction. Thus the natural tendency in this blast's fallout distribution is trending away from the river and the convention center. In fact, almost zero fallout occurred anywhere across the river. Fallout patterns are not necessary predictable or symmetric, subject as they are to prevailing wind currents. Below are two fallout contour maps.

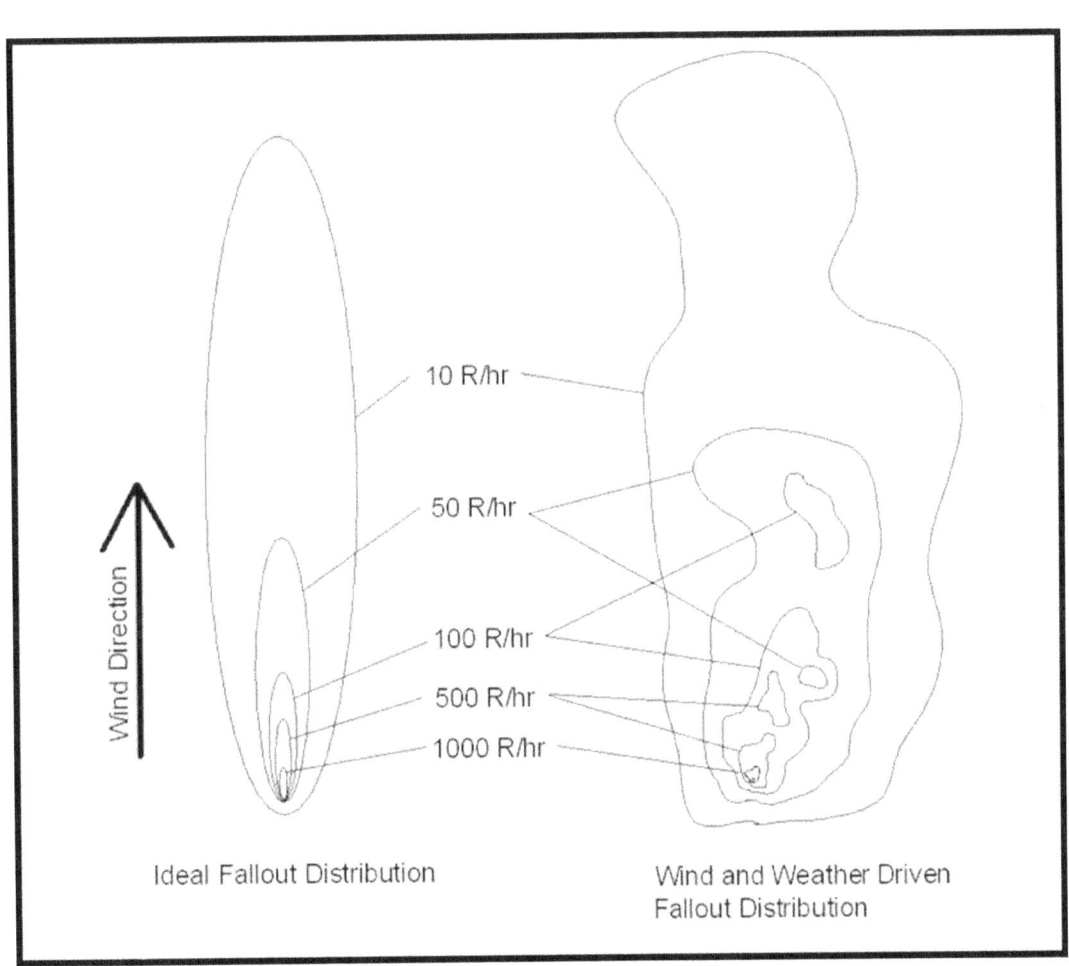

Typical Fallout Distribution – Ideal and Wind Driven

On the left in the graphic of the fallout distribution is an "ideal" plot of where the fallout from an exploded bomb is spread evenly by the wind. As one moves through this fallout zone, the intensity of the fallout changes in a very predictable (and unrealistic) manner. The dose rates are shown for what you would receive as you crossed each boundary line. Keep in mind the dose rates are not constant inside each loop, but gradually increase as one moves inward. Just inside the boundary marked 50 R/hr, for example, you would find 55 R/hr, then 80 R/hr, etc., increasing until you reached the next boundary marked 100 R/hr.

Nature is never that simple. On the right side of the graphic is a more typical fallout distribution. Note there are isolated "pockets" of higher radiation dose rates inside lesser dose rate areas and vice-versa. Inside the 100 R/hr zone is an area that has 500 R/hr, and another that is only 50 R/hr.

Remember that the fallout pattern from a city near you that is struck by terrorists will have an irregular shape, and that the radiation intensity will vary in an unpredictable manner. You cannot know whether you are safe just by where you live in relation to the explosion. Either measure the radiation dose rate yourself, or grab your "go pack" and leave the area. Civil authorities will eventually map these radiation zones and publish them.

The radiation levels around the convention center became very high after the explosion as debris from the mushroom cloud fell back to earth. Those escaping the convention center received very large doses; however, their rapid evacuation from the area and across the bridge limited their doses to serious but not lethal in most cases.

The two police officers are heroes in this story. They knew the roads were impassible to cars and they correctly surmised the presence of fallout. They moved the people out by calmly and quickly directing the exodus by foot across the bridge.

Were there people left behind? Probably. Did they survive? That depends on a number of factors. Perhaps some good Samaritans crossing the bridge located those who were left behind and helped them out of the area, just as Sonny did for the choir member. People do these sorts of wonderful things, and in this case they probably would survive the radiation exposure if they did not linger too long.

Traffic jams are a difficulty you should anticipate if you think you are going to jump in your car and drive out of the wounded city. Debris will be one problem, but there are others: cars running out of gas; no electricity for the gas stations to pump gas; breakdowns; and people just being frustrated and scared, abandoning their cars and blocking the streets when they take to their feet to escape. Can you sit in your car and wait for the traffic to start moving when radioactive material is raining down on you? Think about it. Your car offers very little protection from gamma rays.

The young girl is an example of the walking wounded who will be in shock after the explosion. Most will not survive without the help of others. Help them out of the area or into your shelter if you can. Hopefully you have a shelter.

From history we can look at what these walking wounded will be like. The following is an account of a survivor of Nagasaki. The narrator was working in a factory that was destroyed in the bombing. After describing his escape from the factory ruins he continues….

"I met a classmate in the tunnel. Together we set out for home. Spread out under the sparkling midsummer sun was scene of such horror that it was beyond my ability to take it in." … "The bodies of people and horses were strewn everywhere. All the people were naked, and they were covered with burns and wounds. Their faces were burned dark brown and swollen like balloons. The living were wandering around like ghosts, burns all over them and their skin hanging in tatters."[64]

The Yorksberg Bridge in Sonny's story is one of the over-arching metal, girder types, constructed in the 1950s. Well maintained, it easily withstood the 1 psi overpressure and gust of wind from the blast 1 ½ miles away. There was some damage in the form of broken signs and lights, and in one place where hidden corrosion had worked its way into some supporting metal pieces, a section of guard railing was blown into the river.

Sonny survived. His wife was elated when she received his phone call from South Yorksberg. The young choir girl survived, as did her fiancé. His leg required surgery to put it back together, and he walked with a slight limp for the rest of his life.

The young burned girl was rushed to a hospital burn center for treatment. Her parents were never located, and in spite of posting her photo nationwide, no one came forward to identify her. Nor was she ever able to tell anyone who she was. She had apparently walked out of the city, and was highly contaminated. Her radiation exposure crippled her immune system, and she died of infections related to her burns several weeks later, in spite of the heroic efforts of a hospital's staff to save her. The only thing anyone heard her say was "Momma, where is Listy?"

The photo taken by the bystander at the south side of the bridge became a front-page, full-color photo in all the major newspapers several days later. The photo showed Sonny's bloody face; the choir woman's ripped sleeve and blood-soaked formal gown; the zombie-like, burned, and half-naked 10-year-old girl in Sonny's arms; the pale unconscious youth on the dolly; a line of battered walkers stretching across the bridge behind them as far as the eye could see; and the distant, fire-ravaged city. This image won the Pulitzer Prize for photo journalism that year.

The morning following the explosion, one of the PPF terrorists,[65] safe in a country overseas, held this photo up to his fellow thugs, pointed to it, and grinned, saying, "This is a glorious and wonderful day!"

The photograph of the survivors staggering across the bridge fulfilled the PPF leadership's desired outcome for this event. Photos of distant mushroom clouds do not evoke the fear caused by photos of battered and bloody survivors.

The PPF terrorists made sure their mouthpiece news organization overseas made the most of this photo and attributed this great achievement to the secretive PPF organization. Its prestige among other terrorist organizations worldwide rose enormously in the months following the bombing of Yorksberg. The PPF was flooded with new members seeking to further bloody the United States.

---

[64] Jamestown Foundation, Publication: *Terrorism Monitor*, Volume 2, Issue: 6, by Scott Atran, the chapter titled "A Message to the Young," by Sachiko Masaki, March 24, 2004.
[65] See Appendix D1 for an account of who the PPF terrorists are and how they came to possess a nuclear weapon.

This photo, and several like it taken elsewhere in the ruined city, was the chief cause of fear and panic in other cities. The PPF leadership anonymously released a "letter to the American people" demanding the USA cease all military operations overseas. The letter claimed the terrorists had other such nuclear weapons already positioned and ready to be exploded in other cities if their demands were not met. Welcome to nuclear terrorism.

Quiz on Chapter 7   (Answers are in Appendix A1)

1. Large structures such as auditoriums, convention centers, and theaters may be particularly vulnerable to collapse during the passage of a blast wave. True or False?
2. Although the convention center structure provided some protection from blast and radiation, what factor following an atomic explosion may put you at risk if you remain in the structure?
3. Did the photographer at the end of the bridge ever get his coat back? Explain your answer.
4. Is walking out of an attacked city realistic?
5. Why didn't the Yorksberg Fire Department respond to the fire at the convention center?

Now let's visit another Yorksberg survivor. Will he walk away unscathed because of where he is when the bomb goes off? As in real estate, location, location, location.

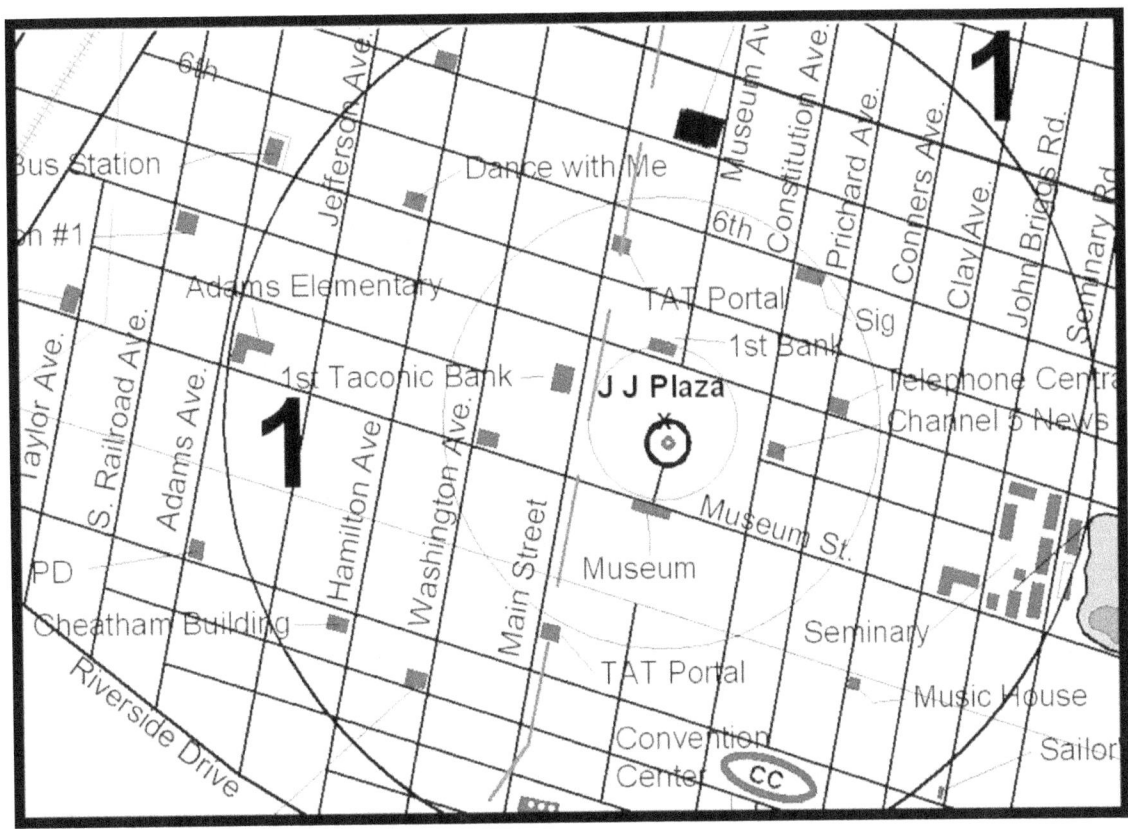

Cheatham Building Construction

8 - Broadrick Edwards – A Good Man in a Hole (0.8 miles)

Dink paused in his inspection of the dewatering line at his feet, removed his left glove, and fished in his pocket for his cell phone, which was buzzing like an angry hornet.

"Water Control, Incorporated, this is Broadrick Edwards," he said, his voice carrying a slight Irish brogue.

"Mr. Edwards, this is Assam Johnson at Market and Fields Construction. How are you this afternoon?"

How does a man named Johnson get a name like Assam?

"Doing well, Mr. Johnson… just a little cold down in this pit."

"Call me Assam, please. You must be on the Cheatham building construction site."

"Yes I am. How can I help you? And by the way, call me Dink. Everybody does."

"I know the excavators opened an underground seam containing water, and for our planning purposes I was asked to check on the effect this will have on our schedule. Can you give me the situation in a few words?"

"Sure. The excavation is basically done, and foundation work could begin the next warm spell we get, except for the water. We have installed a number of well points around the periphery of the excavation and pumps have been running 24/7. Today is the first day we have seen the flow begin to drop off, and if that continues we will have the seam grouted in a day or two."

111

"That sounds good. We will plan accordingly."

"Call me in two days, Assam, just to be sure."

"Will do, and thanks."

Beagle walked up as Dink put the cell phone away.

"She's definitely slowing down," Beagle said. "Another day or two and we can patch'er."

"I just informed Market and Fields. Just in time too. Those steel and concrete boys are chompin' at the bit to get in here as soon as we get a patch of warmer weather."

"I vote for that," Beagle said. Turning his head to the side, he spat a mouthful of tobacco-stained spittle onto the ground.

"You vote for what?" Dink came back.

"Warm weather, boss."

"You're getting to be an old man," Dink chided him. "If you'd just dress—."

Beagle interrupted him. "Not the long johns speech, please. I am wearing them, and I am still cold."

Dink laughed. "Well, we're done here. Get the boys to fuel all the pumps and we'll let 'em run another couple of nights. Let's head back to the shop. You can warm your buns there. I've got a junior high basketball game to referee at 3:30."

"Hot damn!" Beagle said and spat again.

"One more thing," Dink said, "I need you to check the warehouse for the materials we need to patch this sucker. Call Toby Tucker up in Atlanta if we are short of anything; he can have it down here in a day or two. I'm thinking we can start patching at the end of the week."

Dink continued walking along one of the dewatering lines up against the east wall of the excavation, checking for any icing problems.

"Hey Kirby!" Beagle yelled upward.

A head in a parka appeared, peeking over the edge of the excavation. "Yo!" Kirby said.

"The boss says 'Diesel up the pumps and let 'em run all night. Then meet us back at the shop.'"

"Okay, will do," Kirby said, giving a floppy salute.

Broadrick was looking down at some PVC piping along the Hamilton Avenue wall of the excavation, when suddenly the world lit up so bright he had to close his eyes. Instinctively he looked down and turned his face toward the excavation's wall. It was suddenly very warm. A second or two later a great ear-popping blast struck, causing instant pain in both ears, picking him up and throwing him against the excavation's wall. The impact knocked the breath out of him and he fell to the ground across one of his dewatering trenches while the world reverberated with the thunder of the crashing and falling of a huge rain of debris into the excavation.

The enormous brilliance and heat caused him to cringe up against the wall of the excavation. He turned and looked out into the pit, eyes squinting and partly flash-blinded, and watched cars; a bus; several of his dewatering pumps; some kind of a huge radio antenna; along with copious rocks, stones, dust, and debris fall in a deadly rain into the huge excavation. The rain continued as if time stood still, becoming mostly smaller and smaller debris as time ticked by.

Broadrick wondered how long he would survive before something fell on him, and was immediately answered when another of his pumps crashed 10 feet from him and burst into flames.

He smelled diesel and a strange metallic odor he could almost taste, and the dust was so thick he could hardly see the far side of the excavation. He was being peppered by falling dirt and rocks, some whacking his hands, which he had over his head, his safety helmet gone somewhere.

The deadly rain of debris slowed, the heat faded, and he just lay there stunned. His ears ached and rang, his chest hurt, his back hurt from the impact with the wall, and one foot complained. Then he thought of Beagle.

He gingerly tried to stand and found that his foot would support him if he went easy on it, and he called out for Beagle as he staggered away from the dirt wall of the pit that had saved his life.

"Beagle! Beagle!" he said through the dust. His right chest hurt like fire.

Broken ribs?

"Over here, boss," said Beagle.

Dink could barely see Beagle in the dust; he was so covered with dirt as he got up.

"Are you okay?"

"I guess so. How about you, boss?"

"I'm alive. That was one hell of an explosion."

"Maybe a gas line," Beagle said.

"Kirby!" he said as loud as his aching chest would allow. "Kirby, are you up there?" he tried again. There was no reply, and the pain in his chest strongly suggested he needed to seek medical help.

"Let's get out of here," he said, turning toward the scaffold walkway that had been built to allow access down into the pit. "Oh, crap," he said when he saw it had become a twisted pile of steel and wood planks, now unusable.

"Looks like we're trapped," Beagle said.

"Unless we can climb that," Dink said, pointing to the far wall of the excavation, which had slumped in as if a giant fist had hit it.

He studied it. It was mostly loose rock with chunks of the asphalt roadway, slid down in pieces. This slumping debris appeared to be their only chance to get out.

He picked his way across the floor of the excavation with Beagle following. Halfway across to the slumping wall they found Kirby's body. Dink pulled out his cell phone and dialed 911.

"Poor Kirby," Beagle said with tears in his eyes. "Melissa and the kids, who's gonna tell them? ... What's wrong, boss?"

"No cell phone signal." He turned and looked up. The city skyline had been altered and a huge cloud loomed high above them.

"Hell, no gas line could do that," Beagle said.

"I've got a bad feeling about this," Dink said, still eyeing the huge cloud above them. "We need to get out of here fast."

Leaving Kirby's body behind, he ran to the slumped wall and began to climb out of the pit. He could hear Beagle scrambling up the rock and dirt behind him. It was a very difficult climb. The slumped soil was very loose, moving downslope every time he took a step up. Strangely, he found the black pieces of asphalt roadway that had slid down into the pit were very warm to the touch.

About halfway up he stopped to rest for a moment and watched as Beagle climbed passed him. The exertion of climbing had aggravated the pain in his chest.

"C'mon, boss," Beagle said.

He slid back again and again but finally managed to reach the top, and then stood there catching his breath and looking in awe of the immense destruction around him. There was glass and debris all over the streets, light poles leaning at odd angles or flat on the ground, windowless buildings with pieces of their fascia missing, cars rolled over with several of them engulfed in flames, a fire burning in a debris-filled alley across the way, and trees with broken limbs and some caved over as if a powerful fist had smashed them. Two things struck him as odd. First, on several of the apartment buildings he could see window curtains blowing out of the apartment windows, a peculiar sight for Yorksberg in December, and second, there were many rats out on the streets and sidewalks, scurrying here and there. He felt as if he had been transported into some kind of apocalyptic, science fiction movie.

As his eyes took in this grim scene, he began to see the people, mostly bodies lying here and there, but also coming out of the buildings. Their faces were masks of shock and surprise, and for the injured, pain; their eyes searching the devastation around them for meaning or for help.

The city was strangely quiet. The hustle and bustle of traffic was gone. It was replaced by softer sounds, some of them unusual sounds for such a great city. There was the sound of a siren far off, the splattering patter of water spraying out of a broken pipe and impacting on the road, a dog whining in the distance, people crying or calling to one another, no traffic sounds, and somewhere away from where they were standing many car alarms sounding continuously. There were no birds, not even pigeons flying, and no birdsongs.

"C'mon, Beagle," he said. When Beagle didn't respond, Dink looked back at him standing there in the goofy padded hat with large ear flaps that had given him his nickname, and found the man crying. He didn't have to ask why. He just walked back and hooked an arm around the younger man.

"Let's go."

Analysis of Chapter 8

Broadrick Edwards' situation and survival of the bombing of Yorksberg has a distinctive parallel to that of April Thompson, the curator at Yorksberg's Historical Museum described in chapter 1. Both individuals were below ground level, both felt the effects of the explosion, both were injured, and both survived the initial light, heat, and blast.

Broadrick was not protected by a solid, massive structure as April was. He was outdoors; however, he had the advantage that he was three quarters of a mile from the plaza where the bomb-laden truck had parked. This fact provided him with sufficient distance from the explosion, considering he was at the bottom of a two-story-deep excavation and up against the wall closest to the bomb. The heat, light, blast, and initial burst of powerful gamma radiation had passed over him and Beagle.

At street level, above Broadrick, the distance from ground zero was not adequate to assure survival. On the rim of the Cheatham Building excavation, where Kirby was fueling one of the dewatering pumps, the explosion's blast wave overpressure was about 5 psi and the dynamic gust peaked at about 163 mph. This blast impact is more than sufficient to throw men, cars, and dewatering pumps over the edge and into the pit.

Remember that around every nuclear explosion in a city there will be zones of different destruction and lethality. Look at the Yorksberg map and consider the following data taken from Hiroshima and Nagasaki.[66]

Percentage Killed or Injured at Hiroshima and Nagasaki

Hiroshima		
Zone/Distance	Killed (%)	Injured (%)
Zone 1 0 to 0.6 miles	85.5	9.6
Zone 2 0.6 to 1.6 miles	27.3	36.6
Zone 3 1.6 to 3.1 miles	2.1	24.9
At Hiroshima, 74 percent of the population within 3.1 miles of the nuclear explosion survived.		
Nagasaki		
Zone/Distance	Killed (%)	Injured (%)
Zone 1 0 to 0.6 miles	88.3	6.1
Zone 2 0.6 to 1.6 miles	34.3	29.2
Zone 3 1.6 to 3.1 miles	1.1	9.6
At Nagasaki, 78 percent of the population within 3.1 miles of the nuclear explosion survived.		

If you get nothing else out of this table, it should be this: three out of four people living within 3.1 miles of a Hiroshima-sized nuclear explosion in a large city will survive. You will likely be one of those survivors.

---

[66] *The Effects of Nuclear Weapons*, Samuel Glasstone and Philip J. Dolan, United States Department of Defense, 1977, Table 12.09.

These zones of destruction and lethality grow larger if a bomb that can deliver more energy is used. The Yorksberg weapon delivered a blast of about 19,000 tons of TNT. If 100,000 tons of a TNT weapon were used, all the zones described in the table would be enlarged. Zone 1, for example, might extend to one mile or more.

Larger weapons are bigger and heavier, and therefore less likely to be used. If a five-megaton weapon were used, then Zone 1 would extend as far as five miles. Even in this case, there will be Zones 2 and 3 where there will be survivors and injured who will face the same problems caused by our 19 kt Yorksberg bomb. We must always focus on the survivors and help them recover.

So how are people injured by an atomic bomb? How might you sustain an injury if you are walking along a city street when the bad guys strike? Here is a list of ways.

1. Flash burns from the heat and light at the instant of the explosion.
    a. So hot that your skin will be burned before you can react and turn away.
    b. Reduced by rain, fog, dust, or intervening objects.
    c. Diminishes as the distance from the bomb increases.
    d. Can damage eyes faster than your blink reflex if you happen to be looking where the bomb goes off. On a clear day, this damage can occur several miles from the point of explosion.
    e. Likely to be fatal. Close to two-thirds of the deaths at Hiroshima during the first day after the explosion were reported to be badly burned.[67]

    What can you do?
    Dive for cover. You can limit the burns by getting behind something or by wearing light-colored clothing that reflects the radiant heat and keeps it off your skin. You can't avoid these flash burns, but you can dive for cover to avoid heat burns from the rising fireball.

2. Heat radiation burns from the rising fireball.
    a. Able to reach parts of the city that were shielded from the initial flash by buildings – because the fireball rises.
    b. Diminishes with time as the fireball rises away from the city and cools.
    c. Greater and longer effects from larger bombs.
    d. Can burn the skin through clothing by heating the fabric. Dark colors get hotter quicker.

    What can you do?
    Dive for cover. Get out of the fireball's glow and get shielded by something substantial such as behind a wall or in a ditch, anywhere that allows the blast wave and propelled objects to pass over you.

---

[67] Ibid., Section 12.13. Note: some of these deaths were due to the fires the weapon started. It is also thought that the infections resulting from lack of proper medical care played a significant part in the burn deaths.

3.   Clothing on fire.
Dark colors will absorb more heat and may ignite quicker than light colors.

What can you do?
        This is just an ordinary fire. Like any fire, stop, drop, and roll to extinguish the flames. Just remember the blast wave is coming at you at the speed of sound.

4.   Being picked up and thrown by the dynamic blast wave, impacting a building, a tree, a curb, a light post, or any other heavy, non-yielding object.
        a. There is nothing nuclear about these injuries. You could sustain them in a car accident.
        b. You are safer inside than outside, but may still be injured if inside.

What can you do?
        a. It's just a tremendous gust of wind. Close in, it can hit so hard it can kill you, but farther out it will just knock you down. Cheat it by falling prone on the ground, preferably behind something substantial, in a basement, or in a ditch.
        b. If inside, seek an interior room.
        c. Stay away from windows unless you want to be cut to pieces by the flying glass.

5.   Being struck by a vehicle, a dumpster, street signs, mail boxes, or other objects thrown at you by the blast.

What can you do?
Get behind something substantial. Lie down. Even an eight-inch concrete gutter can provide some protection. But move fast. If you start moving when the flash and heat are first seen, you stand a good chance of reducing or eliminating injury.

6.   Being hit by falling objects such as window glass blown out high above you, tree limbs, store signs, and pieces of buildings very close to the point of explosion. Some of these pieces may be thrown a long distance.

What can you do?
Be indoors, or duck indoors, and stay away from windows.

7.   Fires started in apartments and in trash in alleyways, especially if you are trapped in place by debris or an injury that renders you immobile.

What can you do?
You can try to extinguish the fire if it is safe to do so. Just remember that the fire you are concerned with may be one of hundreds, and it might be a better idea to leave. If you are trapped, call for help. Your situation may be hopeless, but you never know. If you are in a typical room and fire blocks your exit, you may be able to bust your way through a sheet rock wall to escape into an adjoining room or hallway.

8.   Burst ear drums, lung, or other internal organ damage due to the overpressure of the blast wave's acoustics in the canyon-like streets of a big city.
If you are close enough for the blast wave to cause internal injuries, you probably received a lethal dose of nuclear radiation emanating from the bomb the instant it exploded. You will also probably be picked up and thrown at more than 100 mph by the blast wave.

What can you do?
In this case, you are not a survivor. There is really nothing you can do except not be so close to where the bad guys set the bomb off.

9.   Nuclear radiation from the instant of the explosion.
The initial flash from the bomb contains intense x-rays, gamma rays, and neutrons. If you are in direct line of sight of the explosion within 0.6 of a mile and out in the open, you will receive more than 1000 R of radiation damage in the blink of an eye. If a weapon of larger explosive power is used, the distance the initial release of radiation can kill you also increases.

What can you do?
Again, you are not a survivor. If you are out in the open and too close, there is really nothing you can do; however, people in the cities bombed in Japan survived if they were that close and inside strong buildings.

10.   Radiation left behind by the explosion, (i.e., fallout).

What can you do?
Get away from it. Leave the city as rapidly as possible, or take shelter as far from the fallout as you can, and with as much shielding between you and the radioactive fallout as possible.

From this list you can see that many of the injuries, such as head injuries, cuts, contusions, burns, broken limbs, and possibly internal injuries, will be the same as those from any accident. Thus many of the injuries a nuclear bomb can deliver to you are nothing mysterious; you would see the same injuries resulting from a car, a train, or an aircraft accident. Most injuries, including serious cuts and broken bones, can be treated hours later and the injured will recover just fine.

Wait a minute! What about the radiation? Doesn't that cause your skin to melt off your bones, create hordes of flesh eating zombies, or cause mutant creatures to attack?

No, no, and no. Such statements are nonsense! You have been watching too many grade-B movies. You need to file that sort of thing away with movies about giant squids attacking ocean liners and gigantic gorillas carrying blond ladies up tall skyscrapers. Scary stories such as these are fun to read or watch in movies, but have little to do with reality. Relax; if you can handle the physical injuries you just read about, then you can handle the radiation too.

Radiation is discussed in many of the other chapters, so it is not discussed in detail here. Suffice to say, try not to stay in too much radiation too long and take care not to eat or breathe much radioactive material. Then if you focus on getting out of the city and get treatment for your physical injuries, you will do well.

Radiation is damaging to the cells in your body, but if you survive the light, heat, and blast, you have already been damaged by the radiation emitted by the bomb at the time of the explosion. That damage occurred in a microsecond and there is nothing you can do about it. That damage became a part of you the instant the bomb lit up the sky. You can reduce further radiation damage from fallout and radioactive dust by moving upwind, far away from the site of the explosion, and cleaning yourself up.

> If you want to increase your chances of survival, leave the zones of destruction and injury as quickly as possible, and take measures to reduce breathing in particles of dust, smoke, and dirt in the air following the explosion.

Broadrick was almost trapped in the open excavation. This would not have been a good thing. Being trapped in the open is not good because of radioactive fallout. He escaped being trapped only because the blast caused one of the dirt walls of the excavation to collapse, and Broadrick was not too injured to climb out. But what would have happened to him if he had been trapped?

After the explosion, dirt and materials thrown up in the air in the mushroom-shaped cloud come raining back down. Broadrick experienced some of this while at the bottom of the excavation, even though he was almost a mile from the blast. Depending on upper winds, this fallout may fall several miles upwind and to the side of the blast, and the finer dust and dirt may fall hundreds of miles downwind of the city.

Each particle of this radioactive debris will be shooting out millions of nuclear-sized particles that can damage cells in your body. In fact, on the ground underneath the drifting mushroom-shaped cloud you can receive significant radiation exposure emanating from the cloud passing overhead. This effect is called "shine". The cloud is basically glowing with intense radioactive emissions. You might think this is not a problem because the cloud is so far above you, but don't forget its huge size. You will be receiving radiation damage from every part of that cloud at once. Don't make the mistake of bathing in the "shine".

This is another reason, besides fallout, that it is not a good idea to stand outside under such a cloud and watch it pass over.

Had Broadrick not been able to climb out of the pit, he would not have been able to put distance between himself and the radioactive fallout particles falling around him. He would have received a lethal dose of radiation.

For our story we assume from his distance from the explosion, the size of the bomb's energy yield, the constant wind, and the short time it took him to walk out of the danger zone, that he did not receive an immediately lethal dose of radiation. Broadrick did not take any action to reduce the amount of radioactive dust he breathed in, however, and this may cause him to continue to sustain radiation damage that could affect him later in life. The lesson is if you want to increase your chances of survival, leave the zones of destruction and injury as quickly as possible (or find shelter), and take measures to reduce breathing in particles of dust, smoke, and dirt in the air following the explosion.

The first thing Broadrick knows of the explosion is a great light that makes him squint his eyes closed, and the heat; the December air was suddenly no longer cold. For many people in the city, especially those outdoors or where they can see light from outside the building they are in, the first thing they will sense of the explosion is the incredible light produced by the nuclear reaction. It is described as brilliant beyond description, with a tinge of blue or purple due to the incredibly high temperatures produced in the fireball. The rise of the intensity of the light is so fast, on the order of milliseconds, that there is no sense of a growing brightness. It will be an instantaneous brightness and instantaneous heat.

For the Yorksberg Explosion

Zone 1	0 to 0.6 miles
Zone 2	0.6 to 1.6 miles
Zone 3	1.6 to 3.1 miles

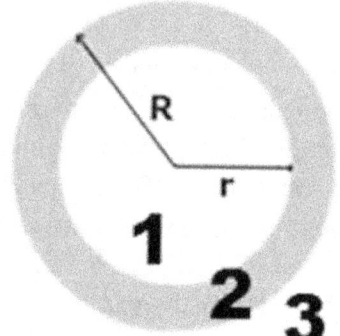

Zone 1 – zone where few survive (r)
Zone 2 – zone of survivable destruction (R-r)
Zone 3 – zone where most survive (>R)

If you are within zones 1, 2, or in zone 3 closest to zone 2, and your bare skin is in direct line-of-sight of a terrorist's nuclear explosion, you will likely receive burns. The closer you are to the explosion and the darker your skin coloring, the quicker your skin will begin burning.

Since Broadrick is up against the wall of the excavation closest to the downtown region of the city, he is effectively in the shadow of that wall, cast by the light from the explosion. He does not receive any of the direct radiation, light, or heat from the blast, but it is still brilliant, and the amount of heat being radiated is so large that he is able to feel the reflected heat radiation (infrared radiation) from the buildings surrounding the excavation. That is also why he later finds asphalt pavement that is still warm.[68]

Broadrick and Beagle get up out of the pit and found not only living people, but also those injured and many dead. The scene of destruction that confronts them is likely to happen all around the city, and moves Beagle to tears.

Rats survive the explosion too. In fact most people have no idea of the huge number of rats that live in a large city. They are secretive creatures that move around mostly at night and have few predators in the man-made canyons of a city. The explosion will shake their world too, and you can expect to see many of them scurrying about afterward.

As people begin moving away from the destruction and as they begin to help others get out, they will likely congregate at schools, churches, police and fire stations, city halls, libraries, and other government buildings. These people will be looking for leadership, someone to step up and give them some directions as to what to do to respond to this unique situation. They may be seeking medical help for the injured, guidance for helping a trapped person, a means of communication to find a loved one, or transportation.

Unfortunately our city, county, and state officials typically ignore training the population to respond to disasters. Instead, our citizens are told to stand back and watch as highly trained paramedics, police officers, and fire department personnel swoop in and do the rescuing, the saving, and the providing of the leadership needed. Our city and county servants do this superbly, but this inadvertently conditions all of us to be spectators and to be ignorant of the knowledge that will be needed in the case of a nuclear terror strike. Fire, police, and medical personnel will be so incredibly overwhelmed following a nuclear attack that knowledgeable leadership will be virtually absent from many areas of the city and suburbs.

Citizens can change this if they want to. You can be part of a knowledgeable, distributed leadership if you will study, make connections with others of a like mind, and plan.

---

[68] Ibid., Section 7.46. Studies of the heat making the surface of polished granite rough in Hiroshima indicate these surfaces reached temperatures of 1,100 °F.

Quiz on Chapter 8   (Answers are in Appendix A1)

1.   How are the ways a nuclear explosion can hurt you different from the ways you might be hurt in an accident?

2.   Suppose you are a Yorksberg city worker standing next to an open manhole ½ mile from a terrorist's nuclear bomb. Suppose also that your reflexes are really fast and when the bomb explodes, during the two seconds you have until the blast wave arrives, you jump into the manhole. Will you survive the attack?

3.   How might the lack of training and leadership among our citizens contribute to the success of the terrorist's attack?

4.   If the heat and radiation from the bomb causes your skin to melt off, or causes mutations such as a dog's head growing out of your arm, what can you do about this?

5.   If you are a mile from a nuclear explosion in a city, what can you do to protect yourself from injury?

In the next section we will look at some people inside a donut shop on 7th Avenue, just inside the one-mile ring around the bomb's explosion at ground zero. You can see it in the top left portion of the map that follows. Will they survive at that distance? Will the donut shop protect those inside? By now you probably think someone will survive. Read "Where Will Authority Be?" to learn what happens.

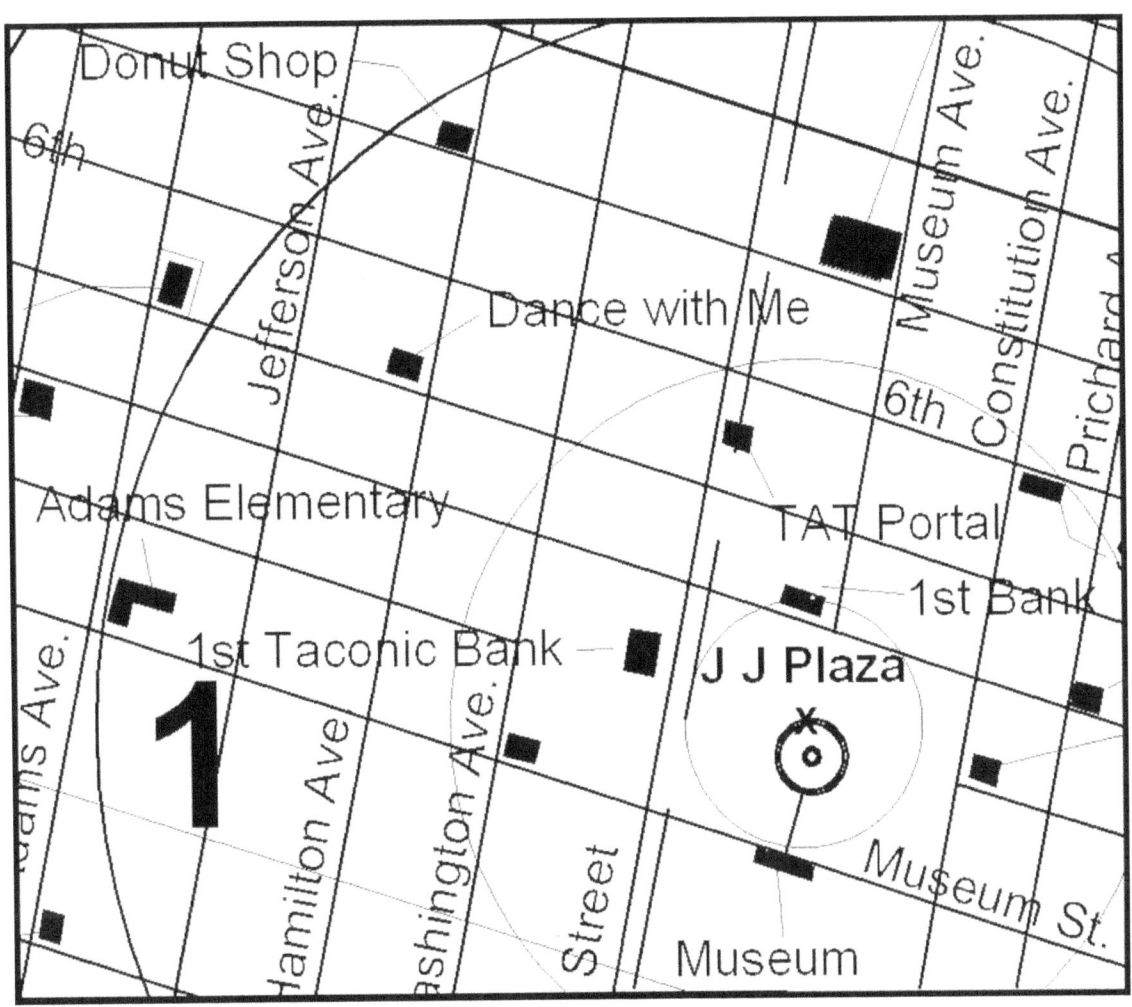

The Donut Shop in Relation to JJ Plaza

9 - Bill Ruffe – Where Will Authority Be? (1.0 mile)

You just never know when a good cop is going to die.

Bill laid the newspaper on the seat.

But why did it have to happen that way? Damn simple traffic stop, a bad tail light, and then a hit and run creates a widow and three fatherless kids.

He keyed the mic on his left shoulder.

"Chief Ruffe is 10-20 at The Donut Hole, 7th and Hamilton." He knew Carla would come back with something on that call.

"10-4, Chief. Bring one for me."

He smiled. He actually didn't like donuts, but keyed the mic twice in acknowledgment.

Looking again at the photo on the newspaper's front page, he took a deep breath, blinked the moisture from his eyes, and got out of the patrol car.

The tinkle of the small bell on the donut shop door and the smell of pastries gave the shop a sweet, warm ambiance on that cold day.

"C'mon in, Chief."

He recognized the voice of the owner of the Donut Hole. "I'll introduce you to some of my neighbors," Mitch said as he waved him toward a booth.

After introductions to two local business owners over a cup of coffee, the group discussed recent crimes in the area that had everyone concerned. As the Chief talked with the men, he watched a young woman he knew only as Jenny saying goodbye to Mitch. She put on a blue scarf and walked to the door. He remembered her from some community work he had done.

A single mom, college student, probably off to class at Yorksberg College.

His eyes were still on Jenny as she stepped out onto the sidewalk, and through the open door he could hear the bells in the church just down the street chime 2:30.

Suddenly everything outside the donut shop flooded with a brilliant blue-white light, and simultaneously the donut shop sound system, which had been playing music, gave a sharp "pop" and died. Through an eye-shielding squint he watched Jenny's shadow shorten as if the sun was rapidly rising. He watched her turn away from the intense light. When her scarf started smoking his instincts kicked in and he started to rise. Someone at the table barely had time to say "What the hell?" before a hard blast shook the whole building and threw him off his feet.

A few seconds later, amid a cacophony of crashes, car alarms, a deep rumble, falling debris, and someone screaming, he found himself on the floor, looking up at the ceiling, which he could see had been transformed into a ruined mass of hanging ceiling tiles and busted fluorescent lamps. His head hurt and he felt that old familiar chest ache of having the wind knocked out of him.

Dust and insulation hung in the air and he had to squint and blink to keep them out of his eyes. As he sat up spitting insulation out of his mouth, the bedlam died off to the distant sound of car alarms and patrons moaning. Someone in back yelled "Fire! Fire!" in a panicky voice.

He got up from the floor, feeling dazed, and surveyed the scene. To his left, one of the two men he had just met lay on the floor and appeared to be dead. A quick pulse check confirmed this.

The other man, now dead and sitting against the wall, had been pinned there by a metal rod that projected through the wall and through his head.

Crying and moaning came from the other side of the donut shop, drawing his gaze. There all the customers were laid out on the floor amid the shattered glass, probably from one of the large front windows, which was now nothing but a large opening letting the cold winter air pour in. Black smoke flowed out of the kitchen area. He could see it spreading across the ceiling and swirling in the incoming cold air.

He had to get help. He'd bet this was probably a gas explosion rather than a terrorist's bomb. Such explosions had happened in other cities, and now it was Yorksberg's turn. At this point it didn't matter, and he reached for his shoulder mic.

"This is Chief Ruffe; I have an emergency at The Donut Hole at 7th and Hamilton. There has been an explosion. Roll Fire and as many EMTs as you have. We have multiple casualties." He paused for the response, but none came.

He found the lack of response from central police headquarters odd. They always responded quickly.

The cook, looking disorientated, staggered out of the smoke-belching kitchen.

"Carla, this is Chief Ruffe. Do you copy me?" Bill said.

This time when he let go of the mic button he noticed the familiar sound of the radio repeater cutting off after his transmission did not happen.

The repeater is down? Power is off there too? What the hell?

Noticing the cook starting to go out the hole where the door used to be, he yelled "Help me get these people out!" The man looked at him, then turned and came back. The two of them began dragging the injured out.

Shouldn't move 'em, but that fire--

A few minutes later they had all the living out in the street. Most of the injuries appeared to be from flying glass. The visible injuries were multiple deep cuts with extensive bleeding. He wondered what the internal injuries would be.

Now outside, he took stock of the scene and quickly realized this could not be a gas explosion. Smoke and dust seemed to be everywhere and cars had been rolled over in the parking lot, including his police vehicle. Several of the cars nearby had interiors on fire, and he could see other fires, especially further downtown, and debris everywhere. Concrete, overturned dumpsters, pieces of signs, pieces of tree branches, leaning power poles, and bricks scattered all over. The street debris would make driving difficult, and it looked worse further downtown.

He spotted a piece of the huge 1st Taconic Bank's sign lying in the street nearby and looked toward the bank's tower a mile from him downtown.

Where did the bank building go? It can't be gone?

He could think of only one thing, and it is unbelievable, unthinkable. He slowly raised his eyes and saw, slightly east of him and high above the city, a towering cloud with a mushroom top that appeared to be blowing northward.

Fine, sand-like particles were beginning to fall all around. He caught one of these in his hand and stared at the small grain for a moment. Suddenly a cold chill ran down his spine and he brushed the grain of sand off his hand. He also brushed his shirt and his hair. He tried to kick them off his shoes, but it was no use. The fine particles continued to rain down on the area.

"We have to leave," he said. His sharp tone caused several of the nearby walking wounded to look at him.

Survivors had collected along the street, holding their wounds, gawking at the cloud overhead and at the donut shop fire, which had enveloped the entire building. Bill yelled at them.

"Come here! All of you, right now."

His voice and the police uniform proved effective and soon he has a good-sized crowd gathered about him.

"Folks, this looks like a nuclear bomb attack. We need to get ourselves and these people away from here quickly. How many of you have cars near here?" Several hands went up.

"Good. Go see if they still work, and if you can, bring them around to here. We'll load the injured."

One of the men standing nearby said, "Shall we take them to the hospital?"

Bill looked up again and pointed to the cloud. "That cloud is out over the hospital. They are going to get peppered with fallout just like here. No, get on the freeway and go south down to Morgensport. There is a county hospital there."

Several of the bystanders seemed to get the idea and move away quickly. The other able-bodied seemed unsure.

"Go now; I need all the cars that still work. Get them here if you can get through the mess in the street. If you can't drive over here, then just come back and you can ride out with someone else."

I just hope they come back with their vehicles and not just leave.

"What is fallout?" a woman said with fear in her voice.

Bill pointed to the cloud. "A nuclear explosion makes the dirt and dust in that cloud radioactive. The dirt and dust will fall back to the ground as the cloud drifts off. Wherever it lands it can kill you if you are near it too long."

The people listening to him looked lost and afraid, and he felt sorry for them. Several of them brushed away the collection of fine dust and sand on their shoulders and heads.

While gathering folks to form a caravan, he walked up 7th Street and spotted Jenny lying at the foot of a metal lamp post. He checked... *no pulse.* He couldn't tell why she died, but the wicked, bloody cut on the side of her head hinted at head trauma. The wound looked awful, and her scarf had apparently burned away, taking part of her coat's collar with it.

Five minutes later several cars and a seven-passenger van were lined up. Bill coordinated the loading and then leaned in to the lead driver and said, "When you get to the hospital, tell them it was a nuclear bomb. They will need to check all of you for radiation. Expect the trip to be slow. Everybody will be leaving Yorksberg and heading in all directions. Be careful."

A dog had been barking, he realized. It had been barking for some time, and he turned around trying to locate it, finally spotting it high up in an apartment about half a block away. Apparently the window had blown out, and the pooch had its head out barking like crazy.

Poor ol' dog. Probably trapped in there. Hope he has some food and water.

He really wanted to set the dog free, but dismissed the idea. There was so much to do, and he had to get out of the area too. A second later a horrible thought hit him.

There must be thousands... no, hundreds of thousands of pets in the building and homes. My God! And there is nothing anyone can do. If the radiation doesn't kill them, they will die of dehydration or starve to death while waiting for their owners to return.

Turning his thoughts from the fate of the doomed, he looked up and down the rubble-filled, fire-smoky avenues lined with broken and twisted trees. Many more people had filled the streets. Officer Ruffe looked at all of them.

Like sheep with no Shepherd.

They stand in little groups, gawking, talking, or helping the wounded.

Standing in a death rain and they don't even know it. They need to be told what to do. The sand falls. That damnable sand falls. Do I stay or get out of Dodge myself?

Analysis of Chapter 9

Citizens will be about their normal activities when the bad guys explode their bomb. In this section we see a police officer working with business owners in the community, all of whom are concerned with crime. This is not the part of Yorksberg Officer Ruffe would normally be in. He is far from his familiar territory and, with no working radio, far from his resources. It will be this way with you and your loved ones right after the blast. You cannot count on being in a particular place or with certain resources that will help you survive the attack.[69] The terrorists will decide when, and you could be anywhere.

You are going to have to do some thinking ahead of time and you are going to have to be resourceful when the event comes and use your knowledge to make the best use of the shelter and escape routes your location presents to you. You will also have to balance distancing yourself from radiation against helping others. This is the situation Chief Ruffe finds himself in.

At the start of the event, the Chief is looking out the window and sees Jenny brilliantly illuminated by the explosion almost a mile from the donut shop. The blast from the explosion travels at the speed of sound, so it takes about five seconds for the blast from the bomb to travel the mile to reach the donut shop. During this time the heat and light from the explosion travels silently at the speed of light and instantly touches the entire city.

---

[69] In a nuclear war, civil defense planners always assumed some warning would come to give a little time. Not much, but in 10 minutes most people can reach a prepared shelter before the missile arrives. Not so in a terrorist's nuclear attack. You will get no warning. You will be where you are and will only have time to respond after the blast, provided you survive it.

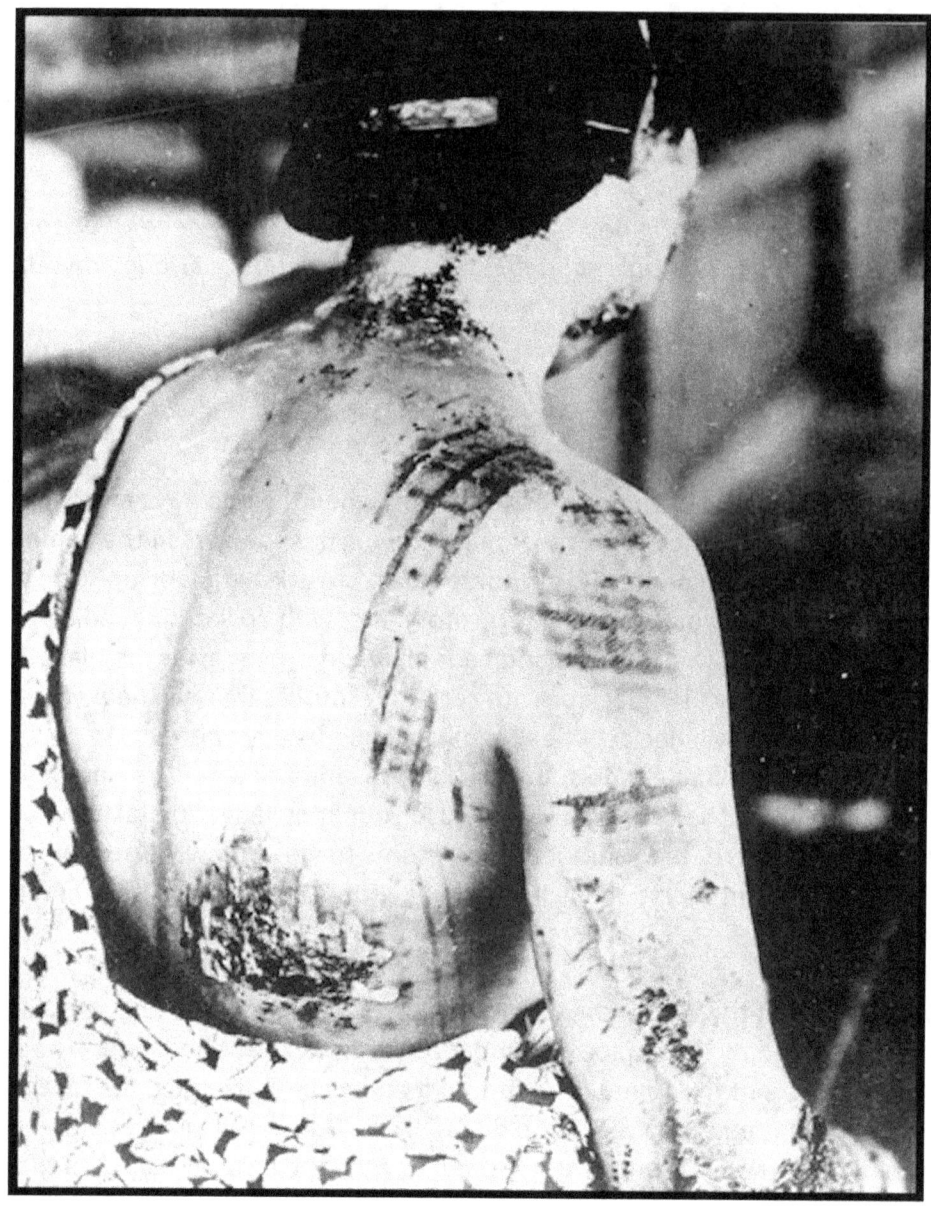

Flash and Heat Burns due to Fabric Heating.[70] Darker portions of the pattern on the fabric reached higher temperatures, resulting in the transfer of the pattern to burn patterns on the exposed skin.

If you wondered why Jenny's scarf started smoking, then you have not yet grasped the enormity of the heat from the huge fireball created by the bomb. Within a second of the start of the explosion, the 19 kt nuclear reaction creates a huge, white-hot fireball, which expands to about 900 feet in diameter. Nine hundred feet straight up is about as tall as a

---

[70] *The Effects of Nuclear Weapons*, Samuel Glasstone and Philip J. Dolan, United States Department of Defense, 1977, Figure 12.72.

75-story building. So although the actual explosion point is not directly visible to most parts of the town, within one second the rising fireball is able to radiate enormous amounts of heat for several miles around to anything in line-of-sight of its brilliance. Take a look at these pictures below (from Japan) to get an idea of what this radiant energy can do in a few seconds.

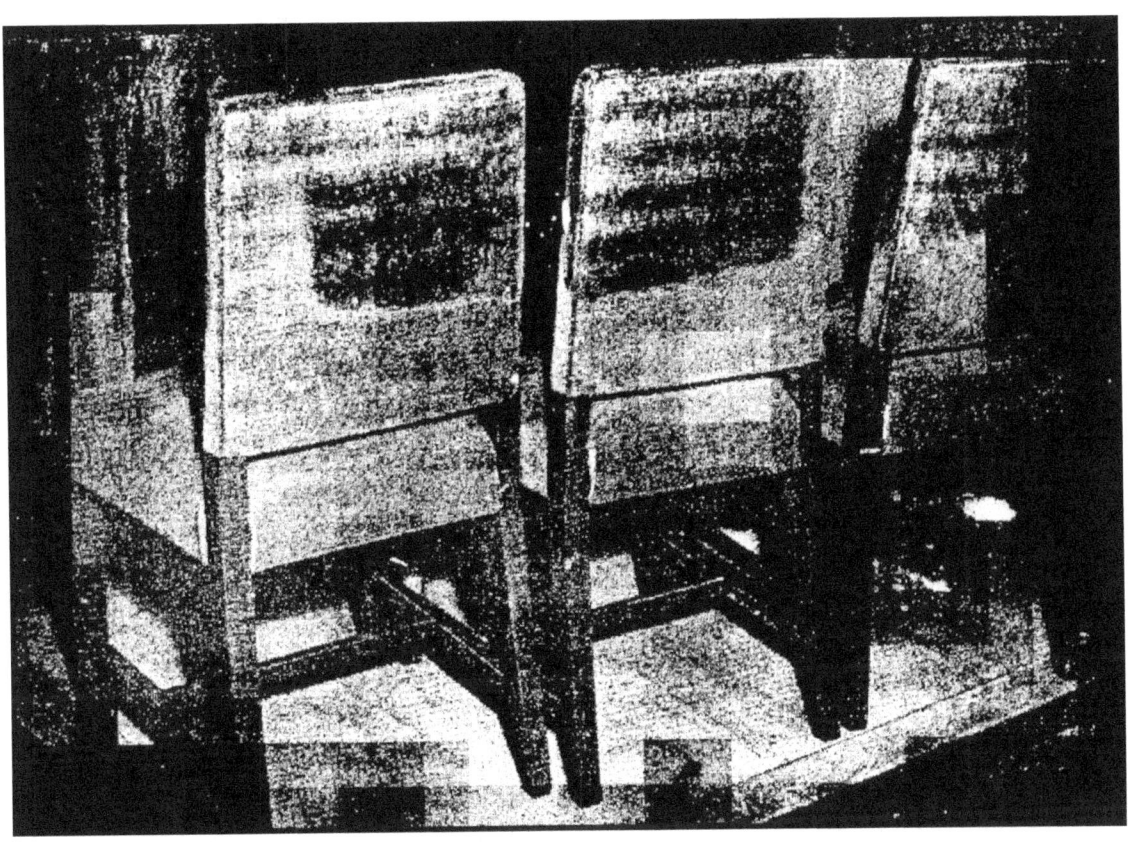

Burns on upholstery exposed to the Hiroshima explosion at a distance of one mile.[71]

This radiated heat is why Jenny's scarf begins smoking seconds before the blast wave hit the donut shop.

---

[71] Ibid., Figure 7.44a.

Charred Poles 1.17 Miles from the Nuclear Explosion at Nagasaki.[72] The portions of the poles that are not charred were shielded from the radiated heat by intervening structures.

The "pop" heard on the sound system in the donut shop is a result of the explosion. Electric power is knocked out due to downed power poles, busted transformers, and the destruction of the central substation, but in addition to this, the explosion causes an electromagnetic pulse (EMP), which caused the "pop" heard on the sound system. This EMP is an extremely fast-rising electrical surge caused by the bomb that can destroy parts of an electrical distribution system. In Yorksberg the EMP is only significant in areas the blast wave will destroy, so we can generally ignore it. The effects of the EMP can be much more significant if the bomb is detonated at a very high altitude.

The blast wave from the explosion impacts the donut shop area but does not directly impact the donut shop's walls because the shop is nestled within many other buildings along the street. This provides the shop with some protection.

If you doubt that Bill could survive the bomb blast one mile from ground zero, consider what was seen at Nagasaki. The Nagasaki bomb (22 kt) released about the same energy yield as the fictional Yorksberg's bomb, but was set off high in the air (about 1640 feet above the ground).[73] Both the Hiroshima and Nagasaki weapons were exploded high

---

[72] Ibid., Figure 7.44b.
[73] Ibid., Section 3.31.

above the ground so that their blast waves could radiate out from the explosion point unimpeded to any point on the ground below, and to reduce radioactive fallout.

Below is a photo[74] showing a wood-frame building that was one mile from ground zero at Hiroshima. The house in this picture was not shielded by any structures, yet it appears that someone inside the lower floor may well have survived, although perhaps with injuries.[75]

The donut shop is a little less than one mile from the Yorksberg "ground zero"; however, there are two significant differences between the house in the Hiroshima photo and our fictional donut shop. First, the Yorksberg bomb is set off sitting in a truck on the ground while the Hiroshima bomb exploded high in the air. Second, while the Hiroshima house had nothing between it and the exploding bomb, the Yorksberg shop had one mile of city buildings between it and the bomb. The intervening buildings provide some blast and heat radiation shielding. Many of the Yorksberg buildings are large concrete and steel structures, so the story was written assuming the heat and light effects, and the blast wave, were attenuated by the intervening structures. Bill's chances of survival, therefore, are better than if he had been in the Hiroshima house.

When the bomb explodes, the rapid expansion of the fireball causes a blast wave to form. This blast wave consists of air compressed into a powerful pressure wave. A pressure wave is essentially a sound wave made of compressed air. This is just air at a higher

---

[74] Ibid., Figure 5.52, upper half.
[75] Ibid., Figure 5.70.

pressure than normal atmospheric pressure. This higher pressure is called the blast wave's "overpressure" and is measured in pounds per square inch (psi).

As the blast wave moves outward from the explosion point, the wave's overpressure decreases. For our fictional 19 kt weapon, here are some approximate overpressure data points at various distances from "ground zero."[76]

Table 2.1 – Overpressure vs. Distance

Distance	Overpressure	Wind Velocity
.51 miles (813 m)	10 psi	294 mph
.76 miles (1220 m)	5 psi	163 mph
.94 miles (donut shop distance)		
1.26 miles (2033 m)	2 psi	70 mph
1.9 miles (3050 m)	1 psi	gust

Note the wind velocity of the blast wave as it passed the donut shop is between 163 and 70 mph. For our story we estimate it is 130 mph. This is enough to throw Jenny into the metal lamp pole and cause fatal injuries.

There are two components of the blast wave that contribute to damaging structures. One is the sudden sharp rise in pressure on a structure due to the blast wave's overpressure, and the other is the peak dynamic pressure, which is the wind's force[77] on structure while the moving air is passing by. This is essentially a gust of wind, and its damage-inducing ability is similar to any wind storm, except the magnitude of the wind is very high within 1 mile of a 19 kt explosion, and that it blows for only a few seconds.

The explosion will throw debris a long distance. In our story, one of the men the Chief was talking to was killed by a piece of debris, and the fire in the kitchen was started when a chunk of concrete smashed in through the roof and into hot grease.

Parts of high buildings, which are physically much higher than a nuclear bomb set off on the ground, will be blasted upward as well as outward. Expect chunks of heavy material to be thrown great distances and arrive back on the ground with deadly force and a high velocity. These flying projectiles can smash through roofs; damage electrical lines; destroy automobiles; sever (and ignite) gas lines where they connect into buildings; bust telephone poles that survive the blast wave; and even penetrate through a roof and first floors to impact in the basement, which might be disconcerting if you have chosen to make the basement your shelter.

---

[76] These numbers are a combination of the sea-level wind velocities of an "ideal shock front" (Glasstone and Dolan, Table 3.07) and Excel spreadsheet calculations using Glasstone and Dolan, Table 3.73c values extrapolated with the scaling formula given in Glasstone and Dolan, page 114. This was done to convert overpressure values from a 1 kt yield to a 19 kt yield. Although by no means precise, this calculation formed a basis against which the fiction in this book could be written with consistency and some degree of accuracy as to the effects of a 19 kt explosion over various distances.

[77] Think of the wind's "force" as the peak load against the structure caused by the inertia of the mass of air flowing by.

This last point is one reason it is a good idea to be against the basement wall closest to the explosion. These chunks of debris will most likely be coming in at an angle, puncturing the structure overhead, flying over you, and ending up smashing against the opposite wall. (Don't store your food and water there.)

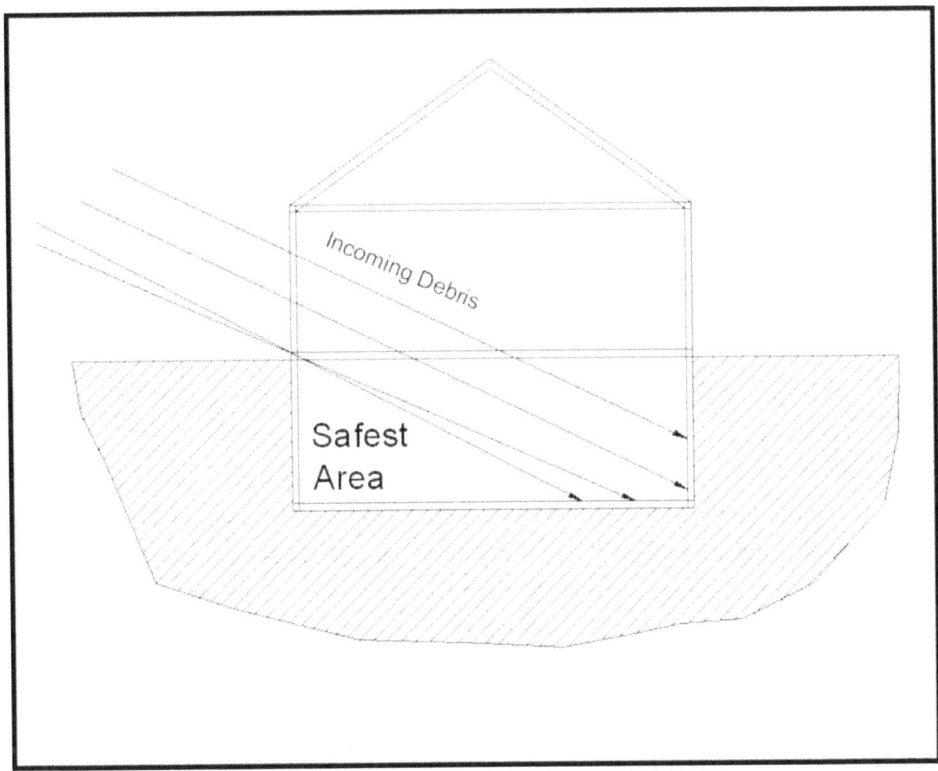

This diagram shows how debris thrown a great distance by
an explosion may enter your shelter at an angle.

Assuming the bad guys will explode their weapon in the center of the city is the only clue you have as to which way the debris will fly. They may park their bomb right outside your donut shop, in which case you don't have to worry about flying debris.

Windows can be a hazard in the vicinity of a nuclear explosion. The explosion creates a very bright light, which creates curiosity. People want to see what is happening outside to cause such a bright light, and may actually walk to a window to look, when they should be diving for cover. Windows are also a weak point in a building's structure; for example, during nuclear testing in Nevada, some reinforced concrete houses were purposefully exposed to a nuclear explosion. The house structure came through well, but the windows were always blasted in.

In a large city there are many streets in the manmade canyons between the tall buildings. These manmade canyons can channel and reflect sound waves. As the blast wave pounds its way across the city, parts of it will reflect off buildings, causing null zones and amplified zones.[78] Null zones are places where reflected waves partially cancel other waves so that the blast is weaker. Amplified zones are where the reflected waves add up with other reflected waves and produce a stronger blast. At the donut shop this is why one plate glass window shatters and explodes inward like a shotgun blast, while the other blows outward. Bill and his companions are seated at the end of the donut shop where the glass blows out. This acoustic effect actually protected him to some extent.

The reflection and interference of the blast wave is based in fact (the physics of sound waves), although no one will be able to do anything but speculate about post-blast damage due to these effects. Many strange things, such as a window that is not damaged when every other window in the block is blown out,[79] will be found in the zone of destruction that no one will be able to explain. Expect that sort of thing, but don't count on it to save you. The window you stand in front of to watch the pretty mushroom cloud rising in the distance will most likely hurt you when the blast wave arrives.

An example of the capricious nature of the blast wave can be found amid the stories told by survivors of nuclear explosions. An example of this is the account of Katsuyoshi Yoshimura, a first-grade student at the time of the bombing of Hiroshima. He watched the bomb fall from the plane. When the blast wave hit, his mother threw herself on top of him and then their house collapsed on top of them. His brother had been sitting outside by the roadside at the time of the blast, watching an umbrella mender work. "He told us later that the blast had thrown the man four or five meters into the air before he crashed to the ground. He had not moved again. Though my brother had been sitting beside the umbrella mender, he had not been blown into the air but had just continued to sit there alone. He was burned on the right side of his head and on his right arm, and later in life still bore the keloids,[80] although he was in perfect health."[81]

You may wonder if what you are reading about a bomb of this size is true to life. For the most part, everything written here is based on actual nuclear test data (see Glasstone and Dolan) and on eyewitness accounts of the effects of the two nuclear bombs dropped on populated areas to end World War II.

After the people Chief Ruffe sent south to the hospital reached the exit at Morgensport, the first sizable city south of Yorksberg, what did they find? Was the civil authority at Morgensport prepared to handle the contaminated injured and vehicles

---

[78] "It is to be expected that the presence of many buildings close together will cause local changes in the blast wave...." Glasstone and Dolan, Section 3.3.8.

[79] The author saw the odd way acoustic (sound) waves can act when the military set off some explosives in an open field as part of a community celebration in Richland Washington in the 1950s. The field was about ¼ mile north of a rectangular city block of stores (with plate glass window fronts) surrounded by a parking lot. None of the stores on the side of the rectangle facing the explosion (north side) were damaged. But one store on the East side and one store on the West side, both right in the middle of the stores lining those sides of the rectangle, suffered shattered windows due to acoustic effects.

[80] A type of scar tissue.

[81] Jamestown Foundation, Publication: *Terrorism Monitor*, Volume: 2, Issue: 6, March 24, 2004, by Scott Atran, in the chapter titled "Weeds by the Roadside" by Katsuyoshi Yoshimura.

pouring south along the interstate? Here are some steps that should be taken to reduce and control the spread of radioactive contamination:

1. The interstate lanes moving traffic toward the bombed city should immediately be closed to all but authorized traffic. Sightseers, trucks carrying goods bound for Yorksberg, or trucks just intending to pass by the city should be rerouted. If traffic is not stopped, fallout on the highway will be picked up by the tires and transported everywhere.

2. Traffic flowing out of the bombed city will thoroughly contaminate the interstate pavement, but it cannot be stopped. Stopping the exodus will result in the death or injury of those at the Yorksberg end of the traffic jam. Those folks need to get away from the heavily contaminated city. The highway can be cleaned later.

3. Vehicles with injured should be allowed to exit the freeway in communities with hospitals as long as the hospital or other city facilities can accommodate them. This will require good communication (i.e., a plan) between the medical folks and the police/state troopers controlling the flow of traffic into the cities along the interstate.

4. Before the explosion, city authorities should decide which facilities can be sacrificed in the event of a nearby nuclear explosion. The critically injured and highly contaminated must have a place to go for treatment. That place will likely be rendered unusable for many years, due to radioactive contamination. Is that what you want to happened to your hospital? You might be able to save it if you plan ahead for this event (i.e., provide the means to decontaminate patients before bringing them into the hospital).

5. The non-critically injured should be decontaminated before being treated. This suggests they be allowed to wash or shower, but brings up the logistics nightmare of contaminated clothing and disposal of contaminated wash water. Any facility used to wash the clothing will be seriously contaminated and eventually rendered unusable (if radiation dose rates become too high). Also, you will probably not be able to set up enough of these decontamination resources to handle the influx of injured. That is another reason the exits from the interstate into the city might have to be closed when the local medical resources are swamped. Traffic must continue to move down the road to allow other communities to help with the injured.

Consider also that if contaminated wash water from decontamination operations is allowed to drain into the city waste water treatment system, the sewer lines and that sewage treatment system will become radioactive. This will affect everyone who works with the treatment plant or who repair sewage lines, for years to come. It would be better to capture the decontamination water and store it for cleanup later. The science of removing radioactivity from water has been perfected at Nuclear Power Plants. It can be done safely and the clean water returned to the environment.

6. Vehicles that are dangerously contaminated should be routed to a field or a parking lot to undergo cleaning prior to continuing into the city. The contaminated dirt in the field or the parking lot asphalt can be cleaned up or hauled off and buried later. Be aware of where your radioactive wash-water goes.

These steps are just a start at examining the needed response of communities near a bombed city. Much of those activities are highly dependent on authorities having the proper radiological equipment in sufficient supply. If you can't measure the contamination, you will be in deep trouble. You don't want to have to abandon your city for many years due to dangerous levels of radioactive contamination brought to you by the exodus from the bombed city. To try to prevent this from happening, vehicles attempting to exit the freeway to enter your city must be screened with a radiation instrument. Those found to be severely contaminated must be directed off the road and sent to a designated parking area to be cleaned up or quarantined.

To get an idea of the scope of the disaster, imagine tens of thousands of cars exiting the contaminated city, going everywhere, even out of state, to hotels, to friends' houses, and to hospitals. The cars are contaminated, inside and out; the people are contaminated, and their clothing is contaminated with highly radioactive materials. Some of them are hazardous to even be near. When they enter their friends' houses and shake hands, the friends' hands may receive radioactive dust, which the friends may ingest the next time they pick up sandwiches to eat. Homes, hotels, hospitals – everywhere these contaminated people go will be contaminated. The cleanup will be inconceivably costly, as will be the health consequences. It would be better to have a plan in place to control this radioactive mass exodus, rather than to spend years and billions of dollars cleaning it up afterward. Are your hospitals and public officials ready? Why don't you ask them what their plans are?

What happened to Jenny? For those of you who just have to know what happened to everybody, Jenny was accelerated to approximately 45 miles per hour by the impulse of the blast wave, and was stopped when she hit a metal pole. She died instantly due to severe head trauma.[82] Her children were safe in school on the south side of the river when the bomb exploded. They ended up in state custody with thousands of other children orphaned by the Yorksberg attack.

The barking dog Bill sees stirs up difficult memories. Those of you who live in New York may remember the news articles about the starving or dead pets found in the homes and apartments of those who died in the 9/11 attacks. Their owners had perished, and in the aftermath of the attack, few thought of the fact that those who lived alone might have had a dog or a cat depending on them for food and water. The situation will be worse after a nuclear terror strike. Radiation will keep would-be rescuers at bay, and will kill many of these helpless animals.

The rain of tiny sand-like particles gently falls all over Yorksberg north of the river. This is the fallout of the larger, heavier particles from the blast, which have a special significance to those who intend to survive. They fall within 10 to 20 miles of the detonation point, subject to upper air winds. These innocent-looking little grains of sand will be lethal to anyone who remains in the area too long.

---

82 Chief Ruffe noted that Jenny's scarf had burned. Charring, smoldering, and even ignition of materials at Hiroshima and Nagasaki were noted up to 1.25 miles from ground zero (Reference 1, Figure 7.63). Dark colors absorb more of the radiated heat energy than light colors. That is why the scarf charred and burned but Jenny's light-colored coat and pants did not.

<u>Quiz on Chapter 9</u>   (Answers are in Appendix A1)

1. True or false? Clothing can be ignited by the heat from a rising nuclear fireball.
2. What are the two main components of the blast wave?
3. Why are windows a hazard following the explosion of a nuclear bomb in a city?
4. True or false? Hospitals far from our major cities do not need to prepare for nuclear terrorism.
5. After a nuclear explosion, small, sand-like particles lofted by the heat of the explosion rain out of the mushroom cloud. What is the significance of these sand grains?

The terrorists do not discriminate about who they attack. Women, children, rich bankers, bums in the back alleys, and even taxi drivers are in their sights the instant they press that button. Sometimes whether or not the bad guys get you has to do with being in the right place at the right time. One of the taxi drivers in Yorksberg's downtown area survives. To find out how, read the next chapter called "Right Place, Right Time." What a difference a cup of coffee makes!

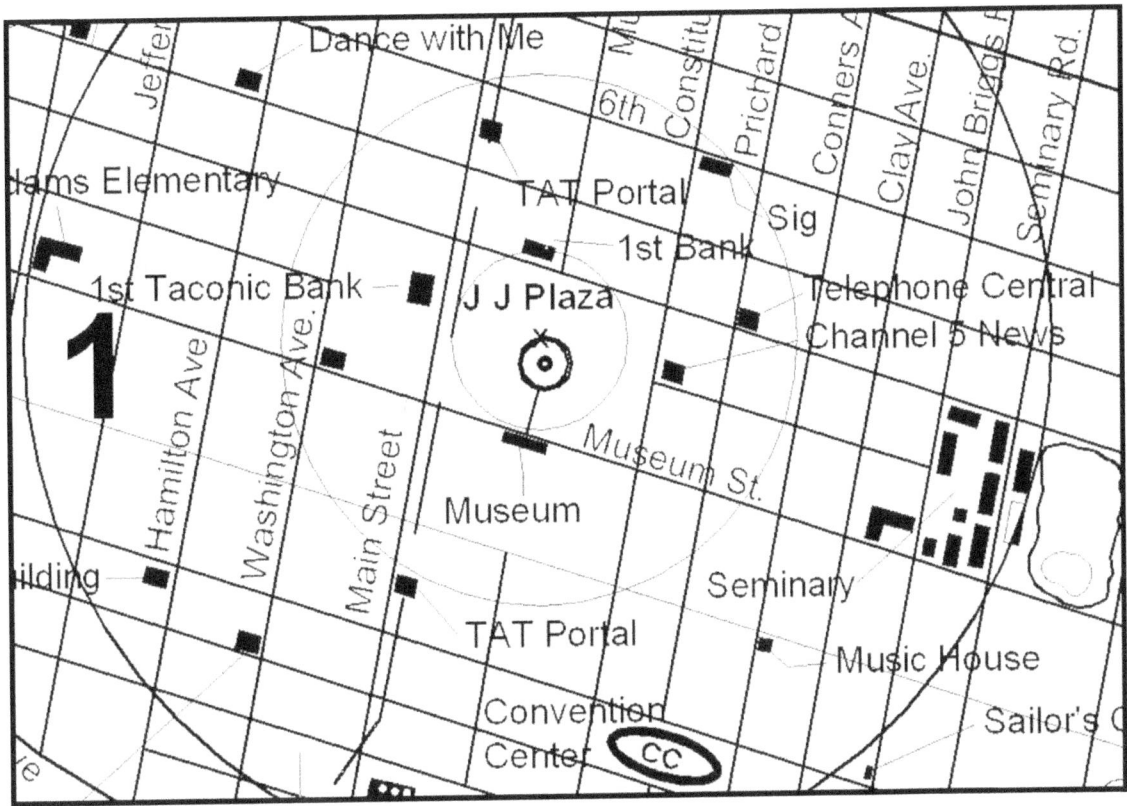

10 - John Burnes – Right Place, Right Time (1.0 mile)

"That's what I tell everybody now, something as small as missing a little cup of coffee can make the difference between life and death," John Burnes said with a solemn face.

"Do you mean skipping a cup of coffee saved you, Mr. Burnes?" Chevy Norick said while adjusting the mic clipped onto the taxi driver's hospital gown.

"Shoot yes, that's exactly what I mean. I ain't a toasted crispy-critter and pushing up daisies because I didn't get that cup of java I wanted. And please, don't call me Mr. Burnes; just John will do."

He watched as the camera man gave an okay sign to Chevy. "One minute, Mr. Norick," the camera man said and ducked behind the television camera.

"Okay, John. This is it; Mark will give us the sign and then we will be live. The audience would like to hear what happened to you in Yorksberg. Just tell it like it happened, and then I will ask a few questions."

"Will they see this in Jamaica?"

"All over the world," Chevy said.

He could hear the national newscaster's voice. "And now we will take you to the Allendale County Hospital, 150 miles west of Yorksberg, where one of its citizens, who was less than one mile from ground zero, will tell his story. The American hero tonight on our Nuclear Terror series is Mr. John Burnes, a 26-year-old, recently naturalized citizen from

Jamaica, who was working as a taxi driver on that fateful day. Our correspondent is Chevy Norick. How is John doing tonight, Chevy?"

The camera man pointed at Chevy and a red light at the front of the camera came on.

"Good evening, Rod, and America. I am pleased to report that Mr. Burnes is well. The doctors say his injured knee is mending and he expects to be out of the hospital soon."

Chevy turned from the camera toward John.

"John, please give us an account of your experience that day in Yorksberg."

"Thanks, Chevy, for the chance to tell my story, and hey there, Jamaica! My wife and kids are watching, I hope."

Chevy smiled. "I am sure they are. How about starting with what you were doing that afternoon."

"I was doing what I call a prowl. In the mornings most of the taxi traffic is carrying people to work, or to the airport. In the evenings, it's mostly meeting incoming flights. Midafternoons are slow, so I just prowl the city, or park my cab and wait for my dispatcher, Ronda Grabels, to radio me a fare."

"So Ronda got you a fare?"

"Shooowee! She did; God bless her. That call saved me. See I usually stop downtown for a hot cup of coffee, especially on cold days like that day. There is a little spot on 4th Avenue, just off the plaza where those crazies put the bomb. I buy a cup of java and park. You know, maybe read a little, and wait for a call. Well that day at about 2:30 Ronda called me to a fare at the Baptist Seminary, right on Seminary Road."

"How far from the plaza do you think that was?" Chevy said.

"Like that fella said a moment ago, 'bout a mile. I took 4th Street because I love that drive; it has lots of large oak trees on either side, and they kinda reach out over the road. Very beautiful... that is, it was very beautiful, John said as he blinked moisture from his eyes. Recovering, he continued.

It was a good fare. Sometimes you have to wait on folks. This one I could see standing out front as soon as I made that right turn on Seminary. The professor and his wife were on the curb. Those folks told me they were bound for San Diego to see their son. 'Good afternoon,' I said it like that, you know, with the island accent. Folks seem to like that. The man, he was a professor you know, caught the accent and said, 'Good afternoon, young man... Jamaica, right? So I flashed him my whites—" as he said this he smiled a big white-toothed grin, "—and I said 'You got it, mon.' I got a smile from him for that!"

"And then what happened?"

"I put the professor's bag in Nellie, that's my cab, and I remember hearing the seminary's bells begin to chime the half hour. All of a sudden, everything got so bright it hurt my eyes. The professor said 'electric arc' or something like that.

Squinting for a second or two, I could see the shadow of a building coming down the wall across the street. It was like some big moon was rising; only this weren't no moon!"

"How long did that last?" Chevy prompted.

"Not long, maybe a few seconds, and the odd thing was it was suddenly warm. You know, that was a chilly day, but I could feel heat coming from the building across the street. Then everything went crazy...moving I mean...and I was shoved toward the building by this wind, and the air was filled with all kinds of stuff. The professor and his wife went down with me. I remember the ground shaking, and even after things calmed down, there were car alarms going off, and stuff hitting the ground.[83] It was crazy, like a tornado, only real fast and ya couldn't see it coming."

"Is that when you were injured?"

"I guess so. I don't remember actually getting hurt, but when I got up my knee hurt like... well, bad. Odd thing was they said it was a bomb that blew up, but I don't remember hearing the explosion,[84] yet my ears were ringing and my nose was bleeding. My fares got it worse than me. The professor's wife, bless her soul, was dead there on the steps; that poor lady had her head crushed, and the professor, his leg was broke real bad. This big piece of the top of the building fell on them. You know, one of those concrete fancy borders up on the edge. That sucker just missed me."

Tears welled up in his eyes again and he had to pause. He accepted a tissue Chevy offered.

"Go on."

"Well, people came running out of the building, and across the street there was this fire in one of the offices... oh, and fires in several cars up at Museum Street. A big oak tree was laid over on its side right up the street, tar paper rolls and shingles scattered around, and a delivery van turned over. There were paper towels and little boxes everywhere. I remember seeing the upper windows across the street were gone, just holes, you know, in the side of the building."

"You mentioned cars on fire. Did your cab burn too?"

"No, but she sure got walloped. Nellie's rear window was gone, just a bunch of glass all over inside. A hammer broke it I think. I found it in the car afterward. Belonged to the roofing crew that was up on the building above us. Poor guys, must have been blown off. I saw a body with a tool belt lying in the street near Nellie."

Choking up and with moisture back in his eyes, John said, "Why did they do it, Mr. Norick? Why?"

"That is a question we are all asking, John. Perhaps we will never know. Sick, twisted men." He paused. "Tell us how you got out of the city?"

"Well, we loaded the professor, and a couple of other people who got banged up, into Nellie, and I tried to drive out. Museum Street was blocked by a power line, so I went on down to 2nd, and from there was able to get to Ocean Avenue. I had to go around stuff, even drove across the lawn at one place to get to Ocean Avenue. I was going to the hospital

---

[83] Those who have heard the space shuttle's sonic booms in a residential neighborhood will recall the booms are shortly followed by a number of startled barking dogs and car alarms. These "sonic booms" are a type of blast wave.

[84] In the book *Hiroshima* by John Hersey, in a chapter called "A Noiseless Flash," he reports the experiences of a Mr. Matsuo, whose house was two miles from ground zero. He says "Almost no one in Hiroshima recalls hearing any noise of the bomb. But a fisherman... heard a tremendous explosion... he was 20 miles from Hiroshima...." Undoubtedly there was much noise, but in the overall shock of the event this is apparently not prominent. The blast knocked Mr. Matsuo's house down and affected a group of soldiers working nearby as follows: "...the soldiers were coming out of the hole, where they should have been safe, and blood was running from their heads, chests, and backs. They were silent and dazed."

up on Hospital Road, but when I looked, there was this huge cloud and dust and it just didn't seem right. Something about that cloud scared me, you know, like poison gas maybe. I figured the hospital would be a mess just like the city, so I just bailed out and went north as fast as I could.

I got to a hospital about 20 miles north of the city, but the police came almost immediately and made everyone move west. I guess they expected the cloud would drift over and drop radioactive stuff there too."

"Any final comments for the nation?" Chevy said.

"Well, that's about it, except thanks to all the nice folks that got me cleaned up, and the doc that is fixin' my knee. God bless you all."

"That was a fascinating account. Thank you very much. Could you tell America what you plan to do now? Will you continue to drive a taxi?"

"That is very sad," John said. "They took Nellie. She's sitting in a field near here, with a bunch of other cars, with police tape all around, won't let nobody in. My picture, my wife and kids you know, is in the sun visor, and they won't let me get it. A cop told me they are going to have to bury Nellie." He choked up at this and wiped the tears from his cheek.

"We understand your loss," Chevy said, "and I am sure you'll get some new pictures of the family. Perhaps one of our viewers will step up and find a new taxi for you."

He then turned to the camera.

"Thank you, John Burnes, our American nuclear terror survivor for today. This is Chevy Norick, reporting from the Allendale County Hospital. Back to you, Rod."

The light on the camera went off, and the sound of Rod's voice could be heard going on to other news.

"That was great, John," Chevy said. "You told it well."

"That was harder than I thought it would be," John said. "But you see about the coffee? If I had not got that fare call and stayed for a cup of java, I would have boiled along with the coffee."

Analysis of Chapter 10

John Burnes survives because he is in a good place at the right time and because he moves out of the area quickly, satisfying one of the two options for folks who have the misfortune to be looking up at a mushroom cloud: get in a shelter or leave the area quickly.

If you are able to look up at a rising mushroom cloud above you, remember that you must either quickly get into a protective shelter or quickly leave the area. "Leave the area" means to travel 20 or 30 miles crosswind or upwind from the direction the mushroom cloud is moving. If you move downwind in the direction the mushroom cloud is moving, the radioactive fallout will just rain on you later.

The reader will note that John drove the same direction the mushroom cloud was moving when he went north on Ocean Avenue. Normally this is not a good idea because it will keep you under that constant "rain" of radioactive dirt and dust the cloud has lifted up. John could not go any other direction, however, and was able to drive faster than the cloud drifted. The authorities knew it would catch up with him when he stopped at a distant hospital, and they made him move west.

Finding a quality shelter will be difficult since most current civil defense leaders (emergency operations folks) are not planning to shelter people. A shelter must allow you to either be a safe distance away from the radioactive dust and debris or it must put substantial mass between you and the radioactive material. Three feet of earth is a good barrier, but the shelter should also have food, water, clean air (a filtration system) and a place to sleep. You may have to stay there a week or more. It will also help for you to have some kind of radio communication, with plenty of batteries, so you can contact the authorities to ask them to help you get out of the radioactive zone. All the components needed to make a good shelter is the reason leaving may be the better option.

One of John Burnes' strengths is his knowledge of the streets of Yorksberg. He knows the streets as well as a taxi driver or perhaps a policeman with years of experience. If you are new to a city, learn the streets as quickly as possible. You don't have to know them all, just the key ones and the interconnections that can get you out of town as rapidly as possible in the event of a nuclear attack.[85] Often, there are routes through the city that will parallel or bypass the clogged arterial roads. You might have to drive several miles farther out, but you will be moving outward from the city while the main roads are jammed with people trying to leave.[86]

The first thing people outdoors will know when the bad guys light off their weapon of terror is the bright flash of the explosion. The light travels at the speed of light and is instantly seen even 100 miles away. The radiant heat is just as fast, but the sound wave of the explosion travels at the speed of sound. This "blast" wave is the energy from the explosion that destroys buildings, trees, cars, people, and anything in its path. It travels outward from the point of explosion like the rings of ripples that travel outward from a rock tossed into a quiet pond. The blast wave is exceedingly strong at first and gradually weakens as it moves outward.

This is why the professor has time to make the comment about an electric arc (his guess as to what made the bright light) before the blast reached the Seminary. It is the quickness of the onset of the flash and its brightness that prompted him to think of an electric arc. This time delay, between when you see the flash and when the blast arrives, is important to remember because it is all the time you have to take cover.

Here are distances from the blast and the time you will have to take cover from the explosion of a bomb the size used on Hiroshima, Nagasaki, or Yorksberg: one mile, 4

---

[85] Having lived where crowds of more than 100,000 come to watch a space shuttle launch, the author has seen over and over again the massive traffic jams waiting for 45 minutes after the launch to get moving out of the city. All the while, there is a set of lesser roads known by the city's inhabitants that allow them to move quickly across town while everybody else is jammed up. This is the street knowledge of your city you want to have under your belt when the day comes that you must run for your life.

[86] Remember the old joke about how fast you have to run to escape a grizzly bear that charges your group of hikers? You don't have to outrun the bear; you just have to be able to run faster than the slowest member of your group. Radioactive fallout does not chase you like a mean bear, but the slower citizens of your city will receive the most radiation damage. A good rule of thumb for response to a terrorist's nuclear attack is to leave early and move as fast as you can.

seconds; two miles, 9 seconds; three miles, 14 seconds; four miles, 19 seconds; and five miles, 25 seconds. We will revisit this "time to take cover" concept in several of the other chapters.

After the initial flash from the explosion of the bomb, there remains a huge ball of white-hot, incandescent gas surrounding the blast point. It begins rising within seconds of the explosion and will still be glowing when it reaches 30,000 feet above the city. This ball of white-hot gases cools by radiating the heat away as it rises.

Think of the glowing-red heating elements on your electric stove. You can feel that heat even several feet from the stove. If an element on your stove was as hot as the white-hot ball of incandescent gasses, the temperature of a nuclear explosion, the radiant heat would probably severely injure you and set the walls of your entire kitchen on fire within seconds. The ball of incandescent gasses rising from a real nuclear explosion is much larger than your stovetop heating coil. It is on the order of 900 feet in diameter for the Yorksberg-sized bomb, and its radiant heat bathes the entire city as it rises.

John mentioned the building's shadow coming down the building across the street...as if a big moon was rising. How this happens can be seen in the following figure. As the hot fireball at position A rises to position B, the shadow of the closer building appears to move down the adjacent building (A to B).

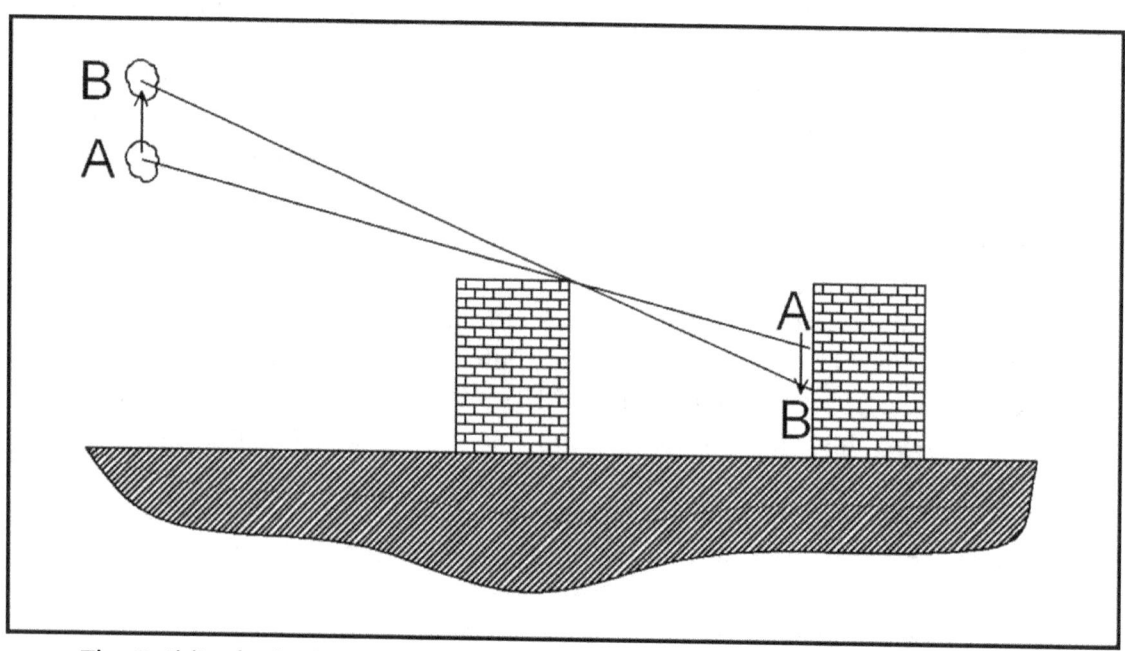

The Building's shadow as seen coming down the wall across the street

What is the blast wave like? You have probably experienced a small version of this during a fourth-of-July fireworks display. When one of the white-flash "thunder-bombs" explodes overhead, a second or two later you heard a loud "boom" that you can actually feel in your chest. It might even shake your clothes. That sound, that boom, is a miniature blast wave passing by you. It is harmless because it is not very strong.

Now imagine a blast wave that can instantly break a tree or a telephone pole in half, or blast in all the doors and window frames of a house, or pick up a car and toss it through the air. The blast wave from a nuclear explosion can do these things even a mile away from the explosion, depending on how powerful the bomb is.

In the case of John Burnes, our taxi driver, the blast wave had to come over one of the Seminary's two-story buildings to get to him. This was to his advantage because he did not feel the direct impact of the blast. Instead, he was actually in the blast wave's shadow of the building. So he and the people standing near him experienced a weaker, refracted blast wave as pressure from above, a reflected blast wave from the building across the street, and suction in toward the nearby building. If it were not for the falling concrete, the blast wave might not have hurt any of the people standing with John.

How could you protect yourself in such a situation? It is not likely that any of us could react fast enough, but if you were near the building's door, a quick duck inside would have sheltered you from falling and flying debris, provided you stayed away from the windows.

The men on the building's roof were exposed to the light and heat with no chance for shelter. They were then blown off the roof by a combination of the blast wave and the burst of wind that followed.

Think of it like this: the passage of the blast wave is like a slap, where one moment the air around you is still and the next instant it is blowing sideways at a high speed. As the blast wave passes you, the wind from the blast slaps you suddenly, gradually slows to zero over several seconds, and then actually reverses for a few seconds. You will experience a hard slap of wind, a gradually decreasing whoosh of wind, and then a softer suction of wind moving back toward the blast zone.

The Seminary is a little less than a mile from JJ Plaza. For the 19-kt nuclear bomb set off in the plaza, we can estimate from nuclear testing that the men on the roof experienced a blast of wind of about 135 mph, which is enough to throw them off the roof. The blast did not kill them, but it did cause their deaths due to the uncontrolled fall to the street below.

In our story, decorative pieces of the upper part of the old Seminary building were knocked loose by the blast. All across the city heavy pieces of material are sent flying by the huge explosion. Quickly taking cover can prevent you from being hurt.

Fire will be a big problem following a nuclear explosion in a city. In this part of our story the only mention of this are the fires started by the radiant heat from the rising fireball, which has set a chair on fire inside a room across the way from where John parked, and inside a car or two. These small fires may just burn out or be extinguished by someone, but in the aftermath of the explosion some fires may grow and rage out of control around the city. After the explosion it is possible to have so many fires set that they create a tremendous, self-sustaining wind that feeds more oxygen to the fires, increasing and spreading them. This is a called a "firestorm," which will continue until the fuel is exhausted.[87]

---

[87] *The Effects of Nuclear Weapons*, Samuel Glasstone and Philip J. Dolan, United States Department of Defense, 1977, Section 7.71: At Hiroshima, about 20 minutes after the explosion, large fires formed. Two hours after the explosion the fires caused an inrushing wind reaching speeds as high as 40 mph. That fires did

During John Burnes' attempts to reach St. Mary's Hospital, he finds the streets littered with obstacles he must get around. Closer to the blast point those who can find a car that still works will discover they probably cannot use it to leave the area because of debris in the streets. If you find yourself in that situation, you should consider abandoning the car and running/walking out if you cannot shelter.

John finds a way out of the downtown area and then makes the decision to get out of town to a distant hospital. As soon as he reaches a hospital to the north of Yorksberg, the authorities begin evacuating it because they know the cloud is drifting their way and the area would soon be contaminated by fallout.

You should know the location of hospitals within 100 miles of your city and the routes that can take you to them. You might want to search out the back roads, the less-traveled minor county roads, since after a nuclear attack the main roads will be clogged with cars.

Be aware of weather conditions so that you know which way is crosswind or upwind, and do not rely on the surface wind alone to guide you. Winds at high altitudes where the bomb's heat carries radioactive materials may be blowing in a different direction from the winds on the ground. If in doubt, look up and see which way the top of the cloud goes. That way you can avoid going to an area that may have to be evacuated later.

You might be interested to know that John's dispatcher, Ronda, survived with burns on her arms received while trying to fight a fire at their office. Interestingly, she has a 23-year-old son, a Navy Seal, who became instrumental in dealing with some of the PPF leaders, as told at the end of this handbook (Appendix D1).

And if you know the American people, you will not be surprised to hear that John Burnes was offered no less than seven taxicabs, and that Nellie II is hard at work.

---

not spread much outside the bombed area is attributed to these winds. This is another reason to exit the bombed area quickly.

Quiz on Chapter 10
(Answers are in Appendix A1)

1. If you are able to look up at a rising mushroom cloud above you, what two choices do you have to make to survive?
2. When leaving the city after a nuclear terror attack, which direction should you not go? Explain why.
3. List the basic necessities needed for surviving in a shelter.
4. Why can a good knowledge of the city streets and traffic flow patterns aid in your survival?
5. If you are 2 miles from the explosion, how long will you have to take shelter before the blast wave arrives? Will the blast wave be a problem 2 miles from ground zero?

Next we will visit an elementary school where, like in most schools, you can survive if you have elementary knowledge. If you would like to know how to protect your children from a nuclear explosion while they are at school, read on. If you do try to take action to protect your kids, you will find the formidable foes of ignorance and political correctness resisting you.

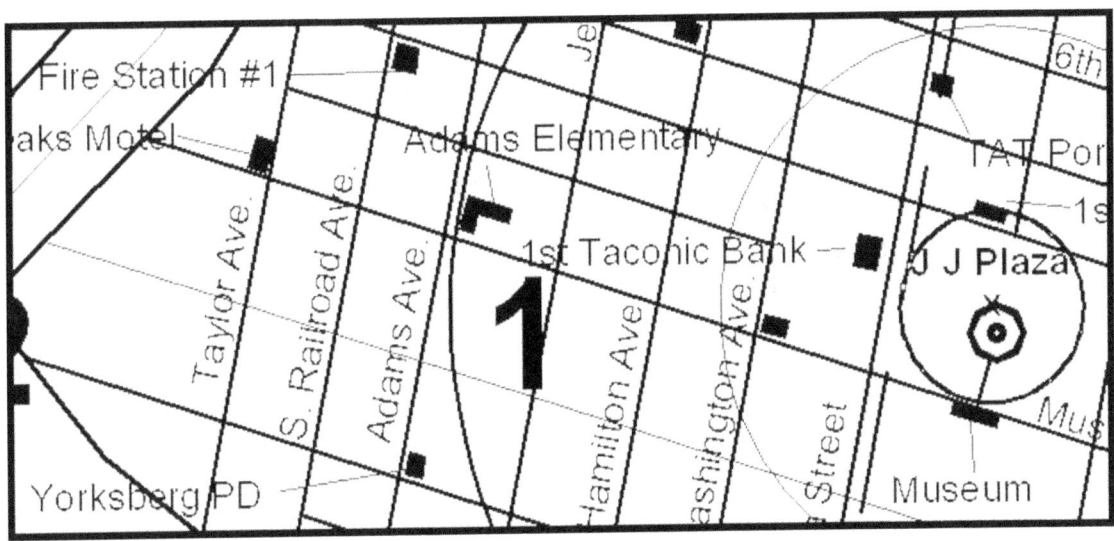

Duck and Cover is Elementary Knowledge

11 - Rachael Miskins – Elementary Knowledge (1.0 mile)

Cameron watched the shapely form of the only eligible young teacher in the school, go into her classroom. "Who is that down in 214?" he said.

Marva chuckled. "That didn't take you long. Ever since you started filling in for Mrs. Beardon I figured you'd eventually notice. That's Rachael Miskins."

"Married?" he said.

"Twenty-three, single, and second year here at Adams Elementary. You're in luck, sort of."

Raising his eyebrows he said, "I think she's attractive. What's this 'sort of?'"

"Pretty, yes, but she's a strange one. Most of the staff avoids her. She has had some problems with parents about some of the things she does in the classroom."

"Wow. A woman of mystery in quiet little Adams Elementary?" He smiled as he eyed the door down the hall. "What makes her strange?"

"I don't want to influence you. You'll find out, probably the first time you talk to her. I will tell you, she refuses to join the union. Pays the dues, but won't join or participate."

"That's odd," Cameron said.

"I've got to get back to the copy room. You just talk to her and you'll see."

Cameron watched Marva walk away, and then glanced back at the mystery woman's classroom. *This Rachael must have a tic or a speech defect or something. Why would the faculty think she's strange?*

Rachael rubbed her head as she walked down to the teacher's lounge, thinking the two aspirins she had taken mid-morning had not helped at all.

Thank God today is one of the days the art teacher comes with her pushcart of art supplies. I have 45 minutes for myself. A cup of tea will help.

She no sooner sat down with her tea and the front page of the local newspaper when a voice caused her to look up.

"Well, look who's here!"

"Good afternoon, Marva," Rachael said, not happy to see the union steward.

Out of the corner of her eye Rachael watched Marva prepare herself a cup of coffee and then sit on the couch opposite her. At that moment another teacher walked up. Another time Rachael might have been interested.

He is attractive.

She took a gulp of tea and burned her tongue.

"May I join you?" he said as he sat down. "I don't think we've met."

"This is Rachael Miskins. Rachael, meet Cameron. He's subbing for Mrs. Beardon while she's on maternity leave. He'll be here for six weeks."

"Glad to meet you," Rachael said. "Now we have two males among Adam's estrogen-saturated halls."

Cameron laughed and Marva, in character, didn't crack a smile.

"Rachael, what brings you into this den of vipers? We hardly ever see you in here." Marva sipped her coffee, her eyes fixed on Rachael.

"Art class and a bit of a headache. I just needed some tea today. Thank God for art."

"I know what you mean," Cameron said. "I love the kids, but sometimes I just need a break."

"Don't we all?" Marva agreed, and then added, "Say, Rachael, it's not too late to sign up. You could remove the blotch from Adams."

"What blotch?" *I really don't want the union push right now.*

"You know we are the only elementary school in the county that does not have 100 percent participation in the union?"

"Not so. Kearny Elementary has two holdouts and I heard that over at Jefferson they are forming a new union."

"Well, that new union stuff will never fly. By the way, are you still scaring those kids of yours with that drill stuff, ducking under the desk and all?"

"What's this?" Cameron said.

"It's a game, Marva, with a purpose. I don't scare any of them. You know this is something I wish all the teachers were doing."

Marva turned to Cameron. "Rachael claps her hands and all the kids do that 1950s civil defense thing… you know, getting down on the floor."

Oh God, she's trying to make me look the fool again. Why don't you just leave me alone?

"Really? I've never heard of this. How does it work, and if you don't mind explaining, why do you have the kids do it?" Cameron said.

Rachael looked at him for any sign of the condescending liberal attitude that kept her out of the lounge, and seeing no sign of it, decided to answer. "It's something my father taught me. At the beginning of the cold war between the U.S. and Russia following World War II, our nation prepared its people for a possible nuclear attack from Russia. In the schools the kids were taught how to quickly protect themselves in the event of a nuclear explosion by getting on the floor and covering their heads. I have made it into a game and they really seem to enjoy it. I think they like the competition and try not to be the last to get into position."

"She gives them candy," Marva said.

She makes it sound like some sort of evil bribe.

"Only if they get down into the safe position within two seconds. I have a couple of kids who don't participate."

Marva gave Cameron an incredulous look. "Safe position, she says. We are talking about nuclear bombs here and she thinks kneeling on the floor makes you safe."

Rachael said nothing at this, sipped some more tea, and rubbed her eyes.

Cameron spoke up. "Marva's right. If someone drops a bomb on us, it won't make any difference what position you or the kids are in. Besides, the cold war is over and Russia is not the threat it was."

There it is again. Ignorance, but maybe he is teachable.

"Cameron," Rachael began, "you are right about getting under a desk not being safe, unless the bomb goes off several miles away. If it does, then the position you are in becomes very important. Do you know what a blast wave is?"

"Oh, here we go again," Marva said, taking another sip of her coffee. "Cameron, you are about to learn more than you want to know about bombs."

"A blast wave is just air pressure from an explosion, I think. At least that's what I remember from my science classes."

My gosh, he knows. How refreshing!

"Right," Rachael said and managed to smile a little. "Now what do you think happens when a really strong wave of air pressure hits a big glass window like the ones in our classrooms?"

"Breaks them?" he answered.

"Not just breaks them. Think about it. Suppose a blast wave of, let's say, 2 pounds per square inch, or psi, hits that window over there." She pointed. "It is roughly 2 feet by 4 feet for each pane. That's 8 square feet that feels the 2 pounds on each square inch. Well, each square foot contains 144 square inches. That's 288 pounds of force on each square foot. Multiply that by 8 square feet and you get about 2000 pounds of force, or over 1 ton of impact, striking the window in an instant. So do you think that will just break the glass?"

"A ton? I didn't realize it would be that much. Is 2 psi a lot?"

"Depends on the explosive force and distance, but no, 2 psi is pretty typical at some point near a big explosion."

"So what happens to the glass?" Cameron seemed really interested.

"Well, basically the window pane shatters into little stiletto-like shards that the impact throws across the room with great force. If the school has installed safety glass the shards are little cubes, but they still fly in. In reports I have read and pictures I have seen, it is common for the entire window and frame to be blown into the building."

"So this blast of flying glass and window frames goes over the crouching kids."

"You got it. I clap my hands once, call 'duck and cover,' and two seconds later all my kids are down in a head-protective position. Marva's children will probably run to the window to see the big explosion, and will be cut to ribbons."

"She's a throwback to the 1950s, Cameron. The cold war is over."

Rachael sensed that Marva did not appreciate the insinuation that her children were not safe.

"She's right, Rachael," he said. "No one is going to attack us with intercontinental ballistic missiles. Besides, I heard they have built intercepting rockets that can stop them if anyone does launch them against us."

"Listen to you," Rachael said. "Why would they build interceptor rockets if they weren't worried about such an attack?"

She noted his silence. She could see the wheels turning in his head. She dug through the newspaper, found the article she had seen earlier, and folded the paper to expose it. She handed it to Cameron.

"Here, look at this."

"Terrorist Group Caught Attempting to Buy Nuclear Bomb Parts,"[88] he read out loud.

"Forget the rockets; these nutcases want to bring a bomb into our cities and set it off. Remember 911?" she said.

He looked at the article. "I see this sort of thing all the time. One of the news magazines I subscribe to had something about this last month."

"What did the article say?" she said.

"I didn't read it," he said.

Surprised by his answer, she thought *At least he's honest.*

Marva stood up. "I'll leave you two to discuss this. I have some work to do. Let me know if you change your mind, Rachael, and Cameron, don't let her scare you."

Cameron rose to go too. "Mrs. Jackson is probably ready to hand my kids back to me. The music always gets them fired up. Thanks for the info. You certainly have me thinking."

"If you ever want a demonstration, come on by. I'm in 214."

Cameron started out the door and then stopped. Turning back in he said, "Say Rachael, you ought to know that some of the other teachers were talking with Mrs. Darby about what you're doing. They think you're scaring the children and the parents."

"That's nonsense. The kids love the game. I don't talk to them about attacks or anything like that, but thanks for letting me know."

Rachael felt anger at this gossip to the principal, but it only made her headache worse, so she closed her eyes, took a deep breath, and tried to think of other things.

At 2 p.m. and with her headache still simmering, Rachael told all the kids to put their coats on.

It's time to burn off some energy. Recess ought to settle them enough to finish off some work before dismissal at 3:30.

As she stepped outside she could see several other classes were out on the playground, and soon she could not distinguish her students among the happily chasing, climbing, running kids.

---

[88] Skeptics are encouraged to read Chapter 3 of *Nuclear Terrorism: The Ultimate Preventable Catastrophe* by Graham Allison. This chapter is titled, "Where Could Terrorists Acquire a Nuclear Bomb?" and it answers its own question well. Times Books. Henry Holt and Company, LLC, 2004. ISBN 0-8050-7651-4.

After about 20 minutes of standing and watching in the cold wind, Rachael felt her headache starting to bloom and had grown tired of the chilly air.

Maybe I'm coming down with something.

Several of the kids were no longer playing, but were standing near her, asking to go in, so she put her whistle to her lips and gave the Room 214 series of tweets. Immediately her kids separated from the playground gaggle, ran to her door, and lined up, at least most did. She rounded up the one or two stragglers and escorted the happy, rosy-cheeked lot of them into the warm classroom.

Coats off and hung up, the warmth lulled them into the typical post-recess quiet. She took advantage of this and instructed them to get out their books for a spelling review to close out the day.

Then she saw Cameron at her door. She walked over and he leaned in and whispered, "Scuttlebutt has it that Principal Darby is going to tell you to stop the drill stuff. Better have your best speech ready for her after school."

"Oh crap," she said a little too loudly.

One of the students nearby said, "Miss Miskins, you said a bad word."

Rachael heard several of the other kids say, "What was the bad word? What did she say?" Many heads were turned toward her.

At the sound of the 2:30 bell for special education students, a blinding, purple-white light filled the room. It appeared to be coming from downtown Yorksberg directly out of the classroom's window.

Without thinking, Rachael clapped her hands once and yelled "Duck and cover!" going down on her knees and covering her head. She could feel heat on her skin as she went down and it scared her.

God help us!

From her head-down position Rachael saw Cameron's shoes duck back into the hall.

A second after she was fully down, she heard a tremendous blast that felt as if it rocked the entire school building. To Rachael the noise sounded extremely loud and for what seemed like an eternity there continued the sound of the school coming apart. Ceiling panels fell, bookshelves toppled, the fire alarm started wailing, car alarms sounded in the parking lot, and several people began screaming.

Rachael looked around her room. Windows along the side of her classroom facing downtown were gone, apparently shattered and blown into the classrooms exactly as she had explained to Cameron. The wall opposite the windows looked as if someone had taken a shotgun to it and blasted its entire length. She knelt there amazed. Even though she had taught this for two years, seeing the aftermath astonished her.

Hearing several of her kids crying brought her back into focus.

"I'm bleeding!" one said.

Another said, "I need a bandage."

Another called, "Miss Miskins, Tommy didn't duck and he got hurt."

Tommy lay still on the floor. His color was an odd whitish-gray. His hand was still warm, but there was no pulse.

CPR came to mind, but the side of his forehead had been caved in and a twisted piece of metal that looked like a piece of a broken window frame, had imbedded itself there. She let the hand drop.

She looked around the room full of crying and scared children. Broken glass and debris covered the floor and desktops, and the room was rapidly growing colder.

What should I do?

Her dad once told her that when one is overwhelmed with tasks, she should pick the most important one and do that first, so she turned and looked for the other student who would not practice duck and cover, expecting her to be dead too. Curiously, the girl appeared to be okay. Seeing her starting to rise with a wide-eyed, shocked look on her face brought on a smile.

"Martha, did you duck this time?" Rachael said to her.

"Yes, Miss Miskins," she said with a tremor in her voice and visibly shaking. "That light scared me and I saw you duck too," she said.

"You did just right," Rachael said, and gave her a hug.

She looked out the window at the huge mushroom-shaped cloud above the city a mile away, and a strong fear came over her. Her father had told her about radiation and she tried to remember the wind direction at recess.

The wind is out of the southwest. If so, most of the fallout will move away from us. But we can't be sure.

"Everyone get up slowly. You did really well! I am so proud of you! Don't touch the glass, and if you have any on your clothing try to shake it out. Don't brush it off with your hands or it might cut you." She said this with as calm a voice as she could muster while shaking glass off herself as an example.

Her voice had a calming effect on the shocked kids. She could see the change in their countenance.

Then she remembered there had been at least two classes out on the playground at the time of the explosion. Glancing outside, she could see many of the kids were down. Those still up were gathering around the fallen. Many were crying and several seemed to be looking toward the school for help. She could hear their voices through the holes where the windows had been. One group looked as if they were attempting to help one of the teachers get up. One little body lay still under the jungle gym.

She shivered in the near-freezing air. "Okay, children," she said as calmly as possible. "You all get an A+ for today. You did exactly right. Susan, please get the first-aid kit from the closet. If you have cuts, form a line here"—she pointed to the floor—"and let me see your cuts. The rest of you get your coats on and get your things ready to go. Bobby, you and Alex get the broom and sweep the glass up against the wall."

That will give them something to do. The room full of kids suddenly flowed into motion with order and purpose.

She put her own coat on and then quickly surveyed the kids' injuries one at a time, cleaned residual glass from their clothes and hair with a small whisk broom, and divided them into two groups: those with superficial cuts and those with cuts likely to require stitches. Amazingly, she found there were zero facial injuries and concluded that bright flash and the tone of her voice had quenched the usual peeking, head turning, and whispering that usually went on during her drills.

I am amazed. The kids kept their heads down.

In five minutes she had checked them all. Only two had cuts that might require stitches. All the rest were taken care of with small adhesive bandages. Only when they all had their coats on did she look out into the dark hallway.

There she found complete bedlam. She could hear someone yelling about a fire in the cafeteria and telling everyone to get out of the school. There were kids with blood on their faces and hands, crying in the cold air, and teachers trying to calm them down and help as they could. One of the teachers trying to help had a deep gash across her face. Principal Darby came down the hall, trying to restore order.

Rachael guessed the injured children crying and bleeding must have come out of the classrooms that were on the same side of the building as her room. A glance told her the rooms across the hall were calm. She could see those teachers holding their children in the rooms, their pale and shocked faces looking out the doors they were holding mostly closed, probably to prevent their own children from seeing the chaos in the hall.

"Where are your teachers?" the principal said to the dazed and bleeding children in the hall. The answers she got sounded more like something a character in a horror movie would say than a kid in school.

"She is lying on the floor and won't get up," one boy said through tears. To Rachael it looked as if he had run through a barbed wire fence, his face peppered with cuts.

It's a miracle he didn't lose an eye.

"Mrs. Jenkens' face is gone," sobbed a little fourth grader. "I want to go home," she wailed. There was blood all across her face and her blouse was soaked.

The school nurse popped out of the next classroom up the hall from Rachael's.

"Mrs. Darby," she called, "we need ambulances and quick. There are multiple bleeders and some have head injuries."

"Mrs. Thompson!" the principal said, "the phones don't work and my cell phone is dead."

"Mrs. Darby, the fire is out. Mrs. Lugar and I put it out with extinguishers." The voice echoed down the hall from the school janitor.

"Thank you, Arnold," Mrs. Darby yelled back, apparently trying to be heard over the wailing.

"We need to set up a triage," Rachael offered. "I'll help. Let's start by getting all the uninjured and lightly injured kids into safe, warm rooms. Mrs. Darby, if you will assign a few teachers to watch them, that will free up teachers to help us. I suggest you move the uninjured kids to the far side of the school from the blast." She pointed to the rooms across the hall from her own. "Let nurse Thompson and me have the rooms on this side."

Soon Rachael could see her suggestion working. It had freed up many teachers. The halls were clear of most of the children, and the first-aid kits from all the rooms had been gathered at one place. She helped move the injured children, whom the nurse judged could be moved, to the intact, warm rooms. She concluded the intact rooms remained relatively warm inside since their windows had not been broken.

By the time they got the injured sorted out, Rachael noted they had only seventeen children and three adults they did not feel comfortable moving. There were several dead and more than one hundred injured. The eye injuries from flying glass were particularly disturbing. They were so unnecessary.

Where they lacked adequate bandages, they created bandages from whatever they could find, and when Rachael saw things were in order, she sought out the principal.

"Mrs. Darby," she said, "We must evacuate this school and get away from the city."

Mrs. Darby started to protest. "Why do you want them moved from the school?"

Rachael took a deep breath and then spoke slowly. "I think that explosion was a nuclear bomb. I know that because no chemical bomb can make light like that. There will be radioactive fallout soon. It may already be falling on the school. We need to transport the children out of the area immediately. I am thinking south or west. The wind is carrying the radioactive cloud to the north, so that is not a good direction to go."

"I don't think I can do that without parental permission or at least an okay from the district superintendent."

Rachael forced her response to be low key. "We don't have time to contact all the parents. Many of them may not be alive, and the school superintendent's office is downtown, right near the explosion. The school district's whole building is probably gone. You are going to have to take charge here."

"I see. Well, there are a few buses out front. I guess we can overload them. It is an emergency after all."

"Now you're thinking," Rachael said with a smile of encouragement. "I'll spread the word to the teachers to load up kids in their cars too and to head out of town. I suggest you get a list of the kids and check them off as they leave."

"We can't leave the injured, and good first aid says we cannot move them." Mrs. Darby said this as a question.

Rachael thought for a moment and then an idea came. She placed her hands on Mrs. Darby's shoulders and explained.

Analysis of Chapter 11

One of the lessons of this chapter is the importance of knowing where you are and what is between you and the site of the explosion. As you can see from the map at the start of this chapter, Adams Elementary is situated about 0.9 miles from "ground zero": John Jay Plaza. This places it in the outer portion of the zone of survivable destruction,[89] and at this distance the school would experience a 3.5-psi blast wave and a 116-mph gust of wind.

What does the blast wave of a 19-kt weapon do a mile away? For an air burst we could expect a 3.5-psi overpressure and at least a 116-mph wind gust. Due to the ground burst nature of the PPF weapon and the intervening buildings, it is likely that Adams Elementary's playground received less than this, so we will assume the school experienced a 3-psi overpressure and 105-mph wind gust. This is sufficient to knock over most people who are not braced for it.

The dry, yellow-brown winter grass on the playground had smoked and erupted in flames in some places from the heat of the rising fireball, but the cold air and the snuffing effect of the passing blast wave of cold air quenched these fires. Several of the children received burns on some portion of their faces or ears from the heat of the explosion. Had the attack occurred during warm weather, it is likely that more skin would have been uncovered and more damage would have resulted.

Were Rachael's duck-and-cover snap drills realistic? Not in the politically correct world of public education today. Drills like this would probably be considered "terrorizing children" and would result in the disciplining or termination of any teacher trying to implement them in his or her classroom. Should we have such drills? The answer is "of course," especially in schools located in large cities that might be hit by terrorist groups.

One of the advantages of doing these drills is the questions this activity will generate in the students. The teacher could introduce snap drills by teaching a history unit on civil defense, and including examples of civil defense from ancient times, World War I, World War II, and the cold war. The unit could emphasize people from all walks of life working together for a common cause against a common enemy. This could lead into the question, do we need civil defense today and if so, why? A science unit that included the nature of explosions and the transference of energy from air pressure to the window glass could be very interesting to older students.

In the author's opinion, the students should be taught the reason for the snap drills, including the terrorist threats, the physics of the explosion (at their level), and how crouching on the floor with their heads covered can protect them from flying glass. Will there be objections? Probably, so be like Rachael and just prepare those who will listen.

Testing has shown that a 2-psi overpressure will instantly shatter window glass into tiny pieces and that these pieces are accelerated by this strong, momentary impulse – think of it as a sharp "slap" of pressured air. Some pieces of glass will be flung into the classroom slower or faster than others, but for a 3-psi overpressure you will do well to consider the

---

[89] See the analysis section for Part 1 Chapter 8, for more discussion of the "zone of survivable destruction."

glass fragments flying in at approximately 75 feet per second (about 50 mph).[90] These fragments may cross over the entire room, with some falling on the students, depending on how tall the windows are and how far the students are from the windows. The danger to the students' faces, and in particular their eyes, is extreme. Why? Because the flash of the bomb's explosion and the rising fireball will cause every child to turn and look out the window. Some students will actually move toward the windows in a natural reflex to get a better view of what is happening. The blast wave will hit the windows seconds after the explosion and blast the shattered glass into the curious, young eyes.

To understand the significance of this, imagine the kids standing along a highway when a truck carrying a broken glass window pane passes by at 50 mph. Just as it passes the children it hits a hard bump and a box full of glass shards falls over and dumps its contents over the waiting children. These shards are moving at 50 mph, so you can imagine the horrible injuries that would result from such an accident.

In fact, not only will the window's glass blow inward with dangerous speed, but the huge impulsive load (instantaneous force) will probably blow entire window frames out of walls and into rooms, along with the glass fragments. This was demonstrated during the 1950s nuclear testing in Nevada. Although it is difficult to see in the "before" and "after" photos that follow, this house experienced only a 1.7-psi peak overpressure. As you can see, all four front windows facing the explosion are gone, frame and all. The dark coloration on the house's exterior wall in the "after" photo is where the paint charred due to the heat from the fireball.

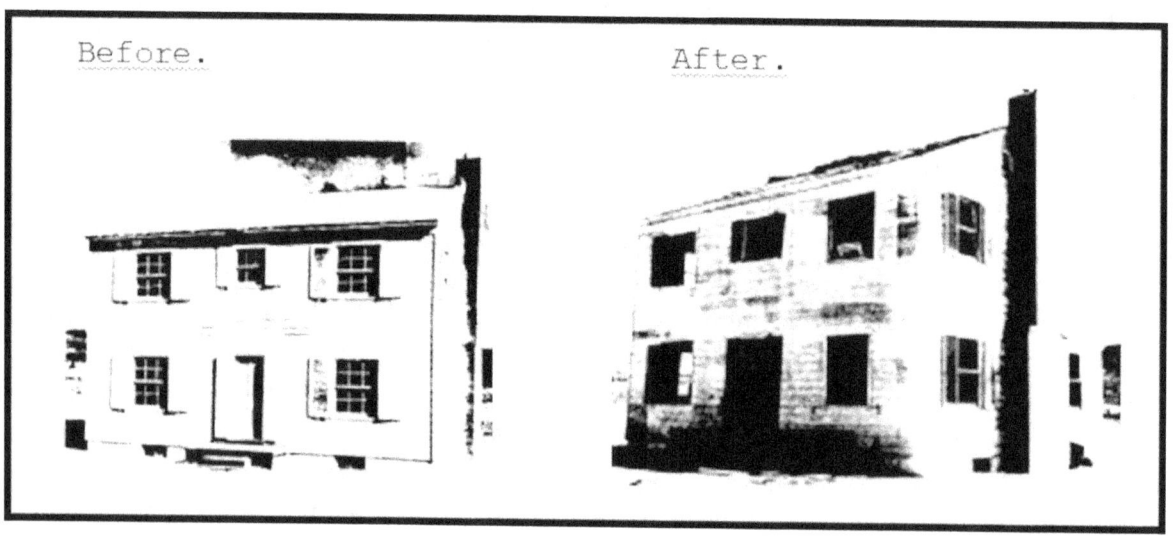

Before and After Photos of Damage. Note that the front windows have been blown in, frame and all. [91]

---

[90] "The Effects of Nuclear Weapons," Samuel Glasstone and Philip J. Dolan, United States Department of Defense, 1977, Section 12.238 (Velocities of Glass Fragments) and Figure 12.238.
[91] Ibid., Figures 5.55 and 5.59.

The angle at which the blast wave hits a window is important. On the map for this chapter, note that only the windows on the downtown side of the short wing of Rachael's school would probably be blown in. North-, west-, and south-facing windows may not be damaged at all. Indeed, in our story, windows not facing the blast were left intact, retaining warmth in those rooms.

Marva's admonition that "She's a throwback to the 1950s—the cold war is over" is a wonderful example of the ostrich phenomenon wherein folks assume there is no reasonable threat and therefore think they do not have to prepare for it. We trust you are well read and there is no need to convince you that the threat of a nuclear strike grows more likely every day, with government-backed state-terrorist organizations working to obtain or create a nuclear weapon.

Unfortunately, today if you mention duck and cover, you are likely to get the comment "That's stupid to think that anyone could survive an atomic explosion by hiding under a desk. Besides, that would scare the children."

If you have read this book you can now see how ignorant such a comment is. And as for scaring the kids, that is nonsense. The author of this book learned to duck and cover at his elementary school in the 1950s, and can tell you the kids clearly understood what the drill was for and were not afraid. They actually enjoyed practicing.

Below you will find some images from 1950s training materials showing the duck-and-cover technique of avoiding flying glass from a nearby explosion. This was taught to school children in the 1950s and should be taught now.

Cover Page of 1950s Civil Defense Training Material

An animated character (Bert) was used to get children interested in learning to duck and cover. A movie was made, which you can still watch today. Just do a Google search for "Bert the Turtle movie," or go to https://www.youtube.com/watch?v=IKqXu-5jw60 .

Inside a classroom near a large explosion
(Interior page of 1950s Civil Defense Training Manual).

This cartoon is an excellent depiction of what happens inside a classroom the instant a blast wave strikes. Remember that if the school is in the survivability zone for any given magnitude nuclear blast, whether it be 20 kilotons or 10 megatons, the result in the classroom is the same. The teacher and children are survivors, and because of duck-and-cover drills, the injuries will be reduced.

Will there be schools too close to the explosion, where everyone instantly dies from heat and blast? That is possible, but this book is about survivors, so those schools are not discussed. And since no one can know which schools will survive, duck and cover should be taught everywhere.

BUT REMEMBER... **DO IT INSTANTLY...** DON'T STAND AND LOOK. DUCK AND COVER!

"Duck and Cover" Can Be Used Inside a Vehicle
(Final Page of 1950s Civil Defense Training Material)

As this third panel shows, the duck-and-cover technique can be used in locations other than a classroom.

In this story, once again the odd light the bomb produces is mentioned. Rachael had never seen it, even though she has seen film footage of nuclear explosions. The film cannot capture the true colors or brilliance of the nuclear explosion light. Its instant appearance, its brilliance, its high-temperature, its purple-blue tinged hues are all clues that startled Rachael to call for the drill and to join her students on the floor.

She had to be fast because the school was, at most, 4 to 5 seconds of blast-wave travel time from John Jay Plaza. If she even thought about it for two seconds, her kids would be caught in their seats or on the way to the floor when the glass shards came flying in. It might be better to teach the kids to go into the safe position if a brilliant light appears outside their classroom's windows, rather than waiting for the teacher's command.

The blast wave knocked down most of those on the playground. Those on the grassy area did not sustain severe injuries because kids run, tumble, and fall all the time on the grass. Several children who had been on the swing, the slide, or the jungle gym, however, had been hurt. These had fallen greater distances or contacted the play equipment as they fell and suffered broken bones or head injuries. One little girl had been blown into the metal jungle gym and lay unconscious from head trauma.

The interplay between Mrs. Darby and Rachael in the hallway is just to get you thinking about how to train your school leadership, and teachers, so that this kind of last-minute improvisation does not have to happen. Mrs. Darby should have already had an emergency plan for this situation that would have given her several options, depending on the severity and nature of the emergency. It would have been in a binder in her office and would have been reviewed with the staff at least once a year.

What do you do with the alive, but seriously injured, children and adults? Do you leave them and depart in order to save the others? Do you stay with them to comfort them until you both receive a lethal dose of radiation? Do you move them and perhaps kill one or two in the process who would have survived had you gotten them better care? Just think of the lawsuits if you did! But you can be sued for doing nothing as well. Like Rachael and Mrs. Darby, you will have to make the best decisions you can and then follow through. An approved emergency plan can help shield you from lawsuits.

When faced with the quandary of moving the badly injured or leaving them to the radiation, Rachael had a good idea. What solution to this problem can you think of?

What are the chances of getting an ambulance under these circumstances? The author believes the chances are very small. Emergency equipment downtown is in ruin or trapped by debris. Thousands of calls for help, if they could get through, would inundate the city services, and the hundred thousand people trying to flee the city will completely jam up the roads. As happened after 9/11, panicky people will abandon their cars stuck in traffic, and walk or run out of the city, stopping traffic completely. With hundreds of children injured, more than one or two ambulances would be needed. At your school the number of casualties may be much larger. You need to have a plan. You are challenged to come up with the most expedient and best plan to extricate the children, and obtain the staff's concurrence ahead of time.

What else did Rachael and Mrs. Darby miss in their planning?

What would the situation have been like if the school had held snap drills for all the children and staff?

Quiz on Chapter 11   (Answers are in Appendix A1)

1. Should duck-and-cover snap drills be practiced by all children in our schools?

2. Suppose a 30-inch by 20-inch window is hit directly on by a 1-psi blast wave. What force will that window experience at the moment of impact? Will it break?

3. Concrete-reinforced houses tested under a nuclear blast survived even under blast overpressures above 4 psi. What didn't survive?

4. How long do the kids have, once duck and cover is sounded, before the blast hits?

5. Some folks will never duck and cover. What rule of nature is this an example of?

Wrap-up of Part 1 – Within One Mile

In Part 1, we have covered a lot of ground. The information imparted to you in the stories and analyses you have read will go a long way toward helping you prepare to survive the attack we all hope never happens. But is there more to learn?

The answer is yes. The remaining chapters contained in the *Nuclear Terror Survival Handbook Part 2* will cover the effects of the bomb beyond one mile, including the following topics:

1. Can a person receive radiant heat burns at more than a mile from ground zero?
2. What are walking wounded?
3. What is a G.O.O.D. pack and why do you need one?
4. Looting following the explosion, and how radiation complicates this illegal activity.
5. How are hospitals, both local and distant, affected?
6. How can contamination be controlled in a hospital?
7. What three serious problems should hospitals within 100 miles of a bombed city be prepared for?
8. What are the six key ideas for decontamination of patients?
9. How will subways be affected by a nuclear explosion? Can they be used as shelters? If so, what modifications need to be made?
10. What are the hazards you will bring to your family when you flee the bombed city and go to stay with them? How can you reduce these hazards?
11. What is the difference between primary and secondary fallout?
12. What happens to a person 15 feet from the bomb when it explodes? It's not what you think.
13. What determines the amount of heat that falls on a surface from a nuclear explosion?
14. Blast overpressure and overpressure-sensitive material.
15. In light of the possibility of a terrorist nuclear attack, what is the best location for the Emergency Operations Center (EOC)?
16. Coordination and equipment sharing with other counties.
17. Chain of command fallback layers.
18. Communications following the attack.
19. The proper location of standby emergency equipment.
20. Shelter design for those who live near and far away.
21. What are the aspects of a well-prepared shelter?

And much more.

You are encouraged to read the stories and analyses of Chapters 12 through 22 contained in the *Nuclear Terror Survival Handbook Part 2* (effects beyond one mile) to further your knowledge. You will enter the lives of eleven more citizens of Yorksberg and experience the nuclear attack from their point of view. Here are a few of the folks we will visit.

Lamar Henderson – a thug who has jumped parole and fled to Yorksberg where he is dealing in illegal substances... until the bomb changes his life's direction in a major way.

Marcus Gingman – the director of Saint Mary's Hospital, who, through a heart patient, learns that technical knowledge about the aftermath of a nuclear explosion is worth its weight in gold.

Tammie Janos – learns the powerful truth that bad things that happen to you, such as a toothache, may be good for you.

Laticia Washington – who travels into the downtown area of Yorksberg to save her daughter and learns that shooting from the hip can be exceedingly dangerous for her relatives who live hundreds of miles away.

Kathy Washington – who sits on a school bus and watches the terrorist press the button that explodes the bomb, and learns some interesting physics about what happened to her and the gasoline in the gas tank on her bus.

Amiee Moller – a mother of two kids living far from Yorksberg who makes a major mistake in dealing with radioactive fallout and must deal with criminals taking advantage of her evacuated neighborhood while her husband is overseas.

End
Part 1
The Nuclear Terror Survival Handbook (within one mile)
See Part 2 for (beyond one mile)

Appendix A1: Answers to the Quizzes

<u>Chapter 1</u>

1. Radioactive materials hurt you by emitting (shooting out) gamma rays that damage your body's cells as these particle-like rays pass through you. Think of the damage as microscopic "paper cuts" through your entire body, each one tiny and by itself inconsequential; however, this damage must be repaired. The damaged cells may die, or may no longer function correctly, and will have to be removed by the body's natural cleanup processes. If millions of these "paper cuts" of radiation damage happen faster than the body can clean up the damage, the whole body may become sick. The damage is cumulative (i.e., it builds up over time). Too much radiation damage can result in parts of the body's systems shutting down and can lead to a compromised immune system or organ failure and death. For more information about radiation, read Appendix B1.

2. Radioactive materials contain unstable atoms that spontaneously fly apart, shooting out small particles at high speeds like tiny bullets. Some radioactive materials also shoot out gamma rays. These powerful particle-like pulses of light damage cells throughout the body. Radiation is the fast-moving small particles and gamma rays.

3. There are several systems of measuring amounts of radiation and damage to human tissue. We measure the damage in "rem." Five hundred rem of radiation damage will kill many of those who receive such damage. Exactly how much it takes to kill any individual depends on the person's health, the amount of exposure, the type and the energy of the radiation, and the medical care they receive. Another measuring system uses the Sievert. One Sievert equals 100 rem, so 5 Sieverts will kill many people.

4. Answer e. all of the above.

5. Mindy's radiation exposure (when she went for help for Mrs. Thompson) damaged her body and compromised her immune system, leading to death ultimately by pneumonia and other infections. It can be argued, however, that ignorance also killed Mindy. With more knowledge, she would have made the better decision to stay in the vault for two days and would have thereby avoided much of the radiation exposure she received. Then she, like Mrs. Thompson, would have survived to live a long, productive life.

Chapter 2

1. Yes, given enough time. Medical care can help too, especially if you receive so much radiation that your body's immune system starts to fail or your small intestine is damaged. Doctors can take mitigative steps to keep you alive while your damaged organs repair themselves.

2. One of the byproducts of the bomb is radioactive iodine. The human body will uptake this radioactive iodine naturally and will concentrate it in certain organs, such as the thyroid gland. There the radioactive iodine will irradiate surrounding tissue and damage cells. Taking non-radioactive iodine pills following the explosion will flood the body with an abundance of good (non-radioactive) iodine, which will out-compete the radioactive iodine for uptake into the organs; thus the body will store less of the radioactive iodine and subsequent tissue damage will be reduced.

3. If you pick a time after the explosion, say one hour, then when seven times that amount of time has passed since the explosion, the radiation will decrease to one tenth of what it was at the one-hour point in time.

4. Radio Amateur Civil Emergency Service. The Radio Amateur Civil Emergency Service (RACES) is a standby radio service provided for in Part 97.407 of the Federal Communications Commission (FCC) rules and regulations governing amateur radio in the United States. (source; Wikipedia)

5. Time (how long you are exposed to the radiation), distance (how far you are from the radioactive material), and shielding (how much material is between you and the sources of radiation).

Chapter 3

1. Being nuclear terror "street-smart" means knowing where the shelters are, formal and informal; knowing what needs to be stocked in a shelter; knowing about the effects of radiation on food; being able to recognize a nuclear explosion early on in the event; learning the "rule-of-seven"; knowing to duck under your desk instead of running to the window to see the pretty light; and knowing the back roads that can get you out and away from the city quickly. Reading this book can help you improve your street-smarts.

2. No, because they would not have been able to extricate themselves from under the pancaked roof panels. The spreading fire and smoke in the collapsed structure, the lack of water (dehydration), and their gradually increasing radiation dose would have eventually killed them within the next several days. Taeya's Star would have sailed without Fletcher, his mother would never know what happened to him, and there would have been two more seats available for Fiddler on the Roof.

3.   No. Instead of sending out a powerful blast wave, it will send a huge water wave ashore, resulting in possible flooding and material damage.

4.   An underwater nuclear explosion can lift a huge amount of water, which creates a wave moving out for some distance from the explosion point, but this wave does not carry the radioactivity with it. You can see this phenomenon of waves by throwing something into them that will float. The object will bob up and down as waves pass under it, but the waves will not drive the object to shore. Wind can drive a floating object to shore, however, so it is possible that radioactivity may come ashore via wind or currents at some time in the future.

   Note that living creatures exposed to the contaminated seawater may incorporate certain radioactive isotopes as they live and grow. These could present a hazard if caught for food at some time in the future.

5.   It is normal for some radioactive fallout to fall within several miles upwind of ground zero even if winds generally carry the radioactive materials off in one direction. This is because the cloud mushrooms out high above the city, and because wind direction can change with altitude.

Chapter 4

1.   Serious. You can see actual damage to a house during an atomic test in Nevada in the image titled, "Music House after the Explosion" in chapter 4. A 5-pound-per-square-inch (psi) blast overpressure wrecked it.

2.   Because the dynamic pressure (induced by wind) follows a blast wave. The 4 – 5 psi blast wave's impact breaks foundational structural points, such as corners and roof connections to the walls, severely weakening it just before the extreme wind gust arrives. The three components of the blast wave are… 1. The blast wave overpressure, 2. The dynamic pressure (load due to the burst of wind flowing by) and 3. A weaker suction wind flowing back toward ground zero.

3.   The fires started at the Music House by the radiant heat energy from the rising fireball were snuffed out by the passing blast wave, and then the cold air of the explosion-created wind suppressed the house's flammable material's temperature to below its flashpoint. Her survival was partially providence, since thermally ignited fires are not always extinguished by the blast wave.

4.   Yes. Thousands of people died at this distance from the bomb, but it is statistically probable that a few percent survived, due to their location and the protection of structures around them.

169

5.   The bomb was set off on the ground and there were quite a few intervening structures and buildings between Stacie and the bomb at the instant of explosion, including the walls of the Music House and the heavy oak staircase.

Chapter 5

1.   Assuming you have enough air, the answer is water. You can live for more than a week without food, but you cannot last long without water. You should store water, not sweet drinks or alcoholic beverages.

2.   Alpha, beta, and gamma radiation.

3.   Alpha and beta. These two types of radiation are stopped by paper, clothing, or the outer layers of your skin.

4.   False. High-rise apartments have a huge exposure to the heat, light, and blast of the bomb. You do not want to be there when the bomb goes off within a mile or two of your building.

5.   The water in the toilet tank (not the bowl) and in the water heater. Dirty water can be used to flush the toilet. Just quickly pour enough in the bowl and it will flush.

Chapter 6

1.   First, in a nuclear war you may get a 15-minute warning. A terrorist's nuclear bomb will give you no warning at all. You will have no time to reach a shelter. Second, a bomb delivered by air or missile in a nuclear war may release much more energy and therefore destroy a much larger part of your city.

2.   Two reasons. First, Jetta was below grade level (in a basement) and therefore shielded by the earth from the direct radiation from the bomb's explosion, and radiation from fallout on the ground. Second, she was rescued by the firemen in fairly short order and taken out of the fallout zone. Good shielding and short exposure (time) saved her from excessive radiation damage.

3.   The fire departments will probably not be able to reach most fires due to huge debris fields and dangerous amounts of radiation. Also, the heat from the bomb will set so many fires the fire department will be overwhelmed. Finally, the broken rubble of wood structures opens up large amounts of wood (fuel) surface area to propagate the fires that are started. Fires will propagate and grow quickly. Also remember that most people die in fires due to the smoke, not from burns. A

trapped person may be some distance from a fire, but be in the smoke emanating from the fire and unable to escape it to get fresh air.

4.   Debris falling into the basement destroyed the stairs or blocked their use.

5.   Radioactive dust will get caught in the fabric of the survivor's clothes (and hair). This radioactive material continuously irradiates anyone nearby. There is no time or facilities to clean this clothing. It will probably be buried so that it cannot harm anyone. Hair may have to be removed because there are no showers or shampoos available for hundreds of thousands of survivors after the attack. Could the survivors wash their hair at some clean location far from the bomb? Yes, but remember that area will then be contaminated too.

Chapter 7

1. True. Blast-wave total forces on a structure are magnified by large surface areas. Most large structures are not designed to withstand huge sideways-impulse loads.

2. Collapse due to the blast wave, and smoke and fire.

3. No, and he lost his shirt, pants, and belt too, contaminated by touching the young girl he took to the hospital. Everyone coming across the bridge was found to be highly contaminated by radioactive material. The photographer's clothing had to be buried in a radioactive waste dump, but he was okay.

4. Yes, if you can walk. In fact, walking may be the only way you can egress due to debris and traffic jams. Remember New York City and 9/11. If you don't know what happened there, do some research. It will paint an image in your mind of the flow of refugees that is just a small part of what an exploded atomic bomb will create.

5. Damaged or trapped equipment, too many fires to fight, many of their personnel dead or injured, and lack of communication. Don't count on the Fire Department to rescue you after a nuclear explosion, and don't wait for rescue if you can move about. Always remember the possibility of silent, tasteless, invisible, radiation. Move upwind or crosswind to the direction the mushroom cloud is moving.

Chapter 8

1.   First, injury by nuclear radiation, which you don't get from a car accident or falling off a ladder. Second, when you are injured in a nuclear explosion in your city you will not have the rapid-response, high-tech teams rushing to whisk you to the

hospital. They may never come, and you will be on your own… except for the helping hand of others and their knowledge of first aid.

2.   You beat the blast wave. It will pass over you. You are sheltered from the fallout, so it will not get you. But you will be dead within a day or two. Why? Because at the instant the nuclear reaction is happening in the bomb (several millionths of a second) humongous amounts of gamma and neutron radiation stream out of the bomb in all directions. This burst of radiation is strong enough to give you a lethal dose in less than the time it takes for you to blink an eye. Your body is damaged beyond hope of repair by the time your brain sees the flash and starts to command you to jump into the hole for safety. A little farther away from ground zero the amount of initial radiation a person would receive will not cause death.

3.   Without training, our citizens will group together after the explosion to help each other, to take pictures of the damage, and to gather into groups and talk about what just happened. They should be running for shelter or getting the heck out of Dodge. Why? Radioactive fallout starts right after the explosion and will kill them if they linger in it. This is the lack of training our city leaders are not currently providing the general public.

4.   Don't worry about this. Heat and radiation do not cause your skin to melt off. Heat can cause a really bad burn, and this might make the skin look tattered, but it doesn't melt. About the dog's head, our first answer is that you would then have a great career working in a carnival, but truthfully, such mutations are from weird science fiction stories and have no place in reality. Radiation can cause mutations, but these express themselves in the form of cells dying or reproducing out of control (cancer). Cancers from radiation usually appear many years (decades) after the exposure, and may not happen at all.

5.   When you see the Godzilla of a flash and feel the heat, quickly get behind some shelter, like a wall, a curb, a building, or inside a building. This will give you some protection from the intense heat and the blast wave. The blast wave travels about a mile in 5 seconds, so you have that long to protect yourself. If you can't shelter, your best bet is to fall to the ground with your head away from the bright light, and cover it with your arms.

Chapter 9

1. True. Dark-colored clothing will get hotter than light-colored clothing. Whether or not it ignites depends on how much heat radiation it absorbs and how flammable the material is.

2. Overpressure and dynamic pressure. Overpressure can be thought of as how much the air in the blast wave is compacted above normal atmospheric

pressure. Dynamic pressure can be thought of as the "push" of the wind as the blast of moving air blows by.

3. Windows are the weakest part of a building exposed to the blast wave. Also, light attracts people, and, if they move quickly to the window to see what that bright light is, they may be hurt if the window glass is blasted in by the approaching blast wave.

4. False. Hospitals far from our major cities will be tremendously affected by the hundreds and thousands of contaminated casualties coming out of a terrorist-attacked city. They should prepare, but most have probably not trained their people. Has your hospital prepared?

5. These grains of sand have been coated with a layer of highly radioactive material from the bomb's fireball. When they fall back to earth, the area in which they fall becomes deadly due to the radiation they emit. Right after the explosion, you cannot live long where these particles have fallen, until several weeks, months, or even years have passed.

Chapter 10

1. You must either quickly get into a protective shelter or quickly leave the city. The dangers to your life in this situation are radioactive fallout and fires. Your best bet is to go into a building (that is not on fire) and downstairs to its basement or an underground storage area. Remember that if you elect to drive out of the city you may get stuck in a huge traffic jam. Your automobile will not provide enough radiation shielding to help you survive.

2. You should **not** go in the same direction the mushroom cloud is drifting. Highly radioactive material will be falling out of the cloud along a path below the cloud's movement for hours. You should go upwind or crosswind from the direction the cloud is moving.

3. The basic necessities are:
    A.   Adequate radiation shielding.
    B.   Drinking water.
    After the above, it would be nice to have the following:
    C.   Food.
    D.   A battery-powered radio and batteries.

4. There will be a huge traffic jam of folks trying to access the highways leading out of town. A delay in leaving a radioactive area increases your exposure to the damaging effects of radiation. If you know a way out that most people are not using, you can move faster and reduce your exposure to the radioactive materials falling from the sky.

5. About 5 seconds per mile or in this case 10 seconds. Sheltering from the blast wave can be as simple as lying behind a curb. Whether or not the blast wave is a problem for you depends on how much energy the bomb released. For the Yorksberg-sized blast, the blast wave will not be very intense at 2 miles. If the device exploded is a 100-kt weapon, then 2 miles may not be safe unless you can shelter.

Chapter 11

1. Yes and the children should be taught why.

2. Thirty inches times twenty inches is 600 square inches. Multiply that by 1 pound per square inch and you get a 600-lb impact. Whether or not it breaks depends on how strong the glass and frame are.

3. The windows. They were blown into the house in every case, just like the windows in your kid's school will be blown in with deadly force. Teach your kids to duck and cover.

4. Calculate 5 seconds per mile from where you think the bomb is likely to be set off. Think like a terrorist. Where would you put the bomb?

5. Darwin's survival of the fittest – nature weeding out the weak-minded, inflexible, and unteachable.

Appendix B1: Radiation and Radioactivity

To understand what really happens in a nuclear explosion you will need some basic background so that what is written here will make sense to you. If you have a degree in a major science (chemistry, physics, engineering, mathematics) and a good understanding of atomic theory, consider this a review or just skip it.

Review of the Basics of the Atomic Theory

The atomic theory of matter is the idea that matter consists of small particles. Over the years the basic particle of matter has come to be called an atom. We now know there are about 118 different kinds of atoms. We call them the basic "elements" of our physical world and have organized them by their properties in the chart called the periodic table of the elements.[92]

Each atom consists of a very small core called the nucleus, which has a positive electric charge, and is made up of protons and neutrons with a surrounding cloud of electrons with a negative charge. The positive electric charge comes from the positively charged protons, while the neutrons carry no charge.

The electrons make up very little of the total mass of an atom. Almost all the mass is in the protons and neutrons at the center of the atom. Protons do not have the same amount of mass as neutrons, but for our purposes we will consider them to have the same mass.

The nucleus is very tiny compared to the entire atom. It has been said that if the nucleus were the size of the head of a pin and you placed it at the center of a football field, the cloud of electrons would extend to the goal posts at either end of the field. The important concept here is that atoms are mostly empty space.

Ions

In most atoms with an equal number of protons and electrons, the net electrical charge is zero and we say the atom is neutral. If a few of the electrons are stripped off the atom, then the atom will have a net positive charge and we call the atom an ion. The term ionized means that some or all the electrons have been removed from a normally neutral atom. Stripping electrons from an atom does not make that atom radioactive or unstable. It just makes it positively charged and it is then called an ion. We say that such an atom is "ionized."

Ions are important because non-radioactive atoms can affect each other in only three ways. One is by a direct collision; one atom collides with another and bounces off, the second is when one atom combines with another to form a molecule (such as a sodium atom combining with a chlorine atom to form salt). The third way is the atom becoming an ion (ionized) by losing some of its electrons and then moving past another atom at high velocity. A neutral atom does not have any electric force field extending into space to interact with other nearby atoms. An ion, however, does have an electric field extending

---

[92]To see the table, go to http://en.wikipedia.org/wiki/Periodic_table

out from it and that electric field can affect surrounding atoms. This is important because ionization of atoms and their subsequent decay back to the non-ionized state (and subsequent x-ray emission) is one of the processes by which the energy released from an atom's nucleus in a nuclear explosion gets transferred out of the bulk of the material. This idea is discussed in more detail in Part 2 of the handbook, chapter 17, titled "Kathy Washington – Kind, Intelligent Eyes (15 feet)," where a young girl fifteen feet from the bomb when it explodes experiences the effect of atoms in the core of the explosion decaying back to the non-ionized state.

Where Does Light Come From?

When an atom has one of its electrons ripped away, the atom is left with one unbalanced positive electric charge in its nucleus. Positive charges attract negative charges, so eventually the ionized atom will attract a free electron, which is strongly attracted to an ion's positive charge. The free electron will be captured by the ion, changing it back to a neutral atom. But free electrons have a bit more energy than the electron when it is bound to an atom. That is why it takes a bit of energy to rip an electron away from an atom. So when the free electron is grabbed by the ion, the extra energy of the free electron has to go somewhere (energy cannot be created or destroyed; it can only change form). The result is the emission of a tiny particle of light, which is called a photon. All light is created by this process of electrons moving from a higher energy state to a lower energy state.

But do all electrons emit the same light photon when they recombine with an ion to make a neutral atom? The answer is no. The energy an electron can have while bound to an atom depends on which position it occupies around the atom's nucleus. The outermost electrons are loosely held. When they are stripped away and then recaptured by an atom into an outer position, only a low energy photon is given off, perhaps a photon of red light, which is the lowest energy photon of visible light. If the electron is snapped into a position closer to the nucleus, then the photon given off will have more energy (perhaps blue light, which is the highest energy visible light). So you can think of the white light (white light is all colors mixed together) from a light bulb as coming from electrons recombining with many levels in the atoms of the hot filament in the bulb. (LED lights work on a different principle, which does not involve heating a material, but does involve an electron moving from a higher energy state to a lower energy state.)

In the larger atoms there are so many positive charges in the nucleus, the electrons around those atoms closest to the nucleus require a large amount of energy to get pulled away. Likewise, when they recombine with the atom by moving to one of those innermost levels, they release such an energetic photon that we call it an x-ray. This is why the hot center of a nuclear explosion emits lots of x-rays. Those x-rays tell us the nuclear fireball is so hot that even the innermost electrons of very heavy elements are being ripped off the atoms and then recombining to emit light in the form of x-rays.

The Nucleus

The simplest atom is the hydrogen atom. It has one proton (very heavy) and one electron (very light). We write the symbol for this element $^1H_1$ where the number to the upper left is the number of protons, representative of the "atomic number" of this element and of its position in the periodic table of elements. The number to the lower right is the total number of protons and neutrons in the atom's nucleus. You might think that to make the next heavier atom you would just add one electron and one proton, like this: $^{2}He_2$, but this will not work. Here is the problem. Remember that the protons are all positively charged. Since similar charges repel, two protons cannot sit close together. Because there are many heavier atoms it is obvious that "nature" has found a way around this repulsion of protons.

The special kind of "glue" that nature uses to keep the protons from flying apart is supplied by the neutrons. Remember that they are the neutrally charged particles in the nucleus. It turns out the next element, helium, is written this way: $^{4}He_2$, where the 2 indicates there are two protons and the 4 indicates there are two protons and two neutrons in the helium nucleus. The two neutrons allow the two protons to coexist together in the nucleus. We can extend this idea to heavier elements like gold, which would be written $^{197}Au_{79},$ indicating that gold is the 79th element (containing 79 protons), but has a total of 197 protons and neutrons in its nucleus. The 118 neutrons (197 – 79) keep the 79 protons from flying apart. You will see why all this is relevant a little later.

Radioactivity (Radioactive Decay)

For most elements there are a certain number of neutrons for which the atom is stable and will last forever. For our example, for gold it is 118 neutrons. So gold $^{197}Au_{79}$ contains 79 protons and 118 neutrons and is stable (i.e., it does not spontaneously fly apart; this means that gold is not radioactive).

An element can actually have more or less neutrons in its nucleus than the exact number it takes to make the atom stable. Atoms of any given element with varying amounts of neutrons are called isotopes of the element. Gold, for example, can form with between 90 and 126 neutrons in its nucleus with its 79 protons. Most of these isotopes (types of gold atoms) are unstable, which just means that sometime after that type of gold is formed it spontaneously ejects part of its nucleus (this is "radioactive decay"). The pieces that come out when it decays are small particles made up of the stuff in the nucleus. These fast-flying particles of matter are called "nuclear radiation" because they radiate away from the nucleus. The particles in nuclear radiation are electrically charged and move very fast. Because they are charged and move fast they can affect atoms they collide with or pass near to.

Radioactive decay can also result in gamma rays being emitted. Similar to the way electrons recombine with an ion and send out a photon of light, photons of light can also come from the atomic nucleus when the energy state of the nucleus drops suddenly to a lower energy.

The "lost" energy when an unstable atom decays can come out in several forms: flying particles or very energetic particles of light we call x-rays (lower energy) or gamma rays (higher energy). Gamma rays are light photons produced within the nucleus of an atom. Gamma rays and x-rays can come out with varying amounts of energy. They have no electric charge, but due to their high energy they can also affect atoms they pass near to or collide with. Unlike the particle forms of radiation (alpha and beta radiation), gamma and x-rays can penetrate most materials.

Remember that the number of positive charges in the nucleus of an atom determines what type of element that atom is. So if either a positive or a negative-charged particle is thrown out of a nucleus, the total number of positive charges in the nucleus changes, and therefore the atom changes to another element. Believe it or not, if an oxygen atom's nucleus kicks out a negative charge from its nucleus it instantly becomes an atom of the hazardous gas fluorine. Likewise, if a zinc atom's nucleus kicks out a positive charge it becomes copper.

Half-life

We will continue to use gold as our example. There are many different types (isotopes) of gold, each containing a different number of neutrons. All the unstable types (isotopes) eventually emit a radioactive particle and change into another element, but they all do so after a certain amount of time has passed. Each isotope has a "half-life," which, assuming you create a large number of these atoms, is just the time it takes until half of the atoms have decayed, (i.e., changed into another element type). There is an isotope of gold with 113 neutrons in its nucleus, for example, that has a half-life of 4.94 hours. If you start with a million of these atoms, then after 4.94 hours you will have only 500,000 gold atoms remaining. Wait another 4.94 hours and you will only have 250,000 remaining. On the other hand, there is another isotope of gold with 108 neutrons, which has a half-life of 8.4 minutes. Start with a million of these atoms and half would decay in the first 8.4 minutes. The shorter the half-life of an isotope the more rapidly the number of unstable atoms decays away. This will be important when we discuss the after effects of the explosion of an atomic bomb.

The question is, when an atom decays or emits atomic particles or gamma rays, where does the atom go? What happens to it? To understand this we have to talk about daughter products, but before we can do that we need to discuss radiation a bit more.

Types of Radiation

For nuclear survival you should understand the nature of the four principal types of nuclear radiation. These are:

Name	Symbol	What is it?	Charge
Alpha[93]	α	An ionized helium nucleus – two protons and two neutrons.	+2
beta[94]	β^+ or β^-	A positive electron (positron) or a regular electron (negative)	+1 or -1
Gamma[95]	γ	A very high energy light wave	0
X-ray	χ	A high energy light wave	0

---

[93] For more detailed information see https://orise.orau.gov/reacts/guide/alpha.htm
[94] For more detailed information see https://orise.orau.gov/reacts/guide/beta.htm
[95] For more detailed information see https://orise.orau.gov/reacts/guide/gamma.htm

Alpha particle: when a nucleus kicks out an alpha particle it is kicking out two neutrons and two protons in one chunk. It is strongly charged +2.

Beta particle: when a nucleus kicks out a beta particle it is kicking out an electron. It can be negatively charged (an electron) or positively charged (a positron).

Gamma ray: a gamma ray is a photon of light that behaves like a particle, but has no electric charge. Gamma rays are the most penetrating of all the types of nuclear radiation.

X-rays: you are familiar with these pieces of light. Your doctor or dentist can make them in his or her office with an x-ray machine and take x-ray pictures of your insides. X-rays, like gamma rays, pass through most materials.

Chains of Daughters

When alpha particles (charged +2) fly out of an atom, two positive charges are removed from the nucleus of that atom, changing the atom's atomic number and therefore changing that element to another type of element. A gold atom with 95 neutrons, for example, is very unstable (half-life 139 milliseconds) and decays by shooting out an alpha particle. Gold (atomic number 79) has only 79 protons, so when two are booted out the nucleus in the alpha particle, the nucleus then only has 77 protons remaining. This changes the atom to an iridium atom. (Iridium is atomic number 77.) Since the nucleus also lost two neutrons in the alpha particle, it has become iridium with 77 protons and 93 neutrons. This atom, which is called a daughter product of the gold atom, is also unstable and decays with a 1.05-second half-life by emitting an alpha and a beta (+) particle. Each radioactive element decays, forming a chain of daughter decay products, all of them unstable and radioactive until finally the number of protons and neutrons is just right and the last atom in the chain is stable (it does not decay and is therefore not radioactive).

You can see this in the following example. Uranium is naturally occurring in the earth's crust as Uranium 238.[96] None of the isotopes of uranium are stable; all are radioactive. We find U238 in the earth's crust because the half-life of uranium 238 is about 4.5 billion years (i.e., it takes a very long time for half of this element to decay). But when it does decay it converts to thorium 234, which begins a long chain of decays (many daughter isotopes) ending in stable lead 206. Symbol Pb, lead, has three stable forms: 206, 207, and 208.

---

[96] 238 is the total number of protons and neutrons in the nucleus.

Here is what the chain looks like for uranium 238. The type of radiation given off is shown in parenthesis.

238U(α) → 234Th(β) → 234Pa(β) → 234U(α) → 230Th(α) → 226Ra(α) → 222Rn(α) →
218Po(β) → 218At(α) → 214Bi(β) → 214Po(α) →
210Pb(β) → 210Po(α) → 214Pb(β) → 214Bi(α) → 210Tl(β) →

or **210Pb(β)** → 210Bi(α) → 206Tl(β) → **206Pb(stable)**
        or   210Bi(β) → 210Po(α) → **206Pb(stable)**
or **210Pb(α)** → 206Hg(β) → 206Tl(β) → **206Pb(stable)**

Notice that lead 210Pb can decay to stable 206Pb several different ways.

Radioactivity That Remains After a Nuclear Bomb Explodes

The atoms in a nuclear bomb's core are primarily uranium 235 before the explosion. This is one of only a few isotopes that can be made to explode. The process of energy release is called fission, meaning the atoms split apart during the nuclear reaction. The triggers that split them are neutrons. When a slow neutron enters the nucleus of a uranium atom, the nucleus will fission or fly apart. The two halves that fly apart may contain any of a variety and number of protons and neutrons, but their sum approximates the weight of the original nucleus. These "fission products" are radioactive and immediately begin decaying into the string of various daughter isotopes. If all the half-lives were on the order of milliseconds, then in a few minutes all the radioactivity produced by splitting of uranium atoms in the bomb would be gone within an hour. Unfortunately many of the fission products have long half-lives, and these result in the debris from an atomic explosion being highly radioactive for a long time after the explosion is over.

The most hazardous daughter products of a bomb explosion potentially affecting human internal exposure are in the short term: radioactive iodine 131 through 135, the most notable being $^{131}I_{53}$. Over longer periods of time, $^{137}Cs_{55}$ and possibly $^{90}Sr_{38}$ are more important. These are dangerous especially if they are ingested through foodstuffs.

How Does Radiation Harm You?

The radioactive materials in the fallout from the mushroom cloud (in the sand-like fallout near ground zero, in the dust remaining near the site of the explosion and in the mushroom cloud) largely come from the fission products created when the uranium core underwent the fission chain reaction. It contains alpha, beta, and gamma emitters. Much of these radioactive materials will emit all three kinds of radiation. To survive you must avoid this material as much as possible. So how can you protect yourself from each kind of radiation?

Protection from Beta Radiation

Beta radiation is just a fast moving electron. It has little weight and a charge of -1 or +1. If a charged particle moves through material with enough energy to knock electrons off the atoms of the material, it may break the bonds in any chemicals it passes through. This includes proteins, cell structure, and DNA in your body's cells. This is how a beta particle can cause damage.

But a beta particle is easily stopped. A sheet of paper or the outer surface of your skin can stop it. So in general, beta radiation is not a direct hazard to you except in one case. That case is if you ingest (eat or swallow) the dust that is emitting beta particles. Each tiny piece of dust may contain millions of radioactive atoms decaying to their daughter isotopes and emitting beta radiation. When you breathe in the dust, or eat something with this radioactive dust on it, the dust may end up imbedded in your body right up against important cells, such as lung tissue, intestinal tissue, or even bone tissue. That tiny speck of dust will sit there and continuously bombard nearby tissue with damaging radiation for as long as it remains. That in turn may kill the cells near the imbedded dust or cause cancer to form by damaging the cell's DNA.

So you should protect yourself from beta-emitting dust by avoiding it, keeping it off your hands when you handle food and out of your nose and mouth.

Simple cleanliness may be hard to maintain after an explosion that wrecks the water and electrical supply systems in your area, so part of your preparations must include assuring you can wash after being contaminated by radioactive dust. Soap and clean water are what you need.

Beta radiation cannot make a material radioactive, so it is harmless if it strikes food or liquids.

Protection from Alpha Radiation

Alpha particles are very heavy compared to a beta particle (electron). The alpha particle is a tiny chunk of matter we call a helium nucleus. The nucleus of the helium atom consists of two protons and two neutrons and is charged +2. The fast-moving alpha particle can do a lot more damage than a beta particle when it flies through materials because its weight makes it harder to stop and because it has a more intense electrical charge. This weight and charge allow it to interact in a stronger manner with surrounding materials and it can therefore rip apart more molecules before it finally slows to a stop; however, it too can be stopped easily by your clothing or a piece of cardboard. As with the beta particle, the real danger from the alpha particle is ingesting the material that is emitting the alpha particles.

So you protect yourself from alpha-emitting dust by avoiding it, keeping it off your hands when handling food, and out of your nose and mouth. Simple cleanliness is important. So, again, part of your preparations must include assuring you can wash after being contaminated by radioactive dust. Soap and clean water are what you need.

Alpha particles do not make the materials they strike become radioactive.

Protection from Gamma Radiation

Gamma radiation is different from beta or alpha radiation. A gamma ray is not a solid particle; it is a form of very high energy light. This high energy light cannot be seen by the human eye.

Light is believed to be electromagnetic radiation, which just means it is made of alternating electric and magnetic fields. Light travels at the speed of light, about 186,000 miles per second. It can behave like a wave or like a particle depending on the situation and how we measure it. For our purpose we will talk about its wave-like nature when we compare gamma rays to other forms of light and we will talk about its particle nature when we talk about the damage it can do.

You probably know that visible light, the type of light we can see, comes in many colors. The strength or energy carried by an individual packet of light is proportional to its frequency: individual pieces of red light (lower frequency) carry less energy than blue light (higher frequency). Lower frequency red light is infrared light that we can "feel" with our skin. When you stand near a hot stove and feel the warmth on your face you are "seeing" infrared light with the receptors on your skin. It can warm your skin, but does not cause sunburn.

Types of Light Radiation

Type of Light –	Can Penetrate	Damage it Can Do
Infrared	Empty space and air.	Can heat a surface. Can burn the skin.
All visible light	Empty space and air.	Generally not harmful if not too bright.
Ultraviolet	Slight penetration into certain surfaces such as skin.	Sunburn. Damages and kills unprotected living cells.
X-ray	Passes through soft tissue and some bone. Stopped by thick materials or heavy materials such as metal plates.	It can burn the skin and do sunburn-like damage throughout a material's volume. Can cause damage that leads to cancer.
Gamma rays	Pass through almost everything.	Causes tissue damage along its path while passing through the human body.

Violet light is more energetic than blue light, but we can still see it.

Ultraviolet (beyond violet) light is even higher energy and can actually penetrate the human skin and cause damage to the tissue. We cannot see ultraviolet light. Sunburn is damage caused to your skin by ultraviolet light.

Add more energy to light and you have a form of light called "soft x-rays." As you increase the energy of the light particles, you get x-rays and then "hard x-rays." X-rays have enough energy to penetrate skin and bone but not thick metal plates. In fact some of the x-rays are stopped by bone, which allows x-ray pictures to be taken, which show the tissue and bone structure inside a person.

If we keep increasing the energy in the light we will eventually have gamma rays. These are so powerful they can pass through anything, although the more massive the material and the greater the thickness the fewer gamma rays get through. When a gamma ray zips through you, it rips electrons off atoms in your tissue, causing the molecules that make up your cells to be broken, split, changed into new molecular compounds, or destroyed. Gamma rays can damage tissue to such a degree that it loses its ability to function normally. You can think of this as like getting a really bad sunburn throughout your whole body, both on the skin surface and deep inside. The cells in the marrow of your bones and the cells that line the intestine to process food for you are particularly sensitive to radiation damage from gamma rays.

So how can you protect yourself from gamma radiation? In a way it is the same as the way you prevent sunburn. Either stay out of the sun or cover yourself with clothing or sun blocker. Unfortunately, gamma rays are so powerful no clothing you could wear will protect you. There is no "gamma blocker" cream. So what you must do is get as far away from the source of the gamma rays (that same radioactive dirt) or put something thick and heavy between you and the radioactive material that remains after the nuclear explosion.

If you are in the area where much radioactive dirt falls, you will want to know about distance, time, and shielding, your keys to survival when dangerous levels of radiation are around you.

How Does Radioactive Decay Help You?

One of the aspects of nuclear terror is the radioactive dirt and dust the explosion of a bomb leaves behind. When the World Trade Center was attacked on 9/11/2001, as soon as the dust cleared, rescue workers were able to move back into the area and search for survivors. There were serious hazards such as silica dust and asbestos in the air, but these can be protected against, using techniques as simple as wetting the area down or wearing a mask.

It will not be this way after an atomic explosion. The area around ground zero (the point of explosion) will be so highly radioactive for some time that anyone spending too much time there will die. So cleanup will be a matter of months or years in some cases, and even then, protective measures will have to be taken for the workers. In addition to this, much of the radioactive dust will be carried high into the atmosphere and blown downwind.

Areas under this cloud downwind of the blast site will be irradiated by the gamma rays coming from the cloud passing high overhead (this is called "shine") and may also receive a rain of tiny radioactive particles that were caught up in the mushroom cloud. This is called fallout. Fallout patterns are discussed in the chapter 7 analysis of what Sonny Summers experiences, in the story called "Caring for Others."

The source of the beta, alpha, and gamma radiation coming from the radioactive dust created by the atomic blast is the decay of the radioactive daughter isotopes. This is both a curse and a blessing of sorts. It's a curse because the radiation is dangerous and a blessing because the radioactivity constantly decreases as time passes. The very process (radioactive decay) that causes the hazard works to assure that eventually most of the radioactivity will be gone.

Appendix C1: Is the Threat Real?

Nuclear bombs are not easy to make. They require years of work; exotic, dangerous materials; precision machining, precise mathematics, and great financial resources. This is why you don't have to worry about your neighbor building one in his basement. You can get an idea of the difficulty of building one of these bombs by reading Tom Clancy's novel *The Sum of all Fears.*[97] Nuclear bombs are precise devices, mathematically precise.

Nuclear bombs must stay together long enough to convert enough nuclear energy into heat energy to make a big explosion. The reaction that drives them depends at least in part on the shape, purity, and density of their uranium metal core. As they begin to explode, these devices tend to blow apart, which stops the power-generating, nuclear reaction. An improperly constructed or poorly designed bomb may not explode at all.

The nuclear material that makes a bomb explode is very expensive to make. You have to make it in a nuclear reactor. Once you have made the material you need, you must separate it from tons of highly radioactive material that will make a bomb fail to work if it is not removed. You must also carefully control the amount and shape of the nuclear material, and the other materials that may be nearby, or a nuclear reaction may spontaneously start.[98]

So you should not worry about your neighbor—unless your neighbor is a nation with the economic resources and scientific brainpower to accomplish the task.

There are such nations in the world, and many of them have made nuclear weapons. Should you lose sleep over them? Not necessarily. Most of those countries' leaders are rational. They have developed those weapons to use only if attacked. They are interested in commerce and trade, the job market, and putting their kids through college. They value human life. That is why a nuclear France, England, and Israel are not nations to lose sleep over.

Who should we worry about?

Unfortunately there are a few nations in the world that are led by men driven by an ideology that is more important to them than life. They are following a revelation given to them by their god, and will even kill their own children for the cause, thinking it is an honor for their children to die. These are the folks worth losing sleep over.

---

[97] ISBN-13: 9780399136313

[98] There have been fatalities in laboratories where scientists failed to control pieces of metal they were experimenting with near a small sphere of nuclear (fissionable) material. To read about these cases, go to www.wikipedia.com and search for the words "demon core." You will find photos there of the lab setup and the story of what happened.

And they do not keep their intent secret. There is at least one country whose leaders have avowed in public their intent to destroy every man, woman, and child in a neighboring country.[99]

> Your city could be their target.

"'God has ordered us to build nuclear weapons,' proclaimed Fazlur Rahman Khalil of Pakistan's Harkat ul-Mujahedeen on the CBS television news show 60 Minutes II."[100]

"According to Pakistani nuclear physicist Pervez Hoodbhoy, Pakistan possesses small, 600kg (1322 lb) nuclear weapons that could be delivered by pickup truck. Such a device delivered by truck or train and detonated in a densely populated area could kill more people by radiation than died in Hiroshima."[101]

It is a fact that there are some people who are serious about exploding a nuclear weapon in one of our cities to hurt and kill as many people as possible. Where will they place their weapon? To answer this question, remember that they are terrorists. They will place the weapon where it will cause the most terror (i.e., where it will get the most press coverage possible). For maximum terror, they need burned and mangled bodies, the more the better, along with enthusiastic media people to photograph the bodies and destruction and to present these images to the world. All they really need is a place with many people. The maximum terror will occur if they bomb a city, the bigger the better. Your city could be their target.

If you live in a metropolitan area, particularly one well known around the world, you are in the nuclear cross-hairs. Here is a list of some of those prime targets that would get a terrorist group much publicity and cheers from millions of their supporters around the world:

New York City – already their target several times over. Can you doubt they would pick you again? Downtown, Times Square, Central Park, the Waterfront?

Chicago – called the "windy city" and known for its industry. Wind spreads radioactive fallout. And who is downwind? Detroit, Cleveland, Buffalo, and Pittsburgh.

---

[99] An example of this is the April 2006 protest in New York by the Islamic Thinkers Society outside the Israeli consulate. Among other chants, the demonstrators yelled, "Zionists, Zionists, you will pay! The wrath of Allah is on its way! Israeli Zionists, you shall pay! The wrath of Allah is on its way! The mushroom cloud is on its way! The real Holocaust is on its way! Israel won't last long … Indeed, Allah will repeat the Holocaust right on the soil of Israel" http://www.investigativeproject.org/328/islamists-message-to-israel-at-new-york-city-rally .

[100] Jamestown Foundation, Publication: *Terrorism Monitor*, Volume 2, Issue 6, March 24, 2004, by Scott Atran.

[101] Ibid.

Los Angeles – multicultural and home of Hollywood. Downwind we find Riverside, San Diego, Las Vegas, and Phoenix

San Francisco – considered the "devil's city" and rich. Downwind we find San Jose, Sacramento, Fresno, and Reno.

Orlando – the playground of the world. Nearby, within reach of the wind, we find Tampa, St. Petersburg, Daytona Beach and Palm Bay.

Dallas – they have seen what you are like (or so they think) on TV. Fallout may reach Oklahoma City, Ft. Worth, San Antonio, Houston, Shreveport, and even New Orleans.

Oklahoma City – they would be kings of oil if they could. North winds take fallout to Dallas and Ft. Worth, or Memphis, Kansas City or St. Louis.

Boston and Philadelphia – foundational to the history of the USA. And nearby? Providence, Springfield, Manchester, Hartford, and even distant New York City.

Washington, DC – seat of American government and power. Downwind we find Baltimore, Harrisburg and Philadelphia.

Seattle – Boeing aircraft plant, Microsoft. Watch out Everett, Bremerton, Tacoma and Olympia for fallout.

St. Louis – construction of military aircraft. Centered by Kansas City, Chicago, Louisville, Nashville, and Memphis. Someone will catch the drift.

Houston – Johnson Space Center – key to the American space program and oil industry, with San Antonio to the west, Dallas/Ft. Worth to the north, and Beaumont and New Orleans to the east.

London – they hate the Brits; they are too free and strong. And the Netherlands, Belgium and Germany to the east, and Paris France nearby also.

Paris – to bring the nation into submission. The wind can take their mess to London, Brussels, Rotterdam, Berlin, Frankfurt, and Switzerland.

Madrid – they want to cow you into submission. Lisbon could be downwind, as well as Morocco, Rome, Milan, and Barcelona.

Berlin – to show that industrious Germans are not invincible. From there European winds can find Hamburg, Warsaw, Prague, Szczecin, Gdansk, Copenhagen, and Vienna.

Rio de Janeiro – another target to make their point. And nearby as the wind blows: Brasilia, Belo Horizonte, Campinas and many more.

Hong Kong – such an energetic bastion of capitalism. From there the wind can reach Macau, Guangzhou, Quanzhou and even Taiwan.

Mumbai– easy to get into and a huge death count. Fallout may visit Navi Mumbai, Pune, Nashik, Ahmedabad, Hyderabad, Nagpur, or Rajkot.

And many other cities full of people.

So, should you and I worry about this? We hope our elected leaders take this threat seriously and take whatever steps are necessary to interdict the delivery of such a weapon into our country. If we trust them to be proficient at this, then worry is something we should avoid. But that does not mean we sit back and do nothing. That is why this book has been written. There are things you can do to prepare for the small probability that your city, or one within 250 miles of you, will someday be attacked with the ultimate terror weapon, the nuclear bomb.

Appendix D1: How the Attack Might Happen

Remember that the people and places in this book are pure fiction, created to allow us to present the effects of a nuclear bomb. The bad guys, the terrorists and their organization (the PPF), are also fiction. This appendix presents a hypothetical account of how the Yorksberg bomb was obtained.

Phase 1:   Planning and Production

The fictional organization we call the PPF is a small group, numbering probably no more than 100 members around the world, but it is growing through the recruitment of new members. This recruitment is assisted whenever the PPF makes the news when taking credit for the destruction of some symbol of human freedom or authority, or killing women and children in parks, hotels, or just along a street. For the sake of our story, we assume the leaders of the PPF meet in secret in a European nation to discuss their options. They all agree they cannot immediately bring down any of the Western nations, but they realize a 911-type incident would raise their notoriety to the level of Al-Qaeda. An atomic bomb exploded in one of the enemy's cities would be perfect. This is attractive to everyone at the table. The problem is obtaining a weapon.

The PPF is not a nation and does not have the resources to manufacture a nuclear weapon. The only alternative is to buy or steal one. So the leaders make a decision to put out feelers to their own cells[102] in other countries and to brother groups operating around the world. They want to find out if someone in the world's criminal underground has a bomb to sell. Money is no problem, since the PPF will be well funded when its plans become known in sympathetic countries.

Note that having the leaders congregate for a strategic planning meeting is risky, and putting out feelers to search for an available nuke is riskier still. Governments of the free world must be constantly vigilant to listen to what these groups and their leadership and cell members are saying to each other. They must constantly screen communications to detect their meetings, their cell activities, and information about other terrorist organizations.

Interdiction Point 1: Watch for people seeking radioactive materials, or attempting to purchase nuclear weapons or the unique parts needed to make such weapons.

Let's suppose the PPF leaders and cell members are sufficiently discreet and their meetings and communications are not discovered. Let's further assume that several PPF

---

[102] The "cell" network is a classic structure for clandestine organizations. Each cell has a limited number of members with very restricted contact with other cells. This provides security for all since the detection and destruction of any one cell leads to a dead end. Other members worldwide are protected from discovery, provided that proper separation exists between cells.

cell members in a nation with nuclear weapons on the Asian continent are actually members of that country's military, and because of their position inside the military they know where weapons are stored and have contacts within the security staff guarding the nukes.

Assume these undercover PPF members learn there are eight small nuclear weapons stored in a bunker on a military base. They also learn there is a ninth nuke mockup used for training. It is supposed to be indistinguishable from the real bombs. It is in fact made of real bomb components and structural pieces with no nuclear material or explosives, and is stenciled "For Training Only."

So they plan to remove the stenciling that identifies the mockup as a training tool, and then substitute it for the real bomb they steal. All weapons will be accounted for the next time a count is made, but one of the "weapons" counted is will actually be the training mockup with the training stenciling removed, so the theft will not be noticed for some time. The real bomb is secreted to a safe house in the countryside and hidden in a box marked "Well Equipment." The device is half the size of an office desk, weighs about 800 lbs, and although not technically exquisite, it is fully capable of releasing the energy equivalent of 19 kt (19 thousand tons) of TNT.

So our fictional terrorist group now has its own bomb. This simple scenario demonstrates that when countering nuclear terrorism one should not assume anything. Authorities must thoroughly investigate any attempt to steal or purchase nuclear weapons. Look behind the information released. Your assumptions may kill you.

Interdiction Point 2: In cases of the theft or movement of nuclear material or parts that could be used to manufacture a bomb, do not assume anything, and investigate deeper into such activities than you think reasonable. And then check everything again. You may discover the training bomb is missing. You must ask why would terrorists want a training weapon? Perhaps to scare people or make threats, or… maybe the training weapon is not missing. Have you checked? It is that kind of deeper and constant inquiry that may stop or detect the theft of a weapon.

It is necessary to uncover new leads and start monitoring these new leads to identify the organizations and the participants. They may try again. They need to be watched for years (or eliminated) and may actually have been successful and have a bomb. Never assume what you hear in the news is the complete truth.

Phase 2: Smuggling the Weapon into the Target City

More meetings are held. Group members are excited about what they have accomplished undetected. Over tea and cigarettes, late into the night, they discuss ideas about which target to hit. Small cities are off their list. Cities in Latin America, Africa, and the Far East are dismissed, but not without some discussion. These cities would be far easier to penetrate with the weapon than American or European countries.

For our fictional account, we assume they decide to attack an American city. The deciding factor is ideology; after all, their purpose is to strike at the heart of the cultural antithesis of themselves. Besides, the Western news media would not cover an attack on Africa, South America, or the Far East with the same frenzied rush as they would an attack on Europe or the United States.

In our fictional scenario, Israel is discussed as a target by the PPF leaders. That small nation state is considered number one on their target list because it is a nation of Jewish people and the religion of the PPF commands them to hate and kill all Jews.[103] But in the end they decide to bypass Israel for two reasons. One is there are many living in Israel and the surrounding nations who are of the PPF's own religion and who would be killed by the blast or fallout. The second reason is the security. Smuggling a weapon into Israel would not be easy and the risk of being caught before finishing the task is recognized as significant. They decide that obtaining such a weapon was a fortunate event and that it must not be squandered by trying to get it across intensely secure borders.

> **Interdiction Point 3**: Professional border security and a reputation for thorough screening of incoming packages for nuclear materials is a deterrent. It may also catch something.

At this point our PPF leaders have a bit of a disagreement. Several want to target London because of their support of the U.S. in the Middle-East wars. They cite the fact that the new European Union will make it easy to move the weapon to London once they get it into one European Union country. And that is easy, provided they carefully pick the country to enter.

The other side of the leadership argues the English Channel is a choke point where the device is at risk – either entering Great Britain via boat or the Chunnel via France. No one likes the idea of two water-to-shore transitions (one transition from the Far East where the bomb was stolen into a European Union country and another transition onto the British Isles). "The Chunnel is too easy to monitor with gamma detectors," one of the leaders argues. Several of the leaders ask him to explain and he says something like this:

> "The atomic bomb always has at its core a fissile material: Uranium or Plutonium. In this bomb it will probably be Uranium considering where the bomb is coming from. These materials are naturally radioactive; that is, they constantly emit high energy gamma rays. Not only that, these gamma rays are of a particular energy or frequency that is like a signature for the material

---

[103] Ibn Ishaq and al-Waqidi report that the prophet said the morning after the murder (of Kab Ibn al'Ashraf), "Kill any Jew you can lay your hands on." Muḥammad Ibn Isḥāq was an Arab Muslim historian and hagiographer. Umar al-Wāqidī was an Arab historian.

and they can be detected far from the weapon. Shielding the bomb with lead would help a little, but that will make the weapon unmanageably heavy, and it will still allow enough gamma rays to get through to be detected. The British and French are sharp and will probably have gamma ray detectors at both ends of the Chunnel. If we send the device into the Chunnel it will probably be detected and trapped in the Chunnel. This is the same reason we cannot send it through any world-class port. Packages, even whole ships, can be quickly scanned for nuclear material gamma signatures."

Someone at this point suggests France as the next easiest option and a short discussion ensues as to which French city would best be hit. But this idea is rejected too on several accounts. First, the French have not supported the U.S. and Britain strongly in the Middle-East wars. Second, there is a significant population of supporters of the PPF religion in France and they are beginning the process of taking over France using social strife and French democracy against itself. France will be converted within 50 years. Bomb one of the major French cities will, on the other hand, probably cause a huge backlash against their religion, to say nothing of the deaths of their own supporters.

So the die is cast. The PPF leaders finally decide, to a man, that the only target to meet their objectives and that has security lax enough to allow success is the United States. "Did not Pearl Harbor and 911 both prove that point?" one of them quips.

Note that any perceived weakness in security will be viewed as an opportunity. Remaining vigilant, active, and strong is a deterrent in itself. If you appear strong you may not even have to fight.

Interdiction Point 4: Maintain strong border security and advertise it.

The bad guys briefly discuss U.S. cities and quickly come to the old favorite, New York City. The general thought is they can finally get rid of that bastion of diversity and prosperity, a worldwide advertisement for all they think is wrong with the Western world, the city that so quickly recovered, spit in the face of the 911 attackers, cleaned up, and rebuilt. Perhaps, they think, with a nuke they can trash it once and for all.

At this point one of the quieter members of the group of leaders speaks up. He disagrees. Having once desired to be a television weather-caster and having studied weather in the United States, he suggests an alternative that would destroy a major city and, if timed right, allow the PPF leaders to place the fallout from the bomb's mushroom cloud directly across a second, and perhaps a third major city. With the prize "three for the price of one," they quickly agree on a target.

They have chosen "Yorksberg,"[104] and locate it on their map along the Eastern seacoast of the United States. It has several major cities to the north and east, allowing for fallout impact hundreds of miles away.

---

[104] Our Yorksberg is purely fictional, so if you know of a real Yorksberg in the USA, understand that is not the city we write about.

In the days following their decision about which city to attack, the PPF leaders investigate various ways to get their package into the States. They figure it does not matter much where it enters since commerce flows freely along the interstate highways to all areas of the United States. The key was to find a way to get it on shore. Some of the ways they discussed included:

Flying it in.
Shipping it to a major port.
Shipping it to a minor port.
Remote coastline delivery.
Across the Mexican border.
Across the Canadian border.

One of them suggested just mailing it to an address in the U.S. He was not serious, but explained that fortunes of diamonds were sometimes just mailed from Europe to the USA in the standard mail system. The security in that was the reliability of the postal service and the anonymity of being one in a hundred million pieces of mail. They discussed the various methods for hours until suddenly one of them came up with a unique twist that immediately caught everyone's attention. It was brilliant, and key to the brilliance of the idea was its simplicity. There was a bit of risk but all the paths they discussed had risks and this new idea was at first glance one of the least risky.

They sent one of their members to visit his relatives in the U.S. and to check on some of the details of their maturing plan. Weeks later he reported in a non-descript email about the "health of his sister and that everything was as they supposed it would be."

The only piece of the puzzle they did not know was whether or not U.S. authorities had gamma ray detectors along the highways. They did not think there were such detectors but decided to use only small "blue road" highways and to stay off the national interstate system.

By October, with the help of money from overseas, they had the device stored in a barn in a rural community in the U.S. It had taken more than a year to steal the bomb and get it placed in the U.S., but time was of no matter to the PPF leaders. Progress was their most important product.

Phase 3: Placement Strategy

Their target presented them with several placement possibilities. There was a body of water, a shoreline of sorts, a sprawling residential area, and a typical old American city downtown area with many large office buildings, a large rail yard, and a few neighborhoods close in that had gone to seed as times and fortunes changed. Within 5 miles of the downtown center were two high schools with more than 1000 students each, 14 neighborhood elementary schools, 2 hospitals, a police headquarters, and a number of city administration buildings including the central Police and Fire Department exchange. There was some history there too, history important to the American story. The PPF leaders did not miss the irony of their strike hitting an American historical landmark.

The PPF leaders decide to detonate their device at street level or in a small airplane flying through the city canyons formed by the tall buildings on either side of the main thoroughfare. The aircraft idea was finally dropped as unnecessarily complicating the attack, although all realized it was a clever idea.

At the center of the city is a plaza surrounded by banks, insurance companies, government buildings, and a large museum. This would be ground zero. Not only would this strike a blow against the rich American companies surrounding the plaza, it would also destroy the emergency services communication center a few blocks from the plaza. Unknown to the PPF leadership was the fact that the Emergency Services communication for Police, Fire, Ambulance, and the Hospital, as well as the two major television stations and several radio stations, all used towers on the three tallest buildings downtown. They could not have chosen better in attacking a population that was unprepared for what was to come.

Phase 4: Detonation Strategy

The PPF leaders had long ago agreed that the dead of winter would be the best time of the year to inhibit Fire Rescue, Police, and Medical Services personnel as much as possible, allow the heat from the blast to set fires miles away through the clear winter air, and to provide the media 10 to 20 miles away with the best possible photo opportunities.

Their weather expert told them exactly which weather patterns would be best for carrying the deadly radioactive fallout to the neighboring cities. If they got the fallout they anticipated, they fully expected it would cause as many, or perhaps even more, casualties downwind as in the target city. It would be delicious bedlam at freezing temperatures.

The team chose 2:30 p.m. as the prime time on a weekday. This would assure the maximum number of residential commuters in the downtown area. Since the city was on the winter cycle of daylight saving time, it got dark about 6 p.m. that time of year. Thus the blast would destroy the downtown and knock out sewer, water, and electric utilities for miles around. The first night after the blast, the city would be dark and cold and full of dead and dying people. With no light or communication services, and high radioactivity in the downtown area, little or nothing would be done until surveys could be completed the next day.

The team decided to alert media personnel to the west of the city a few minutes before the bomb was set off, and several PPF teams from East Coast cells would hit power substations feeding the area to assure that no electric service would survive the attack. This was to plunge the whole state into darkness to further impede help and assistance from outside the city. They expected this tactic to affect home heating and transportation since gasoline could then not be pumped at service stations around the periphery of the city. Care was taken so that the cell members working the nuke explosion would not have any knowledge of the nuclear portion of this coordinated attack.

Phase 5: Follow-up – How They Plan to Increase Your Terror

Following the explosion, the PPF leaders planned to issue press releases to all the major news organizations, both in the U.S. and internationally, taking credit for the destruction of Yorksberg and dealing a lethal blow to their enemy. They also planned to use photographs taken by the press showing suffering and damage in propaganda releases.

Finally, and most important, the follow-up press releases would claim that several other bombs were hidden in American cities, and that these would be exploded if the group's demands were not met. Thus the seeds of terror would be sown.

> Terror, of the enormity of a nuclear attack, can only be resisted by a people who are well grounded in their values, their sense of right and wrong, and their foundational beliefs. But even in a nation like ours, such strengths can be shaken.

What Happened to the PPF?

Some may be curious about what happened to our fictional bad guys, the PPF. Since they are pure fiction, we could just let them get away with their crime, but it might be more satisfying to have their consequences catch up with them. To this end, please read this article that appeared in the *Yorksberg Times* on the anniversary of the bombing several years later.

Leave Us Nothing but Grief and Pain

That was their intent after all. They wanted to make the citizens of Yorksberg and the nation suffer grief and pain, and then live to celebrate their wickedness. They caused the suffering, but the wanton mass murderers who destroyed so many lives that day should have read the poem "To a Mouse," written by the Scot Robert Burns in 1785. In part it says:

> But little Mouse, you are not alone,
> In proving foresight may be vain:
> The best laid schemes of mice and men
> Go often askew,
> And leave us nothing but grief and pain,
> For promised joy!

They had their plans of escape, glory, and the joy of thinking they had gotten away with the most heinous crime in human history, but just as Burns so eloquently wrote, their plans went askew.

Why? Well, hindsight reveals their own arrogance tripped them up. They had planned to be long gone by the time the bomb went off. They dispersed; leaving the country even as the bomb was exploding, traveling to foreign countries that would celebrate their crime with them.

When the bomb exploded, all state and national law-enforcement agencies across the nation immediately went into a very high alert status, but even so the trail was cold for several hours. The PPF leaders were all on planes headed out of the country by 2:30 that cold January afternoon, and one would think that finding them or their underling soldiers would prove to be impossible; however, their best laid plans began to unravel.

For one thing, one of the PPF cell members had purchased an "I love Yorksberg" sweatshirt as a joke, thinking this pretty funny considering what the PPF was going to do. It never occurred to him that this new sweatshirt purchase would be remembered by a man in a quick-stop store less than three miles from the cell's farmhouse hideout during the massive police investigation that followed the explosion. His call to the FBI shortly after the explosion proved to be key to the discovery of the persons responsible. The video from the store's security cameras allowed the man's face to be quickly identified as someone the FBI and Homeland Security had been watching for years. This led to the arrest of his brother as he stopped over in London, attempting to make a connection flight to a country of refuge.

Second, the PPF cell had sent out several of its junior members to plant explosives in power substations around the Yorksberg countryside in order to keep power off and hamper rescue and emergency operations. This went well, except in one case where an alert state patrol officer, as fate would have it, happened by a substation while the perpetrator was climbing over the substation fence on his way out. Seeing the officer's car coming back to investigate, the criminal panicked and took off at high speed. He wrecked his car trying to flee the aroused state police and was captured when found unconscious in the wreck.

The secrecy of the PPF team unraveled from there, with all the team but two captured or killed within a year.

The last two were located and killed in a Special Forces operation similar to the operation that found and killed Bin Laden.

Our own Rhonda Hitching, a dispatcher for the Yorksberg Taxi Service, expressed pride in her son, who led the Seal Team to locate and kill the final two criminals overseas.

So for all the planning, the murderers have been left with nothing but Grief and Pain, which is certainly satisfying to those who lost, loved ones on that dark day. We remember them all.

Appendix E1: Topics Covered in the NTSH Handbook

Nuclear bomb effects discussed in Part 1 and Part 2 of this handbook include the following (but not necessarily in this order):

- ☼ Initial nuclear radiation
- ☼ Flash burns and blindness
- ☼ Shine
- ☼ Fallout
- ☼ Contamination
- ☼ Ground slap
- ☼ X-ray fireball
- ☼ Thermal fireball
- ☼ Thermal radiation and incendiary effects
- ☼ Types of nuclear radiation (alpha, beta, gamma)
- ☼ Blast wave formation
- ☼ Overpressure and dynamic pressure
- ☼ Biological concentration radioactivity
- ☼ Effects of blast wave acoustics
- ☼ Structural damage
- ☼ EMP

In addition to the effects of the bomb, other related topics of importance are discussed, such as:

- ☼ Shielding
- ☼ Sheltering
- ☼ Contamination control
- ☼ Medical facility operation and overload
- ☼ Loss of command and control
- ☼ Loss of communications
- ☼ Special hazards to emergency response personnel and the press
- ☼ Radiation instrumentation
- ☼ Weather during and after a nuclear attack
- ☼ The role of Amateur Radio following a nuclear attack
- ☼ Recommendations to civil defense personnel, Police Departments, Fire Departments, cities, and schools
- ☼ How can "duck and cover" drills save school children from an atomic explosion since the atomic blast destroys everything?

Other more specific areas discussed include:

1. Can a person receive radiant heat burns at more than a mile from ground zero?
2. What are walking wounded?
3. What is a G.O.O.D. pack and why do you need one?
4. Looting following the explosion, and how radiation complicates this illegal activity.
5. How are hospitals, both local and distant, affected?
6. How can contamination be controlled in a hospital?
7. What three serious problems should hospitals within 100 miles of a bombed city be prepared for?
8. What are the six key ideas for decontamination of patients?
9. How will the subway be affected by a nuclear explosion? Can it be used as a shelter? If so, what modifications need to be made?
10. What are the hazards you will bring to your family when you flee the bombed city and go to stay with them? How can you reduce these hazards?
11. What is the difference between primary and secondary fallout?
12. What happens to a person 15 feet from the bomb when it explodes? It's not what you think.
13. What determines the amount of heat that falls on a surface from a nuclear explosion?
14. Blast overpressure and overpressure-sensitive material.
15. In light of the possibility of a terrorist nuclear attack, what is the best location for the Emergency Operations Center (EOC)?
16. Coordination and equipment sharing with other counties.
17. Chain of command fallback layers.
18. Communications following the attack.
19. The proper location of standby emergency equipment.
20. Shelter design for those who live near and far away.
21. What are the aspects of a well-prepared shelter?
22. What does radiation do to food and drink? Is it safe to eat radiation exposed food and drink. What will this do to you?
23. Will the radiation create mutant humans or mutant creatures that can be dangerous for you and your family?
24. How could an atomic attack on a city hundreds of miles from you hurt you if you stay away from the attacked city?
25. If you are safe in a fallout shelter and two other families that know about your shelter want to come in after the attack, should you let them in?
26. What happens to the tens of thousands pets after a nuclear attack? (Should you try to save your pet?)

References

1. *The Effects of Nuclear Weapons*, Samuel Glasstone and Philip J. Dolan, United States Department of Defense, 1977.

2. *Hibakusha. Survivors of Hiroshima and Nagasaki*. Translated by Gaynor Sekimori. Kōsei Publishing Co., Tokyo.

3. Jamestown Foundation, Publication: *Terrorism Monitor,* by Scott Atran, Volume 2, Issue: 6, March 24, 2004.

INDEX

ABOUT THE AUTHOR

Vern Blanchette is a graduate of the University of Alabama (B.S. – Physics/Mathematics) and the University of Texas at Austin (M.Ed.). He has taught in public schools, community colleges, and for General Electric Company in the commercial nuclear power industry. He recently retired as an engineer with URS Corporation at the Kennedy Space Center.

Mr. Blanchette, married with six children, has been writing for more than thirty years, and is an alumnus of the Christian Writer's Conference at Lake Yale, Florida. His unpublished works include several science fiction stories, and a historical romance novel wherein love reaches across the centuries to reveal a treasure hidden for hundreds of years.

Published Works

Safe Schools Now – Arming America's Teachers, begun October 6, 2011, after the Sandy Hook massacre, was his first published work. Dog Ear Publishing, 2013. This book uses facts and four fictional stories to demonstrate the only way to truly protect school children from murderers is to train and arm the school teachers and staff.

An Encounter with the Honey Island Swamp Monster. Createspace, 2016. This is a true story of a strange encounter with something in a dark, Mississippi swamp. Exactly what was that thing?

Why You are Alive on Earth – Why do You Exist? Createspace, 2016. This book answers that question with some amazing revelations. Do you know why you are here, and who and what you really are?

Comments to the author may be sent to Survive@CFL.RR.COM.

NOTES

NOTES

This book was published through Createspace and is available from any decent book store.